高校专门用途英语（ESP）系列教材

AN INTEGRATED COURSE of
Practical English
for Student Naval Aviators

海军飞行实用英语综合教程

主　编　陈　莉

副主编　王淑东　朱紫健

编　者　王学生　张东力
　　　　徐晓娟　李　静
　　　　赵丛丛　明瑞龙

U0275068

清华大学出版社

北京

内 容 简 介

《海军飞行实用英语综合教程》是一本专门用途英语教材，旨在培养和提高海军飞行人员的专业英语能力。

本教材共10个单元，内容主要涉及海军飞行训练、飞机结构、飞行程序以及航空管制与安全等。每单元有3篇课文，均聚焦单元主题；课后练习围绕课文内容对学生的听、说、读、写、译等各项技能进行训练。附录部分包括常用缩略语表和无线电陆空通话基础知识表，便于学生自学和查阅。

本教材主要供在校飞行学员和空中战勤等相关专业的学员使用，也可作航空兵部队官兵的英语学习资料。

本书参考答案和视频资源请在ftp://ftp.tup.tsinghua.edu.cn/上下载。

版权所有，侵权必究。举报：010-62782989，beiqinquan@tup.tsinghua.edu.cn。

图书在版编目（CIP）数据

海军飞行实用英语综合教程 / 陈莉主编. —北京：清华大学出版社，2021.6
高校专门用途英语（ESP）系列教材
ISBN 978-7-302-56068-5

Ⅰ．①海…　Ⅱ．①陈…　Ⅲ．①海军航空－英语－高等学校－教材　Ⅳ．①E153

中国版本图书馆CIP数据核字（2020）第138017号

责任编辑：周　航
装帧设计：子　一
责任校对：王凤芝
责任印制：丛怀宇

出版发行：清华大学出版社
　　　　　网　　　址：http://www.tup.com.cn, http://www.wqbook.com
　　　　　地　　　址：北京清华大学学研大厦A座　　邮　　编：100084
　　　　　社 总 机：010-62770175　　　　　　　　邮　　购：010-62786544
　　　　　投稿与读者服务：010-62776969, c-service@tup.tsinghua.edu.cn
　　　　　质量反馈：010-62772015, zhiliang@tup.tsinghua.edu.cn
印 装 者：天津安泰印刷有限公司
经　　销：全国新华书店
开　　本：170mm×230mm　　　印　张：19.5　　字　数：463千字
版　　次：2021年6月第1版　　　　　　　　　印　次：2021年6月第1次印刷
定　　价：78.00元

产品编号：087312-01

Foreword
前　言

《海军飞行实用英语综合教程》根据海军航空大学《海军生长军官人才培养方案》和《海军飞行实用英语课程实施计划》编写，旨在培养和提高海军飞行人员的专业英语能力。

本教材为综合教程，课文素材主要参考了国外原版航空英语资料和文献，同时也参考了国内外、军内外航空英语相关教材。本教材共 10 个单元，单元内容涉及飞行员素质、海军飞行员训练、飞行日组训流程、飞机的结构与种类、空域和航空管制、基本飞行程序、飞行保障勤务和地面勤务、航母舰载机操作、直升机操作、航空安全等。每单元有 3 篇课文，均聚焦单元主题；课后练习围绕课文内容对学生的听、说、读、写、译等各项技能进行训练。附录部分包括常用缩略语表和无线电陆空通话基础知识表，便于学生自学和查阅。

本教材的编写力图体现"以学习者为中心"的教育理念，遵循专门用途英语教学的规律，以"加大语言输入、注重语言输出、突出飞行特色"为原则，以"夯实飞行学员扎实的航空专业英语基础"为目标，充分考虑海军飞行学员的岗位任职需求，确保取材合适、重点突出、难度适宜、内容实用，既训练学习者航空专业英语阅读能力，又重视培养其专业英语听说能力。

本教材主要供在校飞行学员和空中战勤等相关专业的学员使用，也可作航空兵部队官兵的英语学习资料。

本教材在编写过程中参考了大量资料并得到相关航空兵部队飞行教官的大力支持。外语教研室教授田少华担任主审，同时，海军航空大学及航空基础学院的领导和机关人员也对本书的编写提供了悉心指导，特别是学院外语教研室的各位同事对本书的编写工作给予了真诚的帮助，提供了有价值的建议。谨致谢忱！

由于编者知识、经验和水平所限，书中疏漏之处在所难免，诚望广大读者提出宝贵意见，以便今后修订完善。

编者

2021 年 4 月

Contents
目 录

Unit 1

Unit 2

Unit 3

Unit 1
Becoming a Qualified Pilot

🧭 Warming Up

Task 1 Watch the video clip about how important the English language is in order to become an airline pilot and fill in the blanks.

As it might not come to you as a surprise, it is crucial that a pilot is able to speak English. It is one of the most commonly used *1*_____ languages. And you will be exposed to the English language as soon as you start the *2*_____ training.

While you're flying your Cessna or Piper Archer, you have to speak English on the *3*_____. Pilots use a common language while communicating with each other and *4*_____. This common language is necessary, because confusion should be kept to a *5*_____ in the entire aviation sector.

To give you an example, as a pilot, you have to stick to standard *6*_____. Pilot and ATC use a specific *7*_____: alpha, bravo, charlie, delta, all the way to zulu. Another example is this: when you would like to *8*_____, you simply say the *9*_____, which is usually a registration number of the aircraft, or the airline's name plus a number, and add the words "request descent", which sounds like this: Speedbird 5501, request descent. You don't say: Hey, it's me, a Speedbird 5510 at FL30. And I'd like to go down to the ground now. Can you maybe clear me to a lower level?

As you may understand, it's important to have an *10*_____ understanding of the English language to prevent situations like this. Don't get me wrong, though. I mean you don't need to be a native speaker in order to become an airline pilot. With or without an *11*_____, you just need to be understandable for your colleagues. That's where it's all about.

Every pilot needs to pass an exam. It's called the Language Proficiency Endorsement (LPE). Level 1 to 3 means that you have failed the exam. You pass with Level 4 or higher, and Level 6 is the *12*_____ achievable level. The levels have different validity. Level 4 is valid for 3 years, Level 5 is valid for 6 years and Level 6 is valid for life. So what can you do if you feel like your English is not good enough?

Task 2 Discuss the ways to improve English with a partner. Then watch the video clip and take down the suggestions.

_____

_____

_____

Task 3 Discuss the following questions in groups.

1. Why do you choose to be a pilot?

2. How to become a qualified pilot?

3. What do you think is the biggest challenge on the way to becoming a naval aviator?

⊘ TEXT A

Selecting the Future Pilots

1   Selecting the right individuals for **pilot candidates** is an important step to ensure success in developing a professional pilot. So what kind of person would we ideally expect knocking on the door of a flight school? The candidates should be healthy, self-motivated, have reasonable **psychomotor** skills, and be emotionally stable.

2   There are three characteristics we are looking for and all three have to be present for an individual to become a successful and professional pilot: desire, ability, and means. One needs the desire or internal drive to want to fly and have the **work ethic** to develop the skills to become a pilot. The person also needs to have **innate** characteristics as well as the ability to learn. Finally, they need the means (or opportunity) to obtain the **pilot license**.

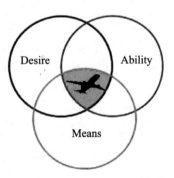

Three Characteristics of a Successful Pilot

Desire

3   Pilot training is not easy. It is a big intellectual, physical, and character-building challenge. Throughout the training, the candidate will be faced constantly with new challenges and exams while **being subject to** an ever-increasing complexity of the skills to be developed. And once the license is received, training will not stop. Nor will taking exams. Throughout the flying career, the pilot will be continuously **screened** and will regularly have to demonstrate his/her skills to an examiner. Not always will the pilot receive classroom training before taking an exam. So self-**tuition** will have to be a quality that the pilot possesses as well. Only candidate with enough self-motivation to carry him through such a **lengthy** training process will succeed.

Ability

4   For the very same reasons, emotional stability that **comes with** the ability for realistic self-reflection is essential. When one starts learning to fly in a multi-**crew** environment, he must possess people management skills in order to function properly as a member of a crew. A clear set of values and rules is part of a stable character. Being able to make decisions without supervision, in other words, having enough self-confidence, is important as well. The ultimate goal is to become a **captain**, which calls for leadership qualities and the ability to **steer** a team. The candidate should thus be an excellent communicator who from the first day of his flying career uses his naturally inquiring mind and his creativity to function properly in a team.

5   The candidate should already have received an education that has given him the ability to master English at a reasonable level as well as mathematics and physics. An academic qualification is not a necessity but rather a (valuable) personal educational **bonus**. Of course, some sorts of tests will determine if these academic qualities are present at a level that is adequate to start **ground school**. As flying also means absorbing information in large quantities, the candidates need to be able to observe and process the data with accuracy and speed, and make correct decisions that result in the appropriate action.

6   Good **coordination** skills should also be present in the candidates. One of the first things to learn will be the relations between speed, height and **engine power**,

and how the **throttle, stick** and **rudder** influence all those **parameters** at the same time. And the real challenge is to continue thinking while learning to move in three **dimensions**. Add on top of that the time dimension and you know that only those with above-average psychomotor skills can succeed.

7　　Obtaining a pilot license is only possible if you are **deemed**[1] medically fit. Medical tests have to be passed and only when achieving a **Medical Class 1 certificate**, the candidate may fly commercial services. Candidates must be screened to ensure they can obtain this Medical Class 1 certificate and being healthy is thus a necessary **precondition**. Next to the medical condition, there are some basic physical requirements (like height) which are determined due to the **cockpit** designs.

8　　The above list is of course non-**exhaustive**. Other dimensions that are considered to be crucial are a certain level of "common sense", i.e., creativity, and **flexibility**.

Means

9　　Everyone knows that pilot training is expensive. Those who don't **have access to** the necessary capital will feel the burden of heavy loans long after they receive their licenses. Those who are not granted loans cannot even enter flight school. And this is not acceptable. Personal wealth or access to money should not be a criterion as it reduces the **pool** of candidates.

Selection Process

10　　Now that we have established the **prerequisites**, and then we look at the selection process. An evaluation will be necessary to check the level of the students when they start, not only to select the right candidates but also to identify which areas the candidate has to focus on more during training. The main objective should be that this process determines with a good level of confidence if training can be concluded successfully. At the same time a longer-term objective of identifying a reasonable potential for lifetime performance should always be kept in mind. These are no easy tasks and the question begs who will be able to run such a selection process and how.

1　deem 常用句型为 "deem+sth./sb.+adj."。

11   The final decision on who to select has to **rest with** the pilots involved in the decision process and with pilots being part of the **decision loop** and the involvement of initial and advanced trainers. Also, the **Training Management System (TMS)** process would have the highest chance of selecting the right candidates. The **instructor** would be **instrumental** in the selection process as they could provide the necessary feedback on how previous candidates have **fared** during training. This feedback should help to refine the selection process. Such **validation** of the selection criteria is important to ensure continuous improvement of the process. As generations develop and come in with their own qualities and **deficiencies**, the prerequisites, the desired pilot **profile** and the training itself will also develop over time.

Vocabulary

Special Terms

captain 机长，舰长，船长；（海军）上校，（陆军或美国空军）上尉

cockpit 驾驶舱，座舱

crew 机组；空勤人员；地勤人员

engine power 发动机功率；发动机推力

ground school 地面训练学校；地面理论课

instructor 教员，教官

Medical Class 1 certificate 一级健康证明书

pilot candidate 候补飞行员

pilot license 飞行执照

profile 轮廓，外形；侧面图，纵剖面图；翼型，型面

rudder （飞机的）方向舵；（船的）舵

stick 驾驶杆，操纵杆

throttle 油门；油门杆

Training Management System (TMS) 训练管理系统

Words and Expressions

bonus	['bəʊnəs]	n.	奖金；红利；（附带的）好处，优点
candidate	['kændɪdeɪt]	n.	候选人；理想对象；求职者
coordination	[kəʊˌɔːdɪ'neɪʃn]	n.	协调，协作；调和；（身体的）协调能力
deem	[diːm]	v.	认为；相信
deficiency	[dɪ'fɪʃnsi]	n.	缺乏，不足；缺陷
dimension	[daɪ'menʃn]	n.	方面；规模，范围；尺寸；维度
exhaustive	[ɪg'zɔːstɪv]	a.	详尽的，全面的；彻底的
fare	[feə]	v.	进展；遭遇
flexibility	[ˌfleksə'bɪləti]	n.	灵活性；弹性；柔性
innate	[ɪ'neɪt]	n.	天生的，与生俱来的
instrumental	[ˌɪnstrə'mentl]	a.	起重要作用的
lengthy	['leŋθi]	a.	长时间的；漫长的
license	['laɪsns]	n.	许可证，执照
parameter	[pə'ræmɪtə]	n.	参数，参量；决定因素
pool	[puːl]	n.	共用的钱 / 物品 / 人力等；池，塘
precondition	[ˌpriːkən'dɪʃn]	n.	前提，先决条件 v. 把……预先安排好
prerequisite	[ˌpriː'rekwəzɪt]	n.	前提，先决条件；必备条件 a. 必须先具备的
psychomotor	[ˌsaɪkəʊ'məʊtə]	a.	心理运动的
screen	[skriːn]	v.	筛选，筛查，审查
steer	[stɪə]	v.	驾驶（船、汽车等）；引导；控制
tuition	[tjuː'ɪʃn]	n.	教学，指导；学费
validation	[ˌvælɪ'deɪʃn]	n.	确认；验证；核实
be subject to...			受……的影响
come with			伴随……发生；与……一起来
decision loop			决策环
have access to			有利用 / 接近……的权利和机会
rest with			取决于
work ethic			职业道德

 **Exercises**

Comprehension of the Text

I. Answer the following questions according to the text.

1. What good qualities should pilot candidates possess?

_____

2. What are the three characteristics of an individual to become a successful and professional pilot?

_____

3. Why is pilot training not easy?

_____

4. If the pilot cannot receive classroom training before taking an exam, what should he do?

_____

5. Why is self-motivation essential to pilot candidates?

_____

6. What is the pilot's ultimate goal? What qualities should he possess to achieve this goal?

_____

7. Is academic qualification important for a future pilot? Why or why not?

_____

8. What may coordination skills involve?

_____

9. What are the requirements for candidate's medical condition?

_____

10. Why is it necessary to check the level of the students when they start training?

_____

11. What are the main objective and the longer-term objective of the selection process?

_____

12. Who will make the final decision on whom to select?

_____

13. Why does the instructor play an important role in the selection process?

_____

14. Do you agree with the statement that the prerequisites of selecting future pilots should never be changed? Give your reasons.

_____

Vocabulary Practice

II. Match the meanings in Column B with the special terms in Column A and translate the terms into Chinese.

Column A	Column B
1. captain _____	a. a movable control surface, usually attached to a vertical stabilizer, by which an air vehicle is guided in the horizontal plane
2. stick _____	b. a person considered likely to become a pilot
3. rudder _____	c. pilot certificate
4. throttle _____	d. Training Management System
5. instructor _____	e. a lever used to control the motion of an aircraft by changing the angle of the elevators and ailerons
6. engine power _____	f. a person who teaches some specialized subjects, such as flying or gunnery
7. ground school _____	g. a school giving courses in aerodynamics, map reading, photography, and other pertinent subjects for aviators
8. pilot license _____	h. an aircraft commander
9. TMS _____	i. a valve in the fuel system of an aircraft for controlling the fuel that flows to the engine
10. pilot candidate _____	j. the maximum power that an engine can put out

III. Complete each of the following sentences with a word from the box. Change the form if necessary.

coordination	screen	parameter	dimension	tuition
license	bonus	precondition	validation	deficiency

1. The police car idled in the driveway for a minute, perhaps taking down the _____ number of Isabel's car, and then pulled away.

2. Good weather is an added _____, but the real appeal is the landscape.

3. The final _____ of the pond were 14ft×8ft.

4. Action groups work in _____ with local groups to end rainforest destruction.

5. A _____ is an important element to consider in the evaluation or comprehension of an event, project, or situation.

6. Vitamin E _____ is often associated with the disease.

7. They have demanded the release of the three prisoners as a _____ for any negotiation.

8. Only those refugees who are _____ out are sent back to Vietnam.

9. I'm not paying next year's _____.

10. A _____ ID is automatically displayed and ready to be sent.

IV. Complete the following short passage with the words from the box. Change the form if necessary.

assess	exercise	airmanship	limitation	performance
existing	instructor	analyze	procedure	safety

An accomplished pilot demonstrates the knowledge and ability to assess a situation quickly and accurately and determines the correct *1*_____ to be followed under the *2*_____ circumstances. He is also able to *3*_____ accurately the probable results of a given set of circumstances or of a proposed procedure; to *4*_____ care and due regard for *5*_____; to gauge accurately the *6*_____ of the airplane; to recognize the *7*_____ of the airplane and avoid approaching the critical points of each. He should also have the ability to identify, *8*_____, and mitigate risks. The development of *9*_____ skills requires effort and dedication of both student pilot and flight *10*_____, beginning with the very first training flight where proper habit formation begins with the student being introduced to good operating practices.

Translating Practice

V. Translate the following sentences into Chinese.

1. There are three characteristics we are looking for and all three have to be present for an individual to become a successful and professional pilot: desire, ability, and means.

_____

_____

2. As flying also means absorbing information in large quantities, the candidates need to be able to observe and process the data with accuracy and speed, and make correct decisions that result in the appropriate action.

_____

_____

3. For the candidate pilots, one of the first things to learn will be the relations between speed, height and engine power, and how the throttle, stick and rudder influence all those parameters at the same time.

_____

_____

4. Obtaining a pilot licence is only possible if you are deemed medically fit. Medical tests have to be passed and only when achieving a Medical Class 1 certificate, the candidate may fly commercial services.

_____

_____

5. As generations develop and come in with their own qualities and deficiencies, the prerequisites, the desired pilot profile and the training itself will also develop over time.

_____

_____

VI. Translate the following paragraph into English.

初级飞行训练和高级飞行训练的总体目标是获得并磨炼（hone）基本飞行技艺（airmanship）。学习驾驶飞机曾经常被比作学习开车。这个类比（analogy）使人产生误解。因为飞机是在三维环境中操作的，所以学习者需要对提升运动技能有更为深入的了解。

_____

_____

_____

_____

🧭 TEXT B

How Do You Become a US Navy Fighter Pilot?

GM[1]

1   The prerequisites to become a **Naval Aviator** are the same as for the Air Force: candidates must be **commissioned officers** and meet a set of strict physical requirements. All **Student Naval Aviators (SNAs)** start at the same place: **Naval Air Station (NAS)** Pensacola[2], located on the Gulf Coast[3] in the Florida **panhandle**.

2   Known as the "Cradle of Naval Aviation", it is here they will go through **Aviation Preflight Indoctrination (API)**. The program is 6 weeks long consisting of 4 weeks of academics and 2 weeks of survival training. **Concurrent** with the academic phase is the swimming course. SNAs will begin each morning learning swimming **survival**

---

1   **GM:** 美国海军飞行员，具有驾驶"大黄蜂"和"超级大黄蜂"战斗机的双重资格，他曾在 4 艘航母上成功着舰 150 多次。

2   **NAS Pensacola:** 彭萨科拉海军航空站，美国海军的第一个航空站，位于佛罗里达州。

3   **Gulf Coast:** 墨西哥湾沿岸地区。

skills that may help save their lives when they operate in the world's waters. The swimming course **culminates** with a one-mile swim in a **flight suit**.

3   The academics are divided into 6 classes **encompassing** a variety of subject areas including **aerodynamics**, weather, and **navigation**. An exam is given at the end of each course and the grades are very competitive. The **survival training** includes classes on basic land survival, survival equipment, physiology, and first-aid. It's not just Navy and **United States Marine Corps (USMC)** student pilots at API; **Student Naval Flight Officers (SNFOs)** are also in the classes. There are also **US Coast Guard** SNAs as well as students from allied nations.

NAS Pensacola

A US Navy T-6B Texan II from TAW-5 on Approach to Land

4   After going through the API, SNAs will be sent to **primary training** to fly T-6B Texan II[1]. **Primary** is at one of two locations: NAS Whiting Field[2] just outside of Pensacola, or NAS Corpus Christi[3], Texas (SNFOs will stay at NAS Pensacola to fly the T-6A Texan II[4]). The T-6B is a relative newcomer in Naval Aviation and replaces the old **workhorse** T-34C Turbo Mentor[5].

5   In Primary, SNAs are put through a fast-paced syllabus of classes, **sims**, and flights. The syllabus starts with **familiarization flights (FAMs)**, and then moves quickly into **aerobatics**, **instruments**, and **formation flying**. Every event is graded. The flying is challenging, but SNAs definitely have fun as well.

---

1   **T-6B Texan II:** T-6B "得克萨斯人" 二型教练机，有纵列座椅配置和涡桨发动机，主要用于训练美国海军和海军陆战队飞行员。

2   **NAS Whiting Field:** 怀廷菲尔德海军航空站，美国海军的两大初级训练基地之一，位于佛罗里达州。

3   **NAS Corpus Christi:** 科珀斯克里斯蒂海军航空站，位于得克萨斯州。

4   **T-6A Texan II:** T-6A "得克萨斯人" 二型初级教练机，单发双座，用于联合初级飞行训练。

5   **T-34C Turbo Mentor:** T-34C "涡轮导师" 教练机，单发双座下单翼，座舱未增压。

6 In the aerobatics phase, SNAs master maneuvers such as the **Aileron Roll**, **Barrel Roll**, **Immelman**, **Split-S**, and **Half-Cuban-Eight**. In instruments phase, students are tortured in the simulator with various emergencies and **partial panel** approaches. In the aircraft, they will learn the fundamentals of Instrument Flight Rules (IFR) flight and **cross-country flight**. In formation flying (many students' favorite phase), they practice **interval takeoffs**, **crossunders**, **lead changes**, **breakup-and-rendezvous** both as the **lead** and **wingman**.

7 There is no doubt that the structure produces **top-notch** aviators. For example, a **private pilot** candidate needs 40 hours to take the private pilot **check ride** before they can follow **Visual Flight Rules (VFR)** to fly in a single engine airplane. In fact, the national average is approximately 60 hours to take the check ride.

8 Contrast that with a Primary graduate. After 70 hours' practice, the pilot is competent enough to fly a high-performance and complex **turbine aircraft** under IFR, as well as fly aerobatics and formation. It is definitely not for the faint of heart! Typically the Primary instructors come from the fleet **Maritime** (P-3[1] and P-8[2]) and Rotary communities, and are among the best their community has to offer.

A McDonnell Douglas/British Aerospace T-45C Goshawk departs NAF El Centro, California.

9 At the end of the Primary, the SNAs will fill out a "**dream sheet**" of what community they want to join. Based on their preferences, their grades, and the needs of the service, they will get their assignments. For the Navy students, they can select Maritime, Rotary, E-2[3]/C-2[4], or jets. The Marines can select Rotary, jets, **tiltrotor** and **props**.

10 Those SNAs selecting jets will transfer to NAS Kingsville[5], Texas or NAS

---

1 **P-3:** 全称 P-3C Orion，P-3C "猎户" 反潜机，四发涡桨，主要用于反潜和海上监视。

2 **P-8:** 全称 P-8A Poseidon，P-8A "海神" 反潜巡逻机，由波音 737-800ERX 改装，高涵道涡扇发动机，开放式任务系统架构，具备反潜战和反水面战能力。

3 **E-2:** 全称 E-2C Hawkeye，E-2C "鹰眼" 预警机，美国海军的全天候舰载空中战术预警和控制系统平台。

4 **C-2:** C-2 "灰狗" 运输机，用于舰上运送，为航母打击群提供重要的后勤保障。

5 **NAS Kingsville:** 金斯维尔海军航空站，美国海军航空兵第二飞行联队总部所在地，位于得克萨斯州。

Meridian[1], Mississippi to fly the T-45C Goshawk[2]. The syllabus is now much more intense than Primary and is divided into two phases: Phase 1, called "**Intermediate**", and Phase 2, called "**Advanced**". Here the instructors are almost exclusively from the F/A-18 community, with some from the E-2/C-2 and AV-8B Harrier[3] communities as well.

11   Phase 1 is like Primary on **steroids**. Here the same things are taught, but refined for jet aircraft with additional advanced concepts. For example, in Primary, the students will fly in **formations** of two aircraft; in Phase 1 they will fly in formations of four aircraft and learn **tactical formation flying (TACFORM)**. E-2/C-2 students will be sent to NAS Corpus Christi for **multi-engine training** after Phase 1.

12   In Phase 2, SNAs get their first taste of true Naval Aviation. Tactical concepts are taught in various phases like advanced TACFORM, **Night Formation**, **Weapons System (WEPS)**, **Air Combat Maneuvering (ACM)**, and the most important one is the **Carrier Qualification (CQ)**.

13   In the TACFORM phase, students learn how to maneuver dynamically from the "**spread formation**" one nautical mile apart. In the WEPS phase, SNAs master the principles of unguided **bombing**, as well as low **altitude** attacks and **Continuously Computed Impact Point (CCIP)** bombing. In the ACM phase, students learn the fundamentals of 1v1 **perch Basic Fighter Maneuver (BFM)**, as well as **neutral high aspect** and 2v1 concepts. Phase 2 contains a lot of work, but still has a lot of fun.

14   For CQ, students will take **Field Carrier Landing Practice (FCLP)** both in Phase 1 and Phase 2 in preparation to go to the boat. A class of a dozen or two SNAs will be assigned to an **Landing Signal Officer (LSO)** to teach them the art of **meatball**, **lineup**, and **angle of attack**. The **landing pattern** will be flown precisely and each **pass** at the field will be graded and **debriefed**. The LSOs will use their judgment to discover trends and **corrective action** for students' performance. When they are ready, they will go to a **fleet aircraft carrier** for their CQ which lasts over the course of a couple of days.

---

1 **NAS Meridian:** 默里迪恩海军航空站，美国海军两个攻击战斗机训练地之一，位于密西西比州。

2 **T-45C Goshawk:** T-45C "苍鹰" 教练机，纵列座椅配置，喷气式发动机，用于海军和海军陆战队飞行员的中级和高级飞行训练，可上舰。

3 **AV-8B Harrier:** AV-8B 鹞式飞机，单座攻击机，可垂直或短距起降，为海军陆战队提供空中支援。

The Wings of Gold

15   The SNAs are **solo** the entire time at the boat, and most likely are suffering from a helmet fire[1] at least on the first day. After 4 **touch-and-goes** and 10 **traps**, if they meet the minimum **boarding rate** and **Grade Point Average (GPA)**, they've qualified and can join the proud few who wear the Wings of Gold[2]. Students always make bets with their LSOs on their performance, and almost lose. These include things as simple as "3 **wire** on the first pass" to the **fabled** IronMan: no **bolters**, **waveoffs**, or 1 wire. It gets **pricey** for the SNAs but worth for the wings!

16   Dream sheets are again submitted for platform and location. For the Navy pilots, they can be sent to one of three locations: NAS Oceana[3] to fly the F/A-18 Hornet[4] or Super Hornet[5], NAS Lemoore[6] to fly the Super Hornet, or NAS Whidbey[7] Island to fly the E/A-18G Growler[8]. USMC pilots will either go to NAS Oceana or **Marine Corps Air Station (MCAS)** Miramar[9] for the Hornet, MCAS Cherry Point[10] or MCAS Yuma[11] to fly the Harrier, and now MCAS Beaufort[12] (and Yuma, too) to fly the F-35B Lightning II[13].

17   The Naval Aviators join these **Fleet Replacement Squadrons (FRS)** (nicknamed "**RAGs**", Replacement Air Group) to learn the **ins and outs** of their fleet aircraft. This is **analogous** to the **United States Air Force's (USAF)** B-Course[14]. The F/A-18 syllabus is divided into four phases: **transition**, **Air-to-Surface**, **Air-to-Air**, and CQ.

---

1 **helmet fire:** "头脑断片",指因高压任务负荷和丧失态势感知而引起的反常心理状态。

2 **Wings of Gold:** "金翼"飞行证章。

3 **NAS Oceana:** 奥西安纳海军航空站,美国海军主要喷气机基地,位于弗吉尼亚州。

4 **F/A-18 Hornet:** F/A-18 "大黄蜂"战斗／攻击机,双发多用途,可上舰。

5 **Super Hornet:** F/A-18 "超级大黄蜂"战斗机,F/A-18 "大黄蜂"的改进升级型,双发多用途舰载机。

6 **NAS Lemoore:** 勒莫尔海军航空站,主要为太平洋舰队提供保障。

7 **NAS Whidbey:** 惠德贝岛航空站,所有美国海军战术电子攻击中队的基地。

8 **E/A-18G Growler:** E/A-18G "咆哮者"电子战飞机,双座"超级大黄蜂"的特种机型。

9 **MCAS Miramar:** 米拉玛海军陆战队航空站,美国海军陆战队第三飞行联队所在地。

10 **MCAS Cherry Point:** 樱桃角海军陆战队航空站,美国海军陆战队第二飞行联队所在地。

11 **MCAS Yuma:** 尤玛海军陆战队航空站,AV-8B 和 F-35B 多个中队的所在地。

12 **MCAS Beaufort:** 博福特海军陆战队航空站。

13 **F-35B Lightning II:** F-35B 闪电 II,联合攻击战斗机的陆战队机型,具有短距起飞垂直降落能力。

14 **USAF's B-Course:** 美国空军基础飞行课程。

18   In Transition, the students will apply what they learned in the T-45C to the Hornet, except now the expectation is that they already know how to fly. The fifth flight is the very first solo. After a few formation flights (including night TACFORM), they will move into **all-weather-radar intercepts**, and **aerial refueling**.

19   In **Air-to-Ground**, the aviators will learn bombing fundamentals as well as how to **strafe** the mighty 20mm gun. Also the **Low Altitude Training (LAT)** phase will be included where the pilots will **hone** their **low-level flying** skills at 200 feet **Above Ground Level (AGL)** and over 480 Knots. Students will develop these skills in the unguided "circle the wagons"[1] **weapons pattern**, before applying what they learned to the art of **Close Air Support (CAS)**.

20   The CAS flights will use traditional methods such as **Initial Point (IP)** to target, as well as low-threat CAS from overhead the target area, and high-threat CAS with a **low altitude ingress** to a **pop attack**. The phase also includes flights that practice the use of smart weapons, such as the GBU-12 Paveway II[2], GBU-38 JDAM[3], and AGM-65E Laser Maverick[4].

21   In Air-to-Air, they will learn modern fighter tactics, starting with basic **2v2 setups** and eventually into 4vX missions such as an **Offensive Counter-Air (OCA)**, **Defensive Counter-Air (DCA)**, or **self-escort-strike**. This phase is also when students try their best at the instructors at BFM, in addition to learning about how to use weapons such as the AIM-9X Sidewinder[5] and AIM-120 AMRAAM[6].

22   Finally, CQ phase is nearly identical to the T-45C, except now the aviators have to land on the boat at night! Those 2 night touch-and-goes and 6 night traps allowed me to not only earn my place in the fleet, but also get my very first gray hair.

---

1 **circle the wagons:** 把篷车围成一圈，引申义为众人合作，严阵以待；本文中指轮式航线。

2 **GBU-12 Paveway II:** "宝石路"II型激光制导炸弹。

3 **GBU-38 JDAM:** "杰达姆"系列联合直接攻击武器。

4 **AGM-65E Laser Maverick:** AGM-65E 激光制导空对地导弹。

5 **AIM-9X Sidewinder:** AIM-9X "响尾蛇"短程空对空导弹。

6 **AIM-120 AMRAAM:** AIM-120 高级中程空对空导弹。

23   After the completion of the FRS syllabus, aviators are sent to fleet squadrons on both coasts, as well as Japan. All in all, it's a very long road to earn those Wings of Gold. Then again, if it were easy…the Air Force would do it!

Fly Navy!

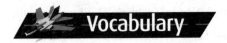 **Vocabulary**

Special Terms

2v2 setup 二对二起始态势设置

Above Ground Level (AGL) 离地高度

Advanced (advanced training) 【口语】高级训练

aerobatics/aerobatic flight 特技飞行

aerodynamics 空气动力学

aerial refueling 空中加油

Aileron Roll 副翼操纵式横滚（飞行特技）

Air Combat Maneuvering (ACM) 空战机动

Air-to-Air 空对空（的）

Air-to-Ground 空对地（的）

Air-to-Surface 空对面（的）

all-weather-radar intercept 全天候雷达截击

altitude 高度；地平纬度

angle of attack 攻角，迎角

Aviation Preflight Indoctrination (API) 飞行前航空教育

Barrel Roll 桶滚（飞行特技）

Basic Fighter Maneuvers (BFM) 基本空战机动

boarding rate 上舰率

bolter 逃逸，拦阻失效后的起飞，触舰复飞；接地后复飞

bombing 轰炸

breakup-and-rendezvous 解散和集合

Carrier Qualifications (CQ) 航母上舰资格认证，航母飞行资质认证

check ride 检查飞行；考核飞行

Close Air Support (CAS) 近距空中支援

Continuously Computed Impact Point (CCIP) 连续计算弹着点

commissioned officer 军官

corrective action 修正的动作

cross-country flight 跨区长途飞行；转场飞行

crossunder 下方交叉（飞行动作）

debrief 飞行后讲评

Defensive Counter-Air (DCA) 防御性防空

dream sheet 分配意愿表

familiarization flight (FAM) 熟悉（机型）飞行

Field Carrier Landing Practice (FCLP) 舰载机陆基着舰练习

fighter 战斗机；歼击机

fleet aircraft carrier 舰队航母

flight suit 飞行服

formation 编队

formation flying / formation flight 编队飞行

Fleet Replacement Squadron (FRS) 舰队补充中队，舰队替补中队

Grade Point Average (GPA) 平均绩点分

Half-Cuban-Eight 半古巴八字（飞行特技）

high aspect 大进入角

Immelman 殷麦曼翻转，半斤斗翻转（飞行特技）

Initial Point (IP) 起始点，出发点；轰炸航路起点

instruments/instrument flight 【口语】仪表飞行

interval takeoff 间隔起飞

Intermediate (intermediate training) 【口语】中级训练

landing pattern 着陆航线；着舰航线

Low Altitude Training (LAT) 低空训练

lead 长机

lead change 长僚机变换

lineup 对准跑道

low altitude ingress 低空进入

low-level flying 低空飞行

Landing Signal Officer (LSO) 着舰指挥官，着舰信号官

Marine Corps Air Station (MCAS) 海军陆战队航空站

Maritime (maritime aircraft) 【口语】海上飞机

meatball / the ball （光学助降系统的俗称）灯球，光球，肉球

multi-engine training 多发飞机训练

Naval Air Station (NAS) 海军航空站

Naval Aviator 海军飞行员

navigation 导航；领航；航行

neutral 均势；中立

Night Formation 夜间编队

night trap 夜间拦阻着舰

Offensive Counter-Air (OCA) 进攻性防空

partial panel 部分航行仪表

pass 航母着舰尝试

perch 设置就位；栖木

pop/pop-up attack 跃升攻击；突袭

Primary (primary training) 【口语】初级飞行训练

private pilot 私人飞机驾驶员

prop 【口语】螺旋桨飞机

Replacement Air Group (RAG) 补充航空大队

self-escort-strike 自我护航打击

sim 模拟器模拟飞行

solo 单飞

Split-S 半滚倒转（飞行特技）

spread formation 墙形疏开队形

squadron （海军或空军的）中队

strafe 低空扫射（或轰炸）

Student Naval Aviator (SNA) 海军飞行学员

Student Naval Flight Officer (SNFO) 海军空勤军官学员

survival training 生存训练

survival skill 生存技能

tactical formation flying (TACFORM) 战术编队飞行

tiltrotor 倾转旋翼机

touch-and-go 触舰复飞；连续起飞

transition 机型改装

trap 拦阻着舰，挂索

turbine aircraft 燃气涡轮式飞机

United States Air Force (USAF) 美国空军

US Coast Guard 美国海岸警备队

United States Marine Corps (USMC) 美国海军陆战队

Visual Flight Rules (VFR) 目视飞行规则

waveoff 复飞

weapons pattern 武器攻击航线

Weapons System (WEPS) 武器系统训练

wingman 僚机

wire (arresting wire) 拦阻索

Words and Expressions

analogous	[ə'næləgəs]	a.	相似的，类似的
concurrent	[kən'kʌrənt]	a.	同时发生的；同时完成的
culminate	['kʌlmɪneɪt]	v.	（在某一点）结束；（以某种结果）告终
encompass	[ɪn'kʌmpəs]	v.	包含；包围
fabled	['feɪbld]	a.	传说中的
hone	[həʊn]	v.	磨炼，训练（尤指技艺）
panhandle	['pænhændl]	a.	突出的狭长行政区域
pricey	['praɪsi]	a.	昂贵的
steroid	['stɪrɔɪd]	n.	类固醇；甾族化合物
top-notch	['tɒp nɒtʃ]	a.	最好的，卓越的
workhorse	['wɜːkhɔːs]	n.	耐用的机器；吃苦耐劳的人
ins and outs			细节；来龙去脉

 **Exercises**

Comprehension of the Text

I. Complete the following table with the information from the text.

Program	Subject	Event	Location	Duration	Participant
API	Academics				
	Survival training				
Primary training: T-6B Texan II	FAMs				
	Aerobatics				
	Instruments				
	Formation flying				
Intermediate phase: T-45C Goshawk	Refined for jet aircraft, advanced concepts				
Advanced phase: T-45C Goshawk	TACFORM				
	Night Formation				
	WEPS				
	ACM				
	CQ				
FRS	F/A-18 syllabus				

II. Answer the following questions according to the text.

1. What is the Naval Air Station Pensacola known as? Why?

_____

2. What is a "dream sheet" used for?

_____

3. How do you understand "Phase 1 is like Primary on steroids" (Para. 11)?

_____

4. What does "the fabled IronMan" (Para. 15) mean?

_____

5. What is the major duty of an LSO?

_____

6. What can you learn from the last sentence of Para. 22?

_____

Vocabulary Practice

III. Complete each of the following definitions with a special term from the box. Change the form if necessary.

aerobatics	bolter	check ride	waveoff	transition	wingman
formation	meatball	altitude	squadron	instrument	aerial refueling

1. A(n) _____ is a pilot who flies at the side and to the rear of an element leader, commonly in a two-plane or three-plane formation.
2. A(n) _____ refers to a grouping or arrangement of two or more airborne aircraft in a pattern arranged for specific purposes, as for attack, security or review.
3. A(n) _____ is a flight on which a pilot or another aircrew member is checked for proficiency in the performance of his duty.
4. The act of refusing a landing to an approaching plane is called _____ .
5. The _____ training refers to the training given a pilot or other crew member as he moves from the operation of one type of aircraft to another.
6. _____ flying is the flying in which navigation is carried out by the use of flight and navigational instruments without visual reference to the ground.

7. In the USAF, a(n) _____ is a unit at a level of command immediately below, and usually subordinate to, a group.

8. _____ refers to the art or action of performing aerial feats with an airplane or glider or an instance of such flying.

9. _____, or the ball, refers to the amber light in the ship's mirror which gives the pilot glideslope information.

10. _____ means an intended arrested landing where the hook fails to engage a wire, so the pilot has to go around for another attempt.

11. A vertical distance from the ground or sea level is called _____, which is usually measured in feet.

12. _____ is a procedure used by the military to transfer fuel from one aircraft to another during flight.

IV. Give the full names of the following abbreviations.

1. API _____   2. SNA _____
3. NAS _____   4. SNFO _____
5. IFR _____   6. VFR _____
7. ACM _____   8. BFM _____
9. AOA _____   10. TACFORM _____
11. LSO _____   12. AGL _____
13. CAS _____   14. FCLP _____
15. FRS _____   16. USAF _____
17. USMC _____   18. CQ _____
19. CCIP _____   20. GPA _____

Listening Practice

V. Watch the video clip about aviation preflight indoctrination and fill in the blanks.

Right now I'm in aviation preflight indoctrination which is 6 weeks of academics and survival training. Yesterday, I had *1*_____ class; basically we learned about all the different types of engines that we could be flying someday. Having an *2*_____ degree, a lot of information was familiar but it's not so much how an engine works but what you do wrong that makes the engine not work is what will stick with us the most. After that we had 3_____ class. "Understanding where you are at and where you wanna go, that's navigation." To finish aviation preflight indoctrination, we have to pass 4_____ tests. And we have to get through the survival training. For the survival training, we learn how to swim through the water if the 5_____ is on fire, if there's debris on fire, just how to conserve our energy, how to flow, you know, waiting for 6_____ to come. Today's challenge is a mile swim in 7_____ suit. So we put flight suits on and 8_____ if you were to crash in the ocean or any body of water, and you have to swim to 9_____, that's one thing that we get tested on. I love swimming, I was on a swim team in high school so I am not nervous and I'm actually really excited for it. I remembered we were about 10_____ through and I was thinking if only I didn't have this flight suit on now I would have been done already. So, it really slows you down.

Translating Practice

VI. Translate the following sentences into Chinese.

1. The prerequisites to become a Naval Aviator are the same as for the Air Force: candidates must be commissioned officers and meet a set of strict physical requirements.

   _____

   _____

2. In Primary, SNAs are put through a fast-paced syllabus of classes, sims, and flights. The syllabus starts with familiarization flights (FAMs), and then moves quickly into aerobatics, instruments, and formation flying.

   _____

   _____

3. Students will develop these skills in the unguided "circle the wagons" weapons pattern, before applying what they learned to the art of Close Air Support (CAS).

   _____

   _____

4. The CAS flights will use traditional methods such as Initial Point (IP) to target, as well as low-threat CAS from overhead the target area, and high-threat CAS with a low altitude ingress to a pop attack.

_____

_____

5. In Air-to-Air they will learn modern fighter tactics, starting with basic 2v2 setups and eventually into 4vX missions such as an Offensive Counter-Air (OCA), Defensive Counter-Air (DCA), or self-escort-strike.

_____

_____

🧭 TEXT C

Ask a Fighter Pilot: What Are My Chances of Making It?

Jack Stewart[1]

1   *I'm a prospective candidate going into the Naval Academy[2] wanting to become an aviator afterwards and I was curious about how many people going into flight school want to be a fighter pilot after becoming an officer? And what is the expectancy of the military to actually maintain combat pilots with the ever-increasing roles of the newer* **drones** *(无人机)?*
                                                                                    —Josh C.

2   Thanks for the question, Josh! First of all, let me commend you on your desire to serve your country. We hear a lot about the "greatest generation" being those who signed up to fight the Nazis and the Japanese in World War II, but I am here to tell you that the greatest generation still exists today. To understand why, I think it's worth putting military service into perspective.

---

1   **Jack Stewart:** F/A18 的假想机飞行员，他也是商业航空公司飞行员。

2   **Naval Academy:** 美国海军学院，美国海军部下属的高等院校，为海军和海军陆战队培养初级军官，位于马里兰州的安纳波利斯。

3   The United States military saw its greatest increase in strength of **active duty personnel** (现役人员) between 1940 to 1945 when it grew from less than half a million to over 12 million. Today, roughly 120 million people (less than half of the total US population) is fit for military service.

4   Over 4 million young men and women reach the age of military service each year, yet we are fighting a global war with an active duty force of 1.4 million. Think about that for a second—just 1% of Americans fit for military service are actually serving. You are in the fortunate minority and I applaud you for ushering in the next greatest generation!

5   To be sure, you and the young men and women who will join the military in the coming years will see the drone fleet continue to grow, although you will probably see a greater increase in the commercial market for drone technology—as much as 19% between 2015 and 2020, compared to 5% in the defense sector. Part of that disparity in growth is due to the fact that the US military has already been operating drones—quite effectively, I might add—in overseas contingency operations since 2001. The Pentagon has acknowledged the value that drones [also known as Remotely Piloted Aircraft (RPA)] provide our combatant commanders and projects a 50% increase in daily drone sorties in the next four years.

6   But, fear not. I predict that the US military will continue to invest in manned aircraft until long after I am gone. Part of the reason is philosophical in that I believe war must continue to have a human element involved to be morally just. But, a larger reason is that drones are very good at some things (such as remaining overhead a target for long periods of time to provide an unblinking eye), but are not ideal for providing support to troops in contact on the ground. Having been on both ends of the radio during Close Air Support missions, I can tell you that there is a psychological effect (positive for our forces and negative for the enemy) to have an A-10, F/A-18, F-16, or other strike platform overhead. A drone just won't do.

7   If you're still not convinced, the published *Naval Aviation Vision*[1] (2014–2025) does not project replacing existing manned aircraft with RPAs and focuses on

---

1 Naval Aviation Vision: 《美国海军航空兵愿景》，其中包括为海军和海军陆战队提供的路线图。

recapitalization（资本额的调整）of assets to meet the demands of the future. That is what we like to call "job security"—Hooray for pilots!

8   You will already be in an elite 1% of Americans serving in the military. Regardless of what warfare community you are assigned to upon graduation, you are serving a vital role. The US Naval Academy Class of 2016 selected 241 **midshipmen**（海军院校学员）for Navy pilot, 79 for Navy NFO, 95 for Marine Corps pilot, and 4 for Marine Corps NFO—almost 40% of the graduating midshipmen pursuing a career in aviation. You will also be competing with newly commissioned officers from the Naval Reserve Officers Training Corps (NROTC)[1] program and Officer Candidate School (OCS)[2] that makes up 75% of all new officers. And, no matter where you go to, you will be competing with all of them. But, how many of you will end up sitting in the cockpit as a fighter pilot?

9   Following D-Day in World War II, the US had a total of 12,200 aircraft in the European theater. Today, the combined US military has roughly 13,000 aircraft—of which only 5,000 are fighter, attack or bomber aircraft. And, although the numbers change from year to year, roughly 400 Navy and Marine Corps pilots earn their Wings of Gold each year after completing the year-long jet training syllabus in either Kingsville, Texas or Meridian, Mississippi.

10   Not to discourage you, but you will defy the odds by becoming a fighter pilot. The US Naval Academy Class of 2019 had 16,101 applicants and admitted 1,191. If history proves accurate, 1,100 will graduate in three years. Of those, 240 will select to be Navy pilots and 80 will enter into jet training. By the time the Class of 2019 reaches the fleet, maybe 50 will be fighter pilots.

11   So, for every 1,000 applicants to the Class of 2019, 3 will become a fighter pilot.

12   Now, that is what I call the greatest generation! Good luck!

---

1 **Naval Reserve Officers Training Corps (NROTC):** 海军后备军官训练团，基于地方高校的美国海军和海军陆战队军官训练项目。

2 **Officer Candidate School (OCS):** 候补军官学校，训练平民或士兵，使其将来能在军队中任职军官。

Exercises

Comprehension of the Text

Decide whether the following statements are true (T) or false (F) according to the text.

(   ) *1.* There is an increase of 5% in the defense sector for drone technology.

(   ) *2.* The value of drones has not been acknowledged by the Pentagon.

(   ) *3.* Owing to a 50% increase in daily drone sorties, the US military will probably not continue to invest in manned aircraft.

(   ) *4.* Drones are ideal for providing support to troops in contact on the ground.

(   ) *5.* The *Naval Aviation Vision* (2014–2025) has projected replacing existing manned aircraft with RPAs.

(   ) *6.* The US Naval Academy Class of 2016 selected almost 40% of the graduating midshipmen pursuing a career in aviation.

(   ) *7.* According to the author, if this pilot candidate dares to defy the odds, he will become a fighter pilot.

(   ) *8.* The percentage of becoming a fighter pilot in the Class of 2019 is 0.3%.

⊘ UNIT PROJECT

Work in groups and draw a flowchart to show the training process that a pilot candidate has to undergo on the way to becoming a US navy fighter pilot.

Oral Practice

Work in groups and discuss the qualities that a good Naval Aviator should possess. And one student from each group will make a 3-minute oral presentation according to the discussion. You may refer to the texts of this unit and the relevant information from the Internet.

Writing Practice

Based on the discussion above, write a composition with at least 150 words on the topic of "Becoming a Qualified Naval Aviator". You may refer to the outline below.

1. the necessity of being a qualified Naval Aviator
2. good qualities that a competent Naval Aviator should possess
3. your resolution to become a qualified Naval Aviator

Unit 2
Naval Aviator
Training

Warming Up

Task 1 Watch the video clip about the traffic patterns and fill in the blanks.

When taking off or landing at airports, pilots use a standardized traffic pattern. The traffic pattern's main purpose is to ensure that *1*_____ flows into and out of the airport in an orderly manner. This makes the airport environment safer since all aircraft should be following the same *2*_____. The basic traffic pattern is similar at all airports, whether it is controlled by a *3*_____ or a non-towered airport. The traffic pattern consists of a rectangular shape made up of five different *4*_____: *5*_____, *6*_____, *7*_____, *8*_____ and *9*_____.

The standard traffic pattern is referred to as *10*_____ traffic. This means that all turns in the pattern are made to the left. A runway could also have a non-standard or *11*_____ traffic pattern where all turns are made to the right. At most airports, the traffic pattern is typically flown *12*_____ feet above the elevation of the airport.

The pilot should enter the pattern on a *13*_____ angle to the downwind leg flying towards the approach end of the runway. When within about one mile of the runway, a turn should be made to enter the downwind leg flying *14*_____ to the runway and in the opposite direction of landing. The pilot should then fly two 90-degree turns: one turn to the base leg and the other turn to the final leg while descending to his *15*_____ point on the runway. This allows them to properly set up for landing and to sequence themselves with other air traffic.

Task 2 Discuss the following questions in groups.

1. As a student pilot, what flight training have you ever received?

2. What do you think of the flight training you have received?

3. Do you have any knowledge about the further training that you will take?

⊘ TEXT A

Naval Aviator Training Pipelines

1   The **Chief of Naval Air Training** (**CNATRA**) headquartered at NAS Corpus Christi, Texas oversees the **Naval Air Training Command** (**NATRACOM**) whose mission is to safely train and produce the world's finest combat quality aviation professionals—Naval Aviators and Naval Flight Officers—and deliver them at the right time, in the right numbers, and at the right cost to the fleet for follow-on tasking in the Global War on Terror.

2   CNATRA conducts seven Student Naval Aviator training **pipelines**—Strike, Rotary, Maritime Patrol, Multi-engine, Tiltrotor, E-2/C-2, and E-6[1]. Strike and intermediate E-2/C-2 training are conducted at Training Air Wing ONE[2] and TWO[3] at NAS Meridian, Mississippi, and NAS Kingsville, Texas. Maritime Patrol, Multi-engine, advanced Tiltrotor, and E-2/C-2 training are conducted at Training Air Wing FOUR[4] at NAS Corpus Christi, Texas. Rotary and intermediate Tiltrotor training are conducted at Training Air Wing FIVE[5] at NAS Whiting Field in Milton, Florida.

Primary Training

3   The foundation of a Naval Aviator's development begins in the primary phase of training. Primary training is conducted in the T-34C at **VT**-27 or VT-28 at Training Air Wing FOUR, VT-2 or VT-6 at Training Air Wing FIVE, or in the new T-6B at VT-3 also at Training Air Wing FIVE.

4   The T-6B replaced the T-34C Turbo Mentor as the primary training aircraft in April 2015. Its digital **avionics** provides fighter-type **maneuverability** with a modern glass cockpit including a **Head-Up Display (HUD), Up-Front Control Panel, Multi-**

---

1 **E-6:** 全称 E-6 MERCURY (TACAMO)，E-6 "水星"（美国抗毁战略通信系统）。
2 **Training Air Wing ONE:** 美国海军航空兵第一飞行训练联队。
3 **Training Air Wing TWO:** 美国海军航空兵第二飞行训练联队。
4 **Training Air Wing FOUR:** 美国海军航空兵第四飞行训练联队。
5 **Training Air Wing FIVE:** 美国海军航空兵第五飞行训练联队。

Function Displays (MFD), **Hands-On Throttle and Stick (HOTAS)**, and a **Global Positioning System (GPS)** with **wide-area augmentation system** and required navigation performance. The T-6B cockpit and avionics **suite** is designed to better **facilitate** the transition to increasingly **sophisticated follow-on training** and fleet aircraft, as well as **keep pace with** emerging **air traffic control** regulations.

5   The T-6B **trainer** is an integral part of the **Joint Primary Aircraft Training System (JPATS)**, a joint venture with the Air Force, which encompasses aircraft, simulators, **courseware**, syllabus and training aids. JPATS utilizes **Training Integrated Management System (TIMS)** to manage and deliver course content. The entire **curriculum** and daily activities of students and instructors are **scheduled** and tracked to ensure accurate and efficient training from the first day of training to **winging**.

6   Simulated instrument training in the T-34C is conducted in **non-visual instrument devices**. T-6B training has been significantly **enhanced** with a suite of **high-fidelity visual simulators**.

Pilot Training Pipeline

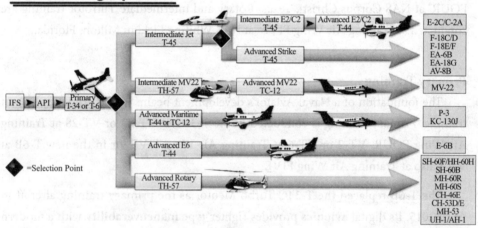

Strike (Tailhook) Training

7   Intermediate and advanced Strike training are conducted in the T-45A and C Goshawk at VT-7 or VT-9 at Training Air Wing ONE or VT-21 or VT-22 at Training Air Wing TWO. This syllabus is the foundation upon which all **tailhook aviators** build their carrier experience. Student Naval Aviators are selected to continue training

in either the advanced Strike or advanced E-2/C-2 pipelines **at the conclusion of** an intermediate Strike syllabus.

8   The Strike pipeline fills fleet seats for the F/A-18A+ through F Hornet or Super Hornet, EA-6B Prowler[1], EA-18G Growler, and AV-8B Harrier in the Navy and Marine Corps. Future F-35 Lightning II pilots will also come from the Strike pipeline.

9   Student Naval Aviators selected for the E-2/C-2 pipeline **at the completion of** the intermediate phase of the Strike pipeline report to Training Air Wing FOUR for Multi-engine training in the T-44A/C[2] or TC-12[3] before receiving their Wings.

10   As CNATRA rapidly moves toward an all T-45C digital **configuration**, all Student Naval Aviators will receive top quality training in a technologically advanced cockpit to **optimally** prepare for fleet **digital/glass cockpit** aircraft of today and tomorrow. With **numerous** cockpit **similarities** to the F/A-18A+ through G series, the digital Goshawk enables the potential future downloading of **Fleet Readiness Squadron** (**FRS**) training at a considerable reduction in cost per **flight hour**. The T-45C is planned to meet CNATRA's Strike training requirements through 2025.

Rotary and Tiltrotor Training

11   Rotary and intermediate Tiltrotor training are conducted in the TH-57B and C Sea Ranger[4] at **HT**-8, HT-18, and HT-28 at Training Air Wing FIVE. The Rotary pipeline provides fundamental and advanced Rotary skills for Student Naval Aviators selected for fleet service in the AH-1 Cobra[5], UH-1 Huey[6], H-46 Sea Knight[7], H-53 Sea Stallion[8], H-60 Seahawk[9] series, HH-65 Dolphin[10], MH-68 Sting Ray[11] in the Navy,

---

1   **EA-6B Prowler:** EA-6B "徘徊者" 电子战飞机。

2   **T-44A/C:** T-44A/C "飞马" 高级海上教练机。

3   **TC-12:** 全称 TC-12 Huron，TC-12 "休伦人" 教练机。

4   **TH-57B and C Sea Ranger:** TH-57B 和 TH-57C "海上游骑兵" 直升机教练机。

5   **AH-1 Cobra:** AH-1 "眼镜蛇" 武装直升机。

6   **UH-1 Huey:** UH-1 "休伊" 多用途直升机。

7   **H-46 Sea Knight:** H-46 "海上骑士" 运输直升机。

8   **H-53 Sea Stallion:** H-53 "海上种马" 运输直升机。

9   **H-60 Seahawk:** H-60 "海鹰" 直升机。

10   **HH-65 Dolphin:** HH-65 "海豚" 直升机。

11   **MH-68 Sting Ray:** MH-68 "黄貂鱼" 直升机。

Marine Corps and Coast Guard. Marine students **designated** for the MV-22 Osprey Tiltrotor[1] receive intermediate Rotary training at Training Air Wing FIVE and then report to Training Air Wing FOUR for Multi-engine training in the T-44A/C or TC-12 before receiving their Wings.

12   CNATRA is pursuing a single type model series TH-57D to **incorporate** the latest digital technology with a **Night Vision Goggles (NVG) compatible** digital cockpit to enhance training by closely **emulating** digital/glass fleet cockpits. The TH-57D will **eliminate** the transition flight **syllabi** between the B and C models and reduce total aircraft **inventory** requirements. The TH-57D will be supported by high fidelity visual simulators that will enable the downloading and the optimal mix of flight and simulator syllabi.

Maritime Patrol, Multi-engine and Advanced Tiltrotor Training

13   Maritime, multi-engine, and advanced tiltrotor training are conducted in the T-44A and C Pegasus and TC-12B Huron at VT-31 and VT-35 in Training Air Wing FOUR. The Maritime Patrol, Multi-engine, and advanced Tiltrotor pipelines provide foundational training for Student Naval Aviators and Air Force pilots selected to fill fleet seats in the P-3C Orion, C-130 Hercules[2], HU-25 Guardian Falcon[3], E-2C/D Hawkeye, C-2A Greyhound, MV-22 Osprey and C-12 Huron[4].

14   Training Air Wing FOUR is slowly **converting analog** T-44As to digital T-44Cs which is the perfect lead-in trainer for the digital/glass cockpit P-8 Poseidon, MV-22 Osprey and C-130J Hercules aircraft. High fidelity T-44C visual simulators are to follow, when funding is available, which will enable the perfect mix of ground and air training, as well as the means to **divest** the entire TC-12 Huron fleet as a training aircraft.

---

1   **MV-22 Osprey Tiltrotor:** MV-22 "鱼鹰" 倾转旋翼机。

2   **C-130 Hercules:** C-130 "大力神" 运输机。

3   **HU-25 Guardian Falcon:** HU-25 "卫兵" 效用机。

4   **C-12 Huron:** C-12 "休伦人" 运输机。

Special Terms

air traffic control 空中交通管制

avionics 航空电子设备；航空电子学

Chief of Naval Air Training (CNATRA) 美国海军航空兵训练总部

digital/glass cockpit 数字／玻璃座舱

Fleet Readiness Squadron (FRS) 舰队预备中队

flight hour 飞行时数

follow-on training 后续训练

Global Positioning System (GPS) 全球定位系统

Hands-On Throttle and Stick (HOTAS) 手不离杆系统

Head-Up Display (HUD) 平视显示仪

high-fidelity visual simulator 高逼真度可视化模拟器

HT (helicopter training squadron) 直升机训练中队

Joint Primary Aircraft Training System (JPATS) 联合初级飞机训练体系

maneuverability 机动性，机动能力

maritime patrol training 海上巡逻机训练

Multi-Function Display (MFD) 多功能工作状态显示仪

Naval Air Training Command (NATRACOM) 海军航空兵训练司令部

non-visual instrument device 非可视化仪表设备

Night Vision Goggles (NVG) 夜视镜

strike training 攻击机训练

tailhook aviator 舰载机飞行员

Training Integrated Management System (TIMS) 训练综合管理系统

trainer 教练机；（地面用的）训练设备，练习器；教练员

up-front control panel 前上方驾驶仪表板

VT (fixed wing training squadron) 固定翼飞机训练中队

wide-area augmentation system 广域增强系统

winging 取得飞机驾驶员资格

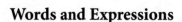

Words and Expressions

analog	['ænəlɒg]	a.	模拟的；指针式的
augmentation	[ˌɔːgmen'teɪʃn]	n.	增大；增强
compatible	[kəm'pætəbl]	a.	兼容的；可共用的
configuration	[kənˌfɪgə'reɪʃn]	n.	构型，结构；配置；布局
convert	[kən'vɜːt]	v.	转换；（使）转变
courseware	['kɔːsweə]	n.	课件
curriculum	[kə'rɪkjələm]	n.	全部课程
designate	['dezɪgnət]	v.	指定；指派
divest	[daɪ'vest]	v.	处理掉；（使）解除；（使）摆脱
emulate	['emjuleɪt]	v.	仿真；模仿
enhance	[ɪn'hæns]	v.	提高；增强
eliminate	[ɪ'lɪmɪneɪt]	v.	消除；排除；根除；（比赛中）淘汰
facilitate	[fə'sɪlɪteɪt]	v.	帮助，促进；促使
fidelity	[fɪ'deləti]	n.	保真度；忠诚
incorporate	[ɪn'kɔːpəreɪt]	v.	将……包括在内，包含
inventory	['ɪnvəntri]	n.	清单；库存
numerous	['njuːmərəs]	a.	众多的，许多的
optimally	['ɒptɪməli]	ad.	最优地；最佳地
pipeline	['paɪplaɪn]	n.	途径；管道
schedule	['skedʒəl]	v.	安排；预定
similarity	[ˌsɪmə'lærəti]	n.	相像性；相仿性
sophisticated	[sə'fɪstɪkeɪtɪd]	a.	先进的；精密的
suite	[swiːt]	n.	一般通用设备；配套件
syllabus	['sɪləbəs]	n.	（ *pl. syllabi* ）教学大纲
at the conclusion of			当……结束时
at the completion of			在……完成时
keep pace with			与……齐头并进，与……步调一致

 Exercises

Comprehension of the Text

I. Answer the following questions according to the text.

1. What are the seven Student Naval Aviator pipelines that CNATRA conducts?

_____

2. What training is conducted at Training Air Wing FOUR at NAS Corpus Christi, Texas?

_____

3. What devices can a pilot find in the modern glass cockpit of T-6B?

_____

4. What does JPATS encompass?

_____

5. Where is the simulated instrument training in the T-34C conducted?

_____

6. What are the Student Naval Aviators selected to do at the conclusion of an intermediate Strike syllabus?

_____

7. From which pipeline will the Future F-35 Lightning II pilots come?

_____

8. Where do the Student Naval Aviators selected for the E-2/C-2 pipeline report at the completion of the intermediate phase of the Strike pipeline?

_____

9. With numerous cockpit similarities to the F/A-18A+ through G series, what is the advantage of the digital Goshawk?

_____

10. What can the Rotary pipeline provide for Student Naval Aviators selected for fleet service?

_____

11. Where do the Marine students designated for the MV-22 Osprey Tiltrotor receive intermediate Rotary training?

_____

12. Why is the CNATRA pursuing a single type model series TH-57D?

_____

13. What are the purposes of Maritime, Multi-engine and advanced Tiltrotor pipelines?

_____

14. What is Training Air Wing FOUR slowly converting analog T-44As to? Why?

_____

Vocabulary Practice

II. Give the full names of the following abbreviations.

1. CNATRA _____   *2.* HOTAS _____

3. HT _____   *4.* HUD _____

5. JPATS _____   *6.* MFD _____

7. NATRACOM _____   *8.* NVG _____

9. TIMS _____   *10.* VT _____

III. Complete each of the following sentences with a word from the box. Change the form if necessary.

courseware	suite	encompass	optimal	similarity
eliminate	intermediate	sophisticated	facilitate	divest

1. The Badminton Club holds coaching sessions for beginners and _____ players on Friday evenings.

2. He argued that the economic recovery had been _____ by his tough stance.

3. As computer systems become even more _____, so do the methods of those people who exploit the technology.

4. Morris executed a(n) _____ of twelve drawings in 1978.

5. This can potentially _____ thousands of schemas and tables and millions of columns from differing databases and files.

6. This paper introduces the reform of the curriculum from the aspects of teaching objective, teaching content, teaching method, and the _____ resource.

7. How to achieve _____ asset allocation is investigated in this paper.

8. The _____ between Mars and Earth were enough to keep alive hopes of some form of Martian life.

9. He attempted to _____ himself of all responsibilities for the decision.

10. He declared war on the government and urged right-wingers to _____ their opponents.

IV. Complete the following short passage with the words from the box. Change the form if necessary.

wings	intermediate	Joint Training	pipeline
primary	navigation	individual	coordination
curriculum	combat	instrument	visual

Upon the completion of the Pre-Flight, Student Naval Aviators and Student Naval Flight Officers proceed to their separate *1*_____ training pipelines. Primary teaches SNAs the basics of flying. The Navy offers the training at either Naval Air Station Whiting Field in Florida, Naval Air Station Corpus Christi in Texas, or *2*_____ with the Air Force at Vance Air Force Base in Oklahoma. All Naval Air Stations use the T-34C Mentor to train, and Vance Air Force Base uses the T-37B to train for Primary. The SNA learns *3*_____ flight, basic instrument flying, the introduction to aerobatics, radio *4*_____ navigation, formation flying, and they has several solo flights. All flight students go through the same *5*_____ for Primary. At the end of the Primary, the SNA requests the *6*_____ they would like to enter. There are 5 pipeline choices: Jet, E2/C2, Maritime Prop, Helicopter and E-6 TACAMO. *7*_____ Flight Training is different for each of the 5 platforms chosen upon the completion of the primary training. Crew learn more about the *8*_____ and air traffic control by flying to other training bases. Intermediate training for the single-seat aircraft, such as the jet platforms, will focus on *9*_____ skills, while for the

multi-seat platforms, such as maritime props, helicopters and E2/C2, will focus on crew
10_____. Advanced flight training is the final stage in earning **11**_____.
Crew learn skills that is specific to the chosen platform such as air to air **12**_____,
bombing, search and rescue, aircraft carrier qualifications, overwater navigation, and
low-level flying.

Translating Practice

V. Translate the following sentences into Chinese.

1. The Chief of Naval Air Training (CNATRA) headquartered at NAS Corpus Christi,
Texas oversees the Naval Air Training Command (NATRACOM) whose mission is
to safely train and produce the world's finest combat quality aviation professionals—
Naval Aviators and Naval Flight Officers.

_____

_____

2. The T-6B cockpit and avionics suite is designed to better facilitate the transition to
increasingly sophisticated follow-on training and fleet aircraft, as well as keep pace
with emerging air traffic control regulations.

_____

_____

3. JPATS utilizes Training Integrated Management System (TIMS) to manage and
deliver course content. The entire curriculum and daily activities of students and
instructors are scheduled and tracked to ensure accurate and efficient training from
the first day of training to winging.

_____

_____

4. Student Naval Aviators selected for the E-2/C-2 pipeline at the completion of the
intermediate phase of the Strike pipeline report to Training Air Wing FOUR for
Multi-engine training in the T-44A/C or TC-12 before receiving their Wings.

_____

_____

5. The Maritime Patrol, Multi-engine, and advance Tiltrotor pipelines provide foundational training for Student Naval Aviators and Air Force pilots selected to fill fleet seats in the P-3C Orion, C-130 Hercules, HU-25 Guardian Falcon, E-2C/D Hawkeye, C-2A Greyhound, MV-22 Osprey and C-12 Huron.

_____

_____

VI. Translate the following paragraph into English.

　　每一种飞机都有其独特的飞行特性，因此，初级和中级飞行训练的目的不是去学会如何驾驶某一种型号的飞机。飞行训练的根本目的是增长知识、积累经验、掌握技能、养成安全习惯，这些方面将构成飞行的基础，在训练中掌握了这些技巧的飞行员会很容易地将技巧应用到任何一种飞机上。

_____

_____

_____

_____

_____

⊘ TEXT B

Flight Missions

1　　Flight missions here mean categories divided according to the nature of flying training contents. This text introduces eight main flight missions: **traffic pattern flight**, instrument flight, aerobatic flight, **navigation flight**, formation flight, **daylight instrument meteorological conditions flight**, **night flight** and **air attack flight**.

Traffic Pattern Flight

2   Traffic pattern flight is a process in which an airplane **takes off**, climbs to a certain height/altitude, and then positions to approach and **lands** on the same runway from which it **departed**. It usually includes five **legs** and four turns. The five legs are **takeoff/upwind leg, crosswind leg, downwind leg, base leg** and **final leg**. The four turns are crosswind turn, **downwind turn, base turn** and **final turn**. If the airplane turns to the left of the **landing "T"** after takeoff, we call it a **left-hand pattern**, while the opposite one is known as a **right-hand pattern**.

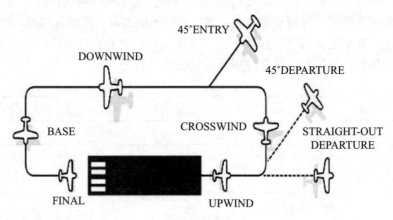

Traffic Pattern

Instrument Flight

3   When the horizon is invisible for any reason, a pilot can't control the **attitude** of the airplane without a suitable instrument. Instrument flight is known as a **hooded flight**, which requires the pilot to fly the aircraft by **cross-checking** and using the radio **navigational aids**. During instrument flight training, pilots are familiarized with the instruments used in aviation, such as the **altimeter, heading indicator, vertical speed indicator, attitude indicator (artificial horizon), airspeed indicator** and **turn coordinator**. Instrument flight is the foundation of instrument meteorological conditions flight, night flight and **over-water flight**.

Aerobatic Flight

4   Aerobatic flight is a kind of **maneuver flight** accompanied by the variation of attitude, speed and height of the plane. In the air, the flying aircraft sometimes **pounce** upon the ground and sometimes soar straight up into the sky. Aerobatic flight can obviously help the pilot improve flying techniques and get control of the air in the **air combat**. At the same time, the aerobatic flight can develop the courage of a pilot, and his steady, rapid and flexible reaction. On the other hand, its diversified **posture** of **rolling** and inverting **enchants** the observers.

Navigation Flight

5   Navigation is the art and science of getting from point "A" to point "B" in the least possible time without losing the way. Navigation flight is defined as a whole process of directing an aircraft to the given place or air zone by locating positions and determining the heading, airspeed and altitude. The navigation method used depends on where the pilot is going, how long the flight will take when the flight is to take off, the type of aircraft being flown, the **onboard navigation equipment**, the ratings and currency of the pilot and especially the expected weather. Since navigation flight runs through the whole flying process for any other flight missions, it is an important flying mission.

Formation Flight

6   The flight of a group of aircraft, which consists of more than two aircraft by maintaining **predetermined interval**, distance and height **separation**, is called formation flight. During the formation flight, the wingman operates his aircraft according to the leader's attempt and change, so the wingman needs to be familiar with the leader's action sequence, orders and operating characteristics. Generally speaking, the same type of aircraft can be in formation. Undoubtedly, formation flight is the basis of **armada** air battle. It is very important for an air force to carry out the principle of "concentrating superiority in force to destroy the enemies one by one".

Daylight Instrument Meteorological Conditions Flight

7   Daylight instrument meteorological conditions flight is a kind of flight in which the pilot flies an aircraft under complex **meteorological** conditions. Generally, it refers to a flight in the cloud or a **low visibility flight**. Daylight instrument meteorological conditions flight requires the pilot to master basic meteorological knowledge, and the pilot must know how to deal with the special unexpected situations that are caused by the meteorological conditions.

Night Flight

8   Night flight means a flight at night. Flying at night, the pilot must fly his aircraft with the help of the instruments and the airport must be provided with night flight facilities. Before the pilots set off on their first night flight, they need to become familiar with at least the basics of airport lighting. At night, they will find visual **glideslope indicators** particularly useful. The most common configuration is the **Visual Approach Slope Indicator (VASI)**. The other common type of visual glideslope indicator is the **Precision Approach Path Indicator (PAPI)**. If there is an air combat, the aircraft will be equipped with **airborne radar** and even **night-vision equipment**.

Air Attack Flight

9   Air attack refers to the attack from the air, i.e., the attack by aircraft, esp. against surface targets. Air attack flight follows the principles of air combat and bombing. It's a flight of attacking the air, ground and over-water targets. By learning the **fundamentals**, the student pilots can master the **fire control** and air attack skills.

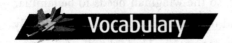
Vocabulary

Special Terms

air attack flight 空中攻击飞行，空袭飞行
airborne radar 机载雷达

air combat 空战

airspeed indicator 空速仪

altimeter 高度表

armada 战机机群；舰队

artificial horizon 人工地平

attitude 飞机姿态

attitude indicator 姿态仪

base leg 四边，基线边，底边

base turn 三、四转弯（连续作三、四转弯）；三连弯

cross-check 交叉检查（根据仪表指示综合判断飞行情况）

crosswind leg 二边，侧风边

daylight instrument meteorological conditions flight 昼间仪表气象条件飞行

depart 起飞；离场

downwind leg 三边，下风边，顺风边

downwind turn 二转弯（转向着陆反航向）

final leg 五边，进场边

final turn 四转弯（进入目标的最后一个转弯）

fire control 火控

glideslope indicator 下滑道指示仪

heading indicator 航向仪

hooded flight 暗舱飞行

instrument meteorological conditions 仪表飞行气象条件

land 着陆，降落

landing "T" T字布；T字灯

left-hand pattern 左起落航线

leg 航线段，（起落航线的）边

low visibility flight 低能见度飞行

maneuver flight 机动飞行

navigational aids 导航设备，助航设备；助航方法

navigation flight 导航飞行；领航训练飞行

night-vision equipment 夜视装备

night flight 夜间飞行

onboard navigation equipment 机载导航设备

over-water flight 水面上空飞行

Precision Approach Path Indicator (PAPI) 精确进近航道指示器

right-hand pattern 右起落航线

roll 滚转；横滚

separation 层次；间距，间隔

take off 起飞

takeoff/upwind leg 一边，离场边，上风边

traffic pattern flight 起落航线飞行

turn coordinator 转弯侧滑仪

vertical speed indicator 升降速度表

Visual Approach Slope Indicator (VASI) 目视进场下滑道指示器

New Words

enchant	[ɪn'tʃænt]	v.	使着迷，使陶醉
fundamental	[ˌfʌndə'mentl]	n.	基本原则；根本法则
interval	['ɪntəvl]	n.	（时间／空间）间隔
meteorological	[ˌmiːtiərə'lɒdʒɪkl]	a.	气象的；气象学的
posture	['pɒstʃə]	n.	姿态，态势
pounce	[paʊns]	v.	猛扑，猛冲；突然袭击
predetermined	[ˌpriːdɪ'tɜːmɪnd]	a.	预先确定的

 Exercises

Comprehension of the Text

I. Answer the following questions according to the text.

1. What flight missions are listed in the Text?

_____

2. What are the five legs and four turns included in the traffic pattern flight?

_____

3. What is the foundation of instrument meteorological conditions flight, night flight and over-water flight?

_____

4. What is the function of the aerobatic flight?

_____

5. What is formation flight?

_____

6. What is the responsibility of the wingman during the formation flight?

_____

7. What does the daylight instrument meteorological conditions flight require of the pilot?

_____

8. In the air attack flight, besides learning the fundamentals, what other skills should the pilots master?

_____

Vocabulary Practice

II. Match the meanings in Column B with the special terms in Column A and translate the terms into Chinese.

Column A	Column B
1. altitude _____	a. (in air traffic control) the spacing of aircraft to achieve their safe and orderly movement in flight while landing or taking off
2. visibility _____	b. the ability, as determined by atmospheric conditions and expressed in units of distance, to see and identify prominent unlighted objects by day and prominent lighted objects by night
3. upwind leg _____	c. Instrument Meteorological Conditions
4. downwind leg _____	d. a flight path in the direction of landing along the extended runway centerline from the base leg to the runway
5. crosswind leg _____	e. a flight path at right angles to the landing runway off its approach end and extending from the downwind leg to the intersection of the extended runway centerline
6. separation _____	f. a flight path parallel to the landing runway in the opposite direction of landing
7. base leg _____	g. a flight path at right angles to the landing runway off its takeoff end
8. IMC _____	h. a flight path parallel to the landing runway in the direction of landing
9. final leg _____	i. the relative orientation of the airplane with respect to pitch, roll and yaw
10. attitude _____	j. the actual height above mean sea level (MSL) at which the aircraft is flying

III. Label the five legs of the traffic pattern.

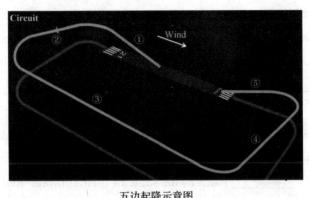

五边起降示意图

① _____   ② _____

③ _____   ④ _____

⑤ _____

Listening Practice

IV. Watch the video clip about the traffic patterns and fill in the blanks.

An airplane that has taken off and is climbing out on runway *1*_____ is on the departure leg. When at a sufficient altitude, the pilot can either depart the pattern or stay in the pattern by turning onto the *2*_____ leg. If they decide to stay in the pattern, the pilot can turn back onto the *3*_____ leg once they have spaced themselves out sufficiently and set up to practice another landing.

There is one additional leg of the pattern which has not been mentioned yet. This leg is called the *4*_____ leg and is also parallel with the runway, but located on the side *5*_____ the downwind. This leg is typically only used if a pilot has to *6*_____ their landing so they can safely space themselves out from other traffic.

Pilots in the pattern announce their positions in reference to these legs. If a pilot announces that they are on the *7*_____ leg and about to turn *8*_____, another pilot on the ground would know that it's probably not safe for them to take off at that time. They'll then wait for the *9*_____ traffic to land before they take off.

At tower controlled airports, ATC may instruct pilots to fly *10*_____ approaches or have pilots enter on the base leg. ATC may even run the left and right patterns simultaneously. At non-towered airports, these procedures are not recommended. Flying the approved full pattern is the best way to avoid traffic *11*_____ when ATC is not there to coordinate *12*_____ arrivals and departures.

As previously stated, standard patterns are flown with all turns to the left. For reasons of terrain, noise abatement or to prevent conflict with other operations, some airports have *13*_____ patterns for some of their runways. Right-hand patterns are depicted on aeronautical charts, noted in an airport facility directories and shown by indicators on the *14*_____ of the airport referred to as segmented circles. A segmented circle consists of a series of panels arranged in a circle, usually in the *15*_____ of the airport with extensions to show the runways and the direction of the patterns if non-standard. In this example, the extension on the left shows left traffic when landing to the east and right traffic when landing to the west.

Translating Practice

V. Translate the following sentences into Chinese.

1. Traffic pattern flight is a process in which an airplane takes off, climbs to a certain height/altitude, and then positions to approach and lands on the same runway from which it departed.

_____

_____

2. Instrument flight is known as a hooded flight. It requires the pilot to fly the aircraft by cross-checking and using the radio navigation aids.

_____

_____

3. Aerobatic flight can obviously help the pilot improve flying techniques and get control of the air in the air combat. At the same time, the aerobatic flight can develop the courage of a pilot, and his steady, rapid and flexible reaction.

_____

_____

4. Navigation flight is defined as a whole process of directing an aircraft to the given place or air zone by locating positions and determining the heading, airspeed and altitude.

_____

_____

5. Daylight instrument meteorological conditions flight requires the pilot to master basic meteorological knowledge, and the pilot must know how to deal with the special unexpected situations that are caused by the meteorological conditions.

_____

_____

🧭 TEXT C

CNATRA's Training Curriculum Today and into the Future

Aviation Training Alignment (飞行训练一致性)

1   CNATRA is aligned under **Commander, Pacific Fleet, and Commander, Naval Air Forces (CNAF)** (美国海军航空兵司令)—in the concept of the **Naval Aviation Enterprise (NAE)** (美国海军航空合作伙伴组织). CNATRA is **dual-hatted** (有双重头衔的) as CNAF Deputy Commander for Training. This alignment enables the ability to **orchestrate** (精心组织) and manage a full **spectrum** (范围) training **continuum** (连续体), not only within the TRACOM but also throughout the NAE from student induction to the completion of Fleet Readiness Squadron (FRS) training.

2   This continuum and alignment enable leadership and training practitioners to **optimize**（使最优化）training content and flow across all phases and pipelines of the entire training spectrum to ensure that the right training is conducted at the right level. Additionally, this continuum and alignment ensure that the most effective and efficient training organization is in place to achieve optimal time for student aviator to train. This continuum and alignment ultimately ensure the production of the world's finest Aerial Warriors for the world's finest air force—the Naval Air Force. Naval Air Force is made up of Naval Aviators and NFOs, who can think, perform, excel under pressure, and deliver in the most demanding aviation environment—**projecting** （投送）power ashore or at sea from the decks of aircraft carriers both day and night.

3   CNATRA and FRS training syllabi are in the process of converting from the old **Navy Standard Score Grading** (海军标准评分) convention we all used (aboves, averages, belows and unsats) to a new **Multi-Service Pilot and NFO Training System (MPTS/MNTS)** (多军种海军飞行员和海军空勤军官训练体系). This new system enables a greater degree of course flow flexibility while providing more objective grading to ensure that the specific and required knowledge, skills, and experiences are developed during each phase of the aviation training. These skills and experiences are linked and tracked through a single network of task lists and learning objectives reaching back from the fleet all the way to a student aviator's first exposure to flight training. MPTS/MNTS enables each stage of the training to be broken down into carefully designed **training blocks** (训练单元) to **incrementally** (逐渐地) build and refine required skill sets. MPTS/MNTS incorporates course training standards that define specific parameters for each maneuver in order to reduce **subjectivity** (主观性) in grading. The end product is targeted proficiency at each level of training to optimize efficiencies and ultimately ensure Student Naval Aviators and NFOs' succeed in follow-on training **venues** (场地).

4   CNATRA has also introduced and incorporated the **Joint Mission Planning System (JMPS)** (联合任务规划系统) to further align training and standards with the fleet. JMPS is a development effort between the Navy and the Air Force to join the

Navy Tactical Automated Mission Planning System (TAMPS) (海军战术自动化任务规划系统) and the **Air Force Mission Support System** (空军任务支援系统) to the **Global Command and Control System** (全球指挥控制系统) and the **Defense Information Infrastructure Common Operating Environment** (国防信息基础设施通用作战环境).

Joint and Combined Training (联合和组合的训练)

5   CNATRA embraces and places a strong emphasis on Joint and Combined Training wherever appropriate and effective. As such, Air Force and International student aviators train alongside Navy, Marine Corps and Coast Guard **counterparts** (职位或作用相当的人) at all Training Air Wings and in all phases of training. 100 Air Force Primary student pilots are trained annually at Training Air Wing FIVE at NAS Whiting Field and over 155 Air Force pilots receive their Wings each year at Training Air Wing FOUR at NAS Corpus Christi following Multi-engine training. **Correspondingly** (相应地), 110–120 Navy and Marine Corps student pilots receive Primary and Multi-engine flight training each year from the Air Force at Vance AFB in Enid, Oklahoma. Air Force Combat System Officer (CSO) students train alongside Navy and Marine Corps NFO counterparts at Training Air Wing SIX in Pensacola, Florida in Strike and Strike Fighter syllabi. CNATRA also trains more than 100 pilots and Undergraduate Military Flight Officers annually from 10 partner foreign countries under the International Military Training program. Student Aviators from Italy, Norway, Germany, Spain, Denmark, **Saudi Arabia** (沙特阿拉伯), Brazil, France, Singapore and India train alongside their American counterparts in Primary, Strike, Rotary and Multi-engine pilot and NFO syllabi.

6   Leadership and instructor positions are filled by officers from the Navy, Marine Corps, Air Force, Coast Guard, and foreign nations in order to facilitate and optimize this Joint and Combined Training. As such, both Navy and US Air Force Squadron command positions are **rotated** (轮换) between Navy, Marine Corps, Air Force and Coast Guard officers. This early exposure to the Joint and Combined environments

adds yet another dimension to the NAE training continuum and CNATRA's "train like you fight" **mindset** (思维模式) by preparing instructors and Student Naval Aviators and NFOs to the reality of today's Joint and Combined war-fighting teamwork.

Training Integrated Management System (TIMS) (训练综合管理系统)

7 Training Integrated Management System (TIMS) was developed as an integral part of the T-6 Joint Primary Aircraft Training System's (JPATS) ground based training system. TIMS combined and replaced five separate TRACOM training management systems and provided a single command-wide management system for both CNATRA and the **Air Force Air Education Training Command** (空军航空教育训练司令部). TIMS is the core of CNATRA's ground based training system and manages all aspects of the undergraduate ground-based flight training activities, which includes scheduling, the creation of grade sheets and flight records, **resource allocation** (资源分配), qualification and **currency** (熟练度) tracking, academics and computer-aided instruction, long-range planning and all training reports. TIMS also provides training connectivity between all CNATRA units using a linked network and has been chosen for the Joint Strike Fighter Program.

Exercises

Comprehension of the Text

Answer the following questions according to the text.

1. What advantage can Aviation Training Alignment bring to CNATRA?

_____

2. What's your opinion about the mindset "train like you fight"?

_____

3. What is the function of the system to which CNATRA and FRS training are converting from the old Navy Standard Score Grading convention?

4. Can you list the foreign countries that participate in Joint and Combined Training in the US?

5. What is Training Integrated Management System? How does it work?

⊘ UNIT PROJECT

 Mind Mapping

Work in groups and draw two maps respectively according to the following topics.

1. the US Student Naval Aviator training pipelines
2. traffic pattern flight

 Oral Practice

Work in groups and discuss one of the eight flight missions mentioned in Text B in detail. And one student from each group will make a 3-minute oral presentation according to the discussion. You may refer to Text B and the relevant information from the Internet.

Writing Practice

Based on Text A in Unit 2, and Text B in Unit 1, write a composition with at least 150 words on the topic of "Training Pipelines of PLA Naval Aviators". You may refer to the outline below.

1. overall introduction (the training you have received and the training you will take)
2. IFS, API and Primary training
3. advanced training (fighter, tailhook, transport, bomber, helicopter)

Unit 3
A Flying Day

◉ Warming Up

Task 1 Watch the video clip about the fighter pilot training and fill in the blanks.

Those guys have to understand that their job, by default, is to *1*_____. That's it. There's no second place when you *2*_____ with people, right. There is no second place when you merge with an *3*_____ aircraft. It's him or you, so by default you win. If you can't win, then this isn't the job for you.

Every time you take off, you have to be *4*_____. You know that every time you drop a bomb, the guys on the ground are counting on you. ...It's a stressful job, but it's stressful to the point that it maximizes your *5*_____ when you are *6*_____. And you get that from the first day of pilot training all the way to hopefully the last sortie you're flying a fighter.

We have a lot of students go downrange. Four months from leaving here, they are in Afghanistan, and they're doing exactly those things like dropping GBU-12s on foes, dropping the GBU-38s or they are down doing *7*_____ in Syria. So we try to make it as *8*_____ as we can for these guys because we know that there is a good *9*_____ that when they leave here just a few months later, they could be downrange doing the same things.

I love being an *10*_____, because I get to *11*_____ those guys as soon as they show up. Those are my guys to turn into *12*_____, so that I know what it's gonna take for those guys to be successful in the air force.

Task 2 Discuss the following questions in groups.

1. What do you know about a fighter pilot?

2. What would a fighter pilot do to get prepared for a mission?

3. Who will be involved during the whole process of a mission?

⊘ TEXT A

A Day in the Life of a Fighter Pilot—Part I

Nate S. Jaros[1]

1   I am often asked what it is like to be a fighter pilot. Sure, we **boast about** how fast we fly, how to shoot missiles, drop bombs, and generally **scorch** around the sky in our hot jets. But honestly, there is a lot more to it than that, including an air of **professionalism** and perfection that is rare in other jobs.

2   Let's take a deeper look into a day in the life of a fighter pilot.

Planning—0600 Local

3   Generally speaking, the squadron's **scheduling shop** will build and publish a schedule for the week. This schedule includes all types of **training rides**, upgrade **sorties** and various other **ground events** and so forth. As a pilot, you can look at the schedule and know with reasonable certainty about what you are doing for that week.

4   Your day begins when you arrive at the squadron. Yep, you have to plan your mission or sortie, and it's not very **glamorous**, unfortunately. When you find yourself scheduled to fly, you need to begin **mission planning**. Depending on what kind of mission you are on, and your position in the **two-ship** or **four-ship**, you will get in touch with the other members of your flight (and possibly any **adversaries** too) and begin planning.

5   Planning for the mission or sortie really hasn't changed **a whole lot** since the days of the first combat pilots. The

Mission Planning

---

1 **Nate S. Jaros:** 美国空军战斗机飞行员，别称 Buster，他驾驶 F-16 C/D/CM 和 T-38A/C 达 2000 多飞行时数，出版著作 *Engine Out Survival Tactics*。

objectives for the mission are identified and that becomes the **bedrock** for the rest of the planning. If it is a **dedicated air-to-ground practice ride**, the pilots will need to begin to plan for that type of mission versus a 4v4 (four versus four) **air-to-air combat training sortie**. Both require detailed and coordinated planning, but they are quite different.

6　　The objectives or goals of the flight are the key to what and how you will begin planning, and thusly what you are trying to get out of the whole event.

Mission Planning on the Computer

7　　Mission planning takes a few hours of your day, possibly more if it is a detailed and complex mission. Today, we typically plan a lot of our missions on a computer and then load the selected **airspace boundaries**, **flight route**, and aircraft communication and **weapons loadout** information onto a **Data Transfer Cartridge** (**DTC**). DTC is a brick-like object (in the F-16) that carries the detailed mission planning data and information. It is loaded into the jet during **ground ops** and transfers all the information you've planned for into the aircraft's computer systems.

8　　In addition to the DTC, you will also generate paper maps and **lineup cards** during mission planning. A lineup card is a piece of paper that contains all the critical information for the mission. Things like the flight's **call sign**, takeoff and landing data calculations, **mission timing**, **code words**, a route overview, **weapon configurations** and all radio frequencies that are expected for the flight are put on the lineup card.

9　　If you have **hot ranges**, more aircraft, or **tanker aircraft** in the mix, there is even more planning required to ensure that all the timing is perfect, and everything is set for the mission.

10　　Print off two or four copies of everything (and load all the DTCs) and you're done! Hopefully, after a couple of hours, your mission planning is complete and you're ready to brief.

The Flight Briefing—0800 Local

11   The flight briefing is quite possibly the most important part of the mission, even more so than the in-flight **execution** to a degree. The flight briefing is where all members of the flight come together and **lay out** the exact details of what will happen, when it will happen and how it will happen for the mission that you are about to fly.

The Flight Briefing

12   For fighter pilots, the brief is a **sacred** event. It is led by the flight lead, who is the pilot in the number one aircraft and who is in charge of the flight. He or she starts the briefing with a **time hack** that is set to exact global time. We do things **down to the second**. If you miss the briefing, you don't fly that day, so don't be late. Briefings usually are set precisely two hours prior to takeoff time.

13   The flight lead briefs the sortie and all the **intricacies**, and no one else speaks, period. There is limited time, so questions are held to the end. The briefing lasts about an hour and consists of two **segments**: the Administration and the Tactical Portion. The Administration is sometimes just called "admin" or more commonly called "motherhood". The motherhood part of the combat brief is fast, just spending eight to ten minutes typically. This is by design, as we like to spend a majority of our briefing time on the tactical stuff. Motherhood encompasses the basics of the ground ops, **radio frequency** plans, **departure** and **recovery** plans, as well as formation positions and a safety review of the rules for the "fight".

14   Contracts are also reviewed. Every flight member has various contracts during different phases of flight. Contracts are important items that you are responsible for, and that every other flight member is expecting you to do, **without fail**. An example contract is to announce when you have one missile or bomb remaining during the fight, which is a very important thing for the rest of the flight members to know!

15   The tactical portion, often called "the Meat" of the mission is where the details of the in-flight execution are discussed. Everything from how you are expected to

release a weapon to a special tactic that the two or four-ship might be working on or practicing, and when to execute that tactic is covered in **excruciating** detail. It is very important that all members understand what will happen and what is expected as lives are at risk.

16   Once the brief is complete, the flight lead **wraps up** with a final review of the flight objectives, and then any and all questions about what is about to happen are **vetted**.

17   It is now about an hour from takeoff time, and time to **suit up** and "step" ! Gather up all the mission materials, dress in your **G-suit**, **preflight** your helmet, and get ready to go out the door.

18   **Stay tuned** for Part II where we will see how the actual inflight execution of the mission develops and later, in Part III we will **dive into** the mission debrief in our Day in the Life of a Fighter Pilot!

Vocabulary

Special Terms

adversary 假想机；假想敌；对手
airspace boundary 空域界限
air-to-air combat training sortie 空对空作战训练飞行
air-to-ground practice ride 空对地练习飞行
briefing 简令；简要说明
call sign 呼号
code word 密语；代码字
Data Transfer Cartridge (DTC) 数据传输盒
departure 离场
flight route 飞行路线，航线
four-ship 四机编队
ground event 地面活动
ground ops (ground operations) 地面操作；地面运转

G-suit 抗荷服

hot range 已准备好投弹的靶场

scheduling shop 飞行调度室

lineup card 飞行任务卡

mission planning 任务规划

mission timing 任务计时

preflight 飞行前检查

radio frequency 无线电频率

recovery 返航；回收

sortie （作战）飞行（任务）；（出动）架次

tanker aircraft 加油机

time hack 校时，对时；计时

training ride 训练飞行

two-ship 双机编队

weapon configuration 武器构型

weapon loadout 武器封装

Words and Expressions

bedrock	['bedrɒk]	*n.*	基石；基础
dedicated	['dedɪkeɪtɪd]	*a.*	专门用途的；有奉献精神的
execution	[ˌeksə'kjuʃ(ə)n]	*n.*	执行；实施
excruciating	[ɪk'skruːʃɪeɪtɪŋ]	*a.*	折磨人的；令人极为不快的
glamorous	['glæmərəs]	*a.*	特别富有魅力的
intricacy	['ɪntrɪkəsi]	*n.*	复杂的细节
professionalism	[prə'feʃənəlɪzəm]	*n.*	专业水平；专业素质
sacred	['seɪkrəd]	*a.*	神圣的；受到尊重的
segment	['segmənt]	*n.*	部分；段
scorch	[skɔːtʃ]	*v.*	（俚）高速疾驰
vet	[vet]	*v.*	检查；仔细审查
a whole lot			很多，许多
boast about			吹嘘

dive into...	投身于……，致力于……
down to the second	精确到秒
lay out	展示
stay tuned	继续关注事情的发展；继续收听
suit up	穿上制服
without fail	必定，务必；无一例外
wrap up	结束，完成

Comprehension of the Text

I. Answer the following questions according to the text.

1. What can a schedule provide for a pilot?

_____

2. What kind of role do the objectives of the flight play?

_____

3. Today, what is the typical way of doing mission planning?

_____

4. What is a DTC?

_____

5. What kind of information does a lineup card usually contain?

_____

6. What will the members of the flight do during the flight briefing?

_____

7. What does the flight lead do to start the briefing?

_____

8. What are the two segments of the briefing?

_____

9. What does "motherhood" contain?

_____

10. What details could be discussed during "the Meat"?

_____

11. What would the flight lead do once the briefing is completed?

_____

12. What will the fighter pilots do about an hour from the takeoff time?

_____

II. **The text introduces the mission planning and flight briefing part of a day in the life of a fighter pilot. Complete the following table with the information from the Text.**

Step	Time	Participant	Task	Function
Mission Planning	0600 Local	pilots, other members of flight, and _____	1. select information about airspace boundaries, _____ , and aircraft communication and _____ 2. load the information onto a DTC 3. generate paper maps and _____	the _____ of the mission
The Flight	0800 Local	pilots, flight lead, and all members of flight	1. lay out all the details in the following mission 2. start with a _____ 3. complete the two segments of the brief: _____and _____ 4. review objectives and vet all relevant questions	the most important part

Vocabulary Practice

III. **Match the meanings in Column B with the special terms in Column A and translate the terms into Chinese.**

Column A	Column B
1. flight briefing _____ *2.* sortie _____	a. a name, letters or numbers used to identify a person or a sub-unit on the radio b. a garment for covering parts of the body below the chest, so designed as to exert pressure to prevent or retard the pooling of the blood below the heart during exposure to abnormal G forces

Column A	Column B
3. G-suit _____	**c.** directed or operating from an aircraft to the surface of the land
4. call sign _____	**d.** Data Transfer Cartridge
5. mission timing _____	**e.** the instruction or lecture given to an aircrew or air passengers before a flight, regarding procedures to be followed, route, weather conditions, target, destination, enemy activity or any other subject pertinent to the flight or mission
6. air-to-ground _____	**f.** to check, test, and prepare for use an aircraft, aircraft engine, bombsight, machine gun or other pieces of equipment previous to a flight
7. recovery _____	**g.** an operational flight
8. DTC _____	**h.** the measurement and recording of the time taken to complete a mission
9. preflight _____	**i.** an area of ground used for shooting practice
10. range _____	**j.** (in air operations) the phase of a mission that involves the return of an aircraft to a land base or platform afloat

IV. Complete each of the following sentences with a word from the box. Change the form if necessary.

tactical	segment	adversary	excruciating	execution
glamorous	dedicated	dive	professionalism	vet

1. "And that was my day, nothing _____. I'm just a fighter pilot," as they used to say.

2. The company hopes to see Intel chips being built into virtually every _____ of computing.

3. If you want to stay relevant, you're going to have to _____ into the domain of the business you're in.

4. The whole search has been so _____, I don't want to go through it anymore.

5. The order of _____ is perceived to be out of order, but is allowed to happen given the current memory model.

6. "We were able to showcase the best airborne _____ command and control platform in the world," he said.

7. All the materials were very thoroughly _____.

8. He is _____ to his duty and always gives priority to the benefits of the squadron, regardless of his personal interests.

9. More than half of Americans in a recent opinion poll viewed China as a(n) _____, compared with 28 percent who saw it as an ally.

10. American companies always pride themselves on their _____.

V. **Complete the following short passage with the words from the box. Change the form if necessary.**

maintenance	squadron	non-standardized	replacement	group
standardization	designated	transition	initiative	mishaps

A lack of standardization and training in both aircraft maintenance and flight operations was cited as a causal factor in a large percentage of 1_____. Several 2_____ programs were initiated in the late 1950s and early 1960s to counter this problem. The first was the Naval Aviation Maintenance Program (NAMP) in 1959. Prior to the NAMP, aircraft 3_____ practices were completely 4_____ across US naval aviation. For example, an aircraft maintenance procedure might be significantly different from one 5_____ to the next, even though both squadrons operated exactly the same T/M/S aircraft on the same base or in the same air 6_____. The NAMP standardized maintenance procedures across all of the naval aviation, or what has been termed since the early 2000s as the entire "naval aviation enterprise".

The second standardization 7_____ began in 1961 with the introduction of the Fleet 8_____ Squadron Program. The purpose of the Program is to indoctrinate newly *9*_____ aircrew (naval aviators, naval flight officers, enlisted naval aircrewmen) and aircraft maintenance personnel into the peculiarities of the specific aircraft. Prior to the Program's concept, qualified pilots *10*_____ to a new aircraft were essentially told how to start it, and then sent to go fly. The final major standardization initiative put in place was the NATOPS (Naval Air Training and Operating Procedure Standardization) Program in 1961.

Translating Practice

VI. Translate the following sentences into Chinese.

1. Depending on what kind of mission you are on, and your position in the two-ship or four-ship, you will get in touch with the other members of your flight (and possibly any adversaries too) and begin planning.

_____

_____

2. Today, we typically plan a lot of our missions on a computer and then load the selected airspace boundaries, flight route, and aircraft communication and weapons loadout information onto a Data Transfer Cartridge (DTC).

_____

_____

3. Things like the flight's call sign, takeoff and landing data calculations, mission timing, code words, a route overview, weapon configurations, and all radio frequencies that are expected for the flight are put on the lineup card.

_____

_____

4. This is by design, as we like to spend a majority of our briefing time on the tactical stuff. Motherhood encompasses the basics of the ground ops, radio frequency plans, departure and recovery plans, as well as formation positions and a safety review of the rules for the "fight".

_____

_____

5. Everything from how you are expected to release a weapon to a special tactic that the two or four-ship might be working on or practicing, and when to execute that tactic is covered in excruciating detail.

_____

_____

VII. Translate the following paragraph into English.

第六飞行训练联队一直致力于不断寻求更优方案以完成使命。通过理论学习、模拟机训练和飞行时间训练等全面化的课程，我们可培养出世界一流的海军飞行军官、武器系统控制军官和国际军事飞行军官。我们团队的奉献精神和专业技能以及对海军和空军航空兵部队的贡献都是首屈一指的。

_____

_____

_____

_____

_____

⊘ TEXT B

A Day in the Life of a Fighter Pilot—Part II

Nate S. Jaros

Stepping to Fly—0900 Local

1   After suiting up, grabbing some coffee or having a quick bite to eat, it's time to join your flight-mates at the **Ops Desk** for the **step brief**. The Ops Desk is where a senior member of the **Fighter Squadron** will be posted daily for the sole purpose of overseeing and sometimes **smoothing** the daily flying operations of the unit. For the day, that pilot is designated the **Ops Sup**. Working with the **maintainers** to ensure that the right jets with the right configurations are ready, dealing with weather

changes, schedule changes, pilot illnesses and **fallout** are among a few of the daily items that the Ops Sup will have to do.

Pilots receive the step brief.

2   It's not very glamorous, but it's essential for the smooth flow of the daily events in a very complex Fighter Squadron schedule.

3   Pilots receive a brief from the Ops Sup before they go out to their jets. In addition to assigning a specific **tail number** that each pilot will fly that day, the Ops Sup briefs the pilots on any updates to weather, airspace, bird conditions, **divert options** and any other important **airfield** items.

4   Following the Ops Sup brief, it's time to step!

5   Pilots now arrive at their jets and greet their hardworking maintainers. **Of note**, most of the maintenance guys have been out on the **flight line** since 0400 or 0500 Local, getting the aircraft **prepped** and ready for flight.

Performing the Walk-Around

6   After greeting the **crew chief** and maintenance guys, we perform a jet "**walk-around**". The walk-around is actually a set of **checklist** procedures where all sorts of items are looked at and checked before climbing in and flying. Careful checks of things like **flight controls**, **hydraulic lines** and tanks, and **weapons settings** are important in the preflight walk-around.

7   After that, it's time to climb in, start the engine and taxi out to the end of the runway.

Getting Airborne—1000 Local

8　　We taxi out our flight (usually a two or four-ship) in order and go to the appropriate runway. There, we are greeted by more maintenance guys who give the jets one final look over, as well as arming up any weapons on board. After that, with **takeoff clearance** received we taxi onto the runway and go…following the briefed departure procedure and formation.

Vipers rejoin after takeoff and head to the airspace.

9　　Somewhere after departure, things get really busy for the fighter pilot. We typically **rejoin the formation** in some **format** and proceed to the **working airspace, tanker track** or wherever the plan was. Along the way we do a "Fence Check"[1] where the aircraft is made ready to fight. Some items in the F-16 Fence Check are setting up the radar and the **targeting pod**, testing **chaff** and **flares**, turning up the volume on the **threat warning receiver** and ensuring that your oxygen and G-suit is working. We'll also turn on the **camera recording system** to "film" everything and all displays for later debrief analysis.

10　　Depending on the loadout, we might also **warm up** missiles and bombs, and do a few checks on them to ensure that they are ready for action.

The Mission—1015 Local

11　　The flight enters the "**fragged**" airspace and it's time to fight. For the next 45 minutes to an hour, we will **put** our fighters **through their paces**. Air-to-air **engagements** against adversaries, **nine G break turns, vertical (up and down) maneuvering** and **air-to-ground bomb deliveries** are all some of the intense and sometimes excruciating things one might do.

1　**Fence Check:** 战区检查，主要是对座舱武器开关进行的检查。根据战术要求，进出敌空域时要进行战区检查。Fence In 为进入战区前的相关检查；Fence Out 为退出战区前的相关检查。训练中进出空域时也要做战区检查。这里 Fence 为缩略语，通常指 fuel（燃油）、engine（发动机）、navigation（导航设备）、communications（通信）和 equipment（设备）。

Raptors drop weapons.

12   Every mission is different. On some sorties, you might do all of the above, but often it is more common to just focus on one segment of the training. We might spend our time doing all air-to-air **intercepts** or basic weapons air-to-ground deliveries. It all depends on what your flight objectives were and what was needed to accomplish for the training on that day.

13   Either way, we will perform whatever we set out to practice, and maybe do it multiple times. Often we have the gas for four or five "sets" of intercepts or air-to-air engagements and may even do some "**dry**" weapons passes releasing simulated weapons in **simulated attacks**.

14   Additionally, everything is being **scrutinized**. If you are an instructor, you are carefully watching and listening to everything that every member does. Did the intercept/attack/engagement go as planned? Did everyone follow briefed contracts? Were there any **gross** errors or **lapses** in safety? These are some important things that are noted.

15   As young wingmen, we are striving to do our best. Wingmen are hoping to be in the correct formation position ALWAYS. We should also be on the correct frequency and be ready to act and **employ** per[1] your Flight Lead's directions and briefed plans. A **solid** wingman should almost be one step ahead of the Flight Lead's plan, and ready to act at all times.

The Return to Base (RTB)—1115 Local

16   Before you know that the formation is getting low on gas and "bingo" fuel[2] is reached… it's time to return to base. "Bingo" fuel is the planned fuel state which allows for a normal recovery back to the airfield or "**pad**" with enough reserve fuel for safety.

---

1   **per:** 同 by、through、according to，意为 "按照，根据"。

2   **"bingo" fuel:** "兵戈" 油量，即最低安全返航油量，"兵戈" 油量是一种特情。

17   The formation **joins up**, fences out and gets headed home. On the way, we safe up any armed up systems and do what is called a **Battle Damage (BD) check**. During the BD check, each aircraft takes a minute to fly behind and under the other aircraft and look for any trouble. **Shrapnel** holes, stuck or hung weapons, hung chaff or flares, leaking fluids and anything else **amiss**. This check seldom **turns up** anything of significance, however, it is important and can become critical later during combat operations.

18   With everything looking good, we come in, land and taxi back to the eager maintenance crew chief who helps get the aircraft **shutdown**, and often prepares it to go back up in an hour or two.

19   It's now about noon and typically we are tired and hungry. There are just a few minutes to fill out the paperwork with maintenance, get out of the **flight gear**, **stow** the helmet and grab a bite to eat as the **flight debrief** is scheduled for exactly one hour after landing.

20   In the next and final segment, we'll discuss the fighter pilot debrief and look at why that is critically important to the combat aviator.

 **Vocabulary**

Special Terms

airfield 机场

air-to-ground bomb delivery 空对地投弹

Battle Damage (BD) check 战斗损伤检查

camera recording system 摄像机录像系统

chaff 箔条，（锡箔片制成用于干扰雷达的）金属反射体

checklist 检查单

crew chief 地勤组组长；飞机机械师

divert option 备降方案；改航方案

dry 模拟的，非实弹的

engagement 交战

Fighter Squadron 战斗机中队

flare 照明弹，曳光弹；红外干扰弹

flight control 飞机操控；（复数）飞机控制／操控系统

flight debrief 飞行后讲评

flight gear 飞行服；飞行装具

flight line 机场维护工作区；飞行路线，航线

hydraulic line 液压管线

intercept 拦截，截击；截获

join up 飞机空中集合

maintainer 维护人员

nine G break turn 9 个过载急转弯

Ops Desk (Operations Desk) 飞行任务调度台，作战台

Ops Sup (Operations Supervisor) 飞行任务主管

pad （小型飞机）降落场

rejoin the formation 重新加入编队

Return to Base (RTB) 返回基地，返场

shutdown 关车；（故障造成）空中停车

simulated attack 模拟攻击

step brief 临机前简令；临机前协同

takeoff clearance 起飞许可

tanker track 加油机航迹，加油机航线

targeting pod 目标指示吊舱，瞄准吊舱

threat warning receiver 威胁警告系统

tail number 机尾数字，机尾号码，尾数

vertical (up and down) maneuvering 垂直（向上和向下）机动

walk-around 绕机检查

weapons setting 武器设置

warm up 加温，暖机；（火箭）准备发射

working airspace 作业空域

Words and Expressions

amiss	[ə'mɪs]	a.	不正常的；错误的
employ	[ɪm'plɔɪ]	v.	应用；运用
fallout	['fɔːlaʊt]	n.	后果；副作用
format	['fɔːmæt]	n.	总体安排；格式，形式
frag	[fræg]	v.	杀伤对手 n. 手雷
gross	[grəʊs]	a.	严重的；总的
lapse	[læps]	n.	疏忽；行为失检
prep	[prep]	v.	预备；把……准备好
scrutinize	['skruːtənaɪz]	v.	仔细查看
shrapnel	['ʃræpnəl]	n.	飞溅的弹片
smooth	[smuːð]	v.	消除 (行动) 障碍；为……铺平道路 a. 平滑的；进行顺利的
solid	['sɒlɪd]	a.	可靠的；固体的；坚硬的 n. 固体
stow	[stəʊ]	v.	妥善放置；把……收好
of note			值得注意的是
put… through its paces			全面测试……的本领或性能
turn up			找到；出现

Exercises

Comprehension of the Text

I. Answer the following questions according to the text.

1. What will be done at the Ops Desk?

_____

2. What are the daily items that the Ops Sup have to deal with?

_____

3. In addition to assigning a specific tail number, what would the Ops Sup brief the pilots?

_____

4. What is the "walk-around" of a jet?

_____

5. Why do things get real busy for the flight pilot after departure?

_____

6. What should be included in the F-16 "Fence Check"?

_____

7. List some of the intense and excruciating things that the pilot might do during the flight.

_____

8. During the mission, what would the instructor do?

_____

9. What is the "bingo" fuel?

_____

10. What would pilots do during the BD check?

_____

II. **This text introduces how the actual in-flight execution of the mission develops in the life of a fighter pilot. Complete the following table with the information from the text.**

Step	Time	Participant	Task	Function
Stepping to Fly	0900 Local	pilots, flight-mates, Ops Sup, _____ , _____	1. _____ the daily flying operations of the unit 2. receive a brief on any updates to weather, _____ , _____ , _____ , and so on 3. perform a jet " _____ " for a careful check of _____ , hydraulic lines and tanks, and _____	This is _____ for the smooth flow of the daily event.
Getting Airborne	1000 Local	pilots, maintainers	1. give the jets one final look over, then _____ 2. after departure, _____ _____ , do a "Fence Check"	/

Step	Time	Participant	Task	Function
The Mission	1015 Local	pilots, _____	1. put fighters through their paces 2. perform whatever were set out to practice, like _____ or _____	/
The RTB	1115 Local	pilots, maintenance crew chief	1. _____ , _____ and get headed home 2. safe up any armed up systems and do BD check 3. _____, get the aircraft _____ 4. fill out paperwork with maintenance, get out of the _____ , stow the helmet	/

Vocabulary Practice

III. Complete each of the following sentences with a word from the box. Change the form if necessary.

stow	format	scrutinize	lapse	maneuver
armed	target	simulated	employ	amiss

1. Our bombers went out today to _____ the enemy ammunition depots.

2. The President switched from set speeches to a question-and-answer _____.

3. Observers of politics in the Arab world and the broader Middle East continue to _____ US's place in the region.

4. This relationship is often associated with a(n) _____ in supervision.

5. A large number of scientific inventions have been _____ for military purposes.

6. Security forces claim that they were suicide bombers, though there was no indication that the would-be suicide bombers were _____.

7. With full-sized planes, the benefit should increase, as more people can _____ their luggage simultaneously along the longer aisles.

8. The pilots flew in the dark arrived at the _____ compound and settled into a hover while the SEALs fast-roped down.

9. Naval aircraft employed torpedoes in the Great War but the chances of a hit on a warship with fast _____ were slim.

10. He had a nose for a situation. If there was something _____, he sensed it easily.

Translating Practice

IV. Translate the following sentences into Chinese.

1. In addition to assigning a specific tail number that each pilot will fly that day, the Ops Sup briefs the pilots on any updates to weather, airspace, bird conditions, divert options and any other important airfield items.

   _____

   _____

2. Of note, most of the maintenance guys have been out on the flight line since 0400 or 0500 Local, getting the aircraft prepped and ready for flight.

   _____

   _____

3. We typically rejoin the formation in some format and proceed to the working airspace, tanker track or wherever the plan was.

   _____

   _____

4. We might spend our time doing all air-to-air intercepts or basic weapons air-to-ground deliveries. It all depends on what your flight objectives were and what was needed to accomplish for the training on that day.

   _____

   _____

5. Often we have the gas for four or five "sets" of intercepts or air-to-air engagements and may even do some "dry" weapons passes releasing simulated weapons in simulated attacks.

   _____

   _____

⊘ TEXT C

A Day in the Life of a Fighter Pilot—Part III

Nate S. Jaros

1   Continuing our three-part series on A Day in the Life of a Fighter Pilot. Now it's time to debrief!

2   Before we dive into the debrief itself, it's important to understand a few things about the fighter pilot debrief. The debrief is not only a **time-honored** (历史悠久的) tradition but a requirement as well. The importance of this traditional discussion cannot be overemphasized. By carefully analyzing everything that occurred during the in-flight execution of the sortie, we can begin to **dissect** (仔细研究) all the actions, see every outcome, and learn where mistakes were made and therefore how to correct them.

3   After all, getting better is the goal of any pilot. And the debrief is the tool to do just that.

Getting Back to the Squadron—1200 Local

4   After getting back to the squadron, we get all the gear off and usually have some paperwork to do briefly. There is a little bit of time to get some food and water, but quickly it is time to begin to prepare for the debrief, which today is scheduled for 1300 Local.

Prepping for the Debrief—1230 Local

5   Fighter pilots don't just gather around a table and talk about what happened. That might happen later in the bar! But in the preparation for the debrief, it is up to each pilot to playback all critical events that occurred during the sortie and take some notes. This is done with the aid of the "tapes" or DVRs that we turned on to record everything at the beginning of the mission.

6   Critical items that will be needed for the debrief are things like the time of any **weapons releases** (武器投放), if they were valid or outside of the parameters at release and maybe any training rule or airspace violations that were committed during the mission. Most fighter pilots take about 20 to 30 minutes to rapidly reconstruct the things occurred and any big highlights, and make notes on key sortie events.

7   Instructor Pilots (IP) use this time to review their tapes as well and prep the debrief room for the debrief. Writing up the flight objectives and gathering notes from the tapes on what happened for everyone are just a few of the items that an IP must do.

A Debrief in Action

The Debrief—1300 Local

8   The debrief starts with another sharp hack of the clock and then it begins. Strict **decorum** (礼节) is adhered to and flight members are only permitted to speak when asked a direct question by the IP or Flight Lead, and even then it needs to be a **succinct** (言简意赅的) answer. Typical "yes" or "no" answers are preferred and nothing more if possible.

9   The debrief is essentially a **massive** (大量的) reconstruction of the day's events. Everything from the briefing is addressed to stepping procedures, radio frequency errors, and basic admin like the takeoff and rejoins, recovery and radio calls are scrutinized and debated.

10   More importantly, the tactics and actions of every flight member are examined and reviewed. The IP or Flight Lead will call up every weapons delivery or key tactical point one by one, and the whole flight will watch it on the screen. Key elements are noted and events are reconstructed to help find out what **transpired** (发生) during the mission and what mistakes were made.

11   **Invariably** (总是), mistakes are made. Usually, the mistakes are not gross or severe, but the IP or Flight Lead point to some minor error in execution or

understanding by a pilot. **Getting "to the bottom" of** (弄清······的起因) that error and understanding why it was made and how it affected the outcome of the mission are the true purposes of the debrief. That is why we spend three or four hours going over every detail and "digging out" the root causes for every missed opportunity or mistake.

12   The debrief is more than a mass of error collections. It is an in-depth analysis of why something went wrong and how we can get better the next time. That is what it means to be a fighter pilot.

The End of the Debrief—1600 Local

13   The debrief is over. Every pilot walks out of the room having learned a little something more for the next time. Maybe they feel a bit more humble and a bit **disheveled** (凌乱的), but they'll be smarter and wiser and certainly more "tactically capable" the next time.

14   It's time to wrap up the day, head home for some rest and get ready to do it again tomorrow!

 Exercises

Comprehension of the Text

I. Answer the following questions according to the text.

1. Why is the debrief not only a time-honored tradition but a requirement as well?

_____

2. According to the author, what is the tool to help the pilot get better?

_____

3. After getting back to the squadron, what will the pilot do before the debrief?

_____

4. What would each pilot do during the preparation for the debrief?

_____

5. What critical items will be needed for the debrief?

_____

6. What must an IP do before the debrief?

_____

7. During the debrief, under which circumstances do the flight members get the permission to speak?

_____

8. What would be scrutinized and debated during the debrief?

_____

9. What would be done to help find out what transpired during the mission?

_____

10. What is the true purpose of the debrief?

_____

II. This text introduces the whole process of debrief. Complete the following table with the information from the text.

Step	Time	Participant	Task	Function
Getting Back to the Squadron	1200 Local	pilots	1. get all the _____ off 2. usually have some paperwork to do	/
Prepping for the Debrief	1230 Local	pilots, _____	1. playback all _____ and take some notes 2. _____ the things occurred and any big highlights, and make notes 3. review the tapes and prep the debrief room; write up the _____ and gather notes	/

Step	Time	Participant	Task	Function
The Debrief	1300 Local	pilots, IP or _____	1. have a massive construction of the day's events 2. examine and review the _____ of every flight members 3. find out what transpired during the mission and _____	an _____ of why something went wrong and how we can get better
The End of the Debrief	1600 Local	Pilots, IP or Flight Lead	have learned something more	become _____, _____ and more "_____"

 UNIT PROJECT

 Mind Mapping

Work in groups and draw a mind map to depict a typical flying day of a flight pilot.

 Oral Practice

Work in groups and discuss how a fighter pilot spends a flying day. One of the group members may act as an interviewer and other group members are interviewees. The interviewer should ask questions according to the time sequence of a pilot's typical flying day. You may refer to the texts of this unit and the relevant information from the Internet.

Writing Practice

Based on the interview above, write a composition with at least 150 words about a typical flying day of a fighter pilot. You may refer to the outline below.

1. mission planning
2. mission briefing
3. mission execution
4. mission debriefing

Unit 4
Airplane Structure and Categories

⊘ Warming Up

Task 1 Watch the video clip about the basic components of an airplane and fill in the blanks.

Airplanes are made up of hundreds, even thousands of parts, from the simplest pieces of wood and fabric to newly designed composite *1*_____, to the most sophisticated of electrical components. Planes come in all *2*_____ and sizes, but they all share the same basic design components.

The basic components of any airplane are the fuselage, the *3*_____, the empennage, the *4*_____ and the *5*_____. The *6*_____ houses the cabin and *7*_____ to hold the pilots, passengers and cargo. The fuselage is considered to be the *8*_____ component of the airplane since all the other components are attached to it. Most airplanes manufactured today use something called semi-monocoque *9*_____. This means that underneath the *10*_____ of the airplane, there are a series of *11*_____ and other supports that help hold the airplane together.

The wings of an aircraft generate *12*_____ as the air flows around them. The wings are shaped to maximize the amount of lift they produce. The wings can be attached to the top, *13*_____ or at the bottom of the fuselage. Most planes have a single set of wings referred to as a *14*_____, but some planes have two or three sets of wings referred to as *15*_____ and triplanes respectively.

Task 2 Discuss the following questions in groups.

1. Can you name the basic parts of an airplane?
2. What generates most of the lift to hold the plane in the air?
3. How many engines does an airplane usually have?

⊘ TEXT A

Major Components of an Airplane

1   Although airplanes are designed for a variety of purposes, most of them have the same major **components**. The overall characteristics are largely determined by the original design objectives. Most airplane structures include a **fuselage**, wings, an **empennage**, **landing gears** and a **powerplant**.

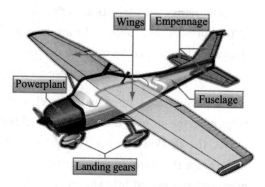

Major Components of an Airplane

Fuselage

2   The fuselage is the central body of an airplane and is designed to **accommodate** the crew, passengers and cargo. It also provides the structural connection for the wings and tail **assembly**. Older types of aircraft design utilized an open **truss structure** constructed of wood, steel or aluminum **tubing**. The most popular types of fuselage structures used in today's aircraft are the **monocoque** (French for "single shell") and **semimonocoque**.

3   As the main body structure to which all other components are attached, the fuselage contains the cockpit or **flight deck**, **passenger compartment** and **cargo compartment**. While wings produce most of the **lift**, the fuselage also produces a little. A **bulky** fuselage can also produce a lot of **drag**. For this reason, a fuselage is **streamlined** to decrease the drag. A

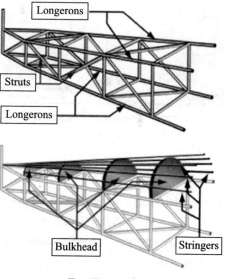

Truss Type Fuselage

streamlined fuselage has a sharp or rounded nose with a **sleek, tapered** body so that the air can flow smoothly around it.

Wings

4   The wings are **airfoils** attached to each side of the fuselage and are the main lifting surfaces that support the airplane in flight. There are numerous wing designs, sizes and shapes used by the various manufacturers. Each fulfills a certain need **with respect to** the expected performance for the particular airplane.

5   The wings are shaped with smooth surfaces. There is a **curve** to the wings which helps push the air over the top more quickly than it goes under the wings. As the wing moves, the air flowing over the top has farther to go and it moves faster than the air underneath the wing. So the air pressure above the wing is less than that below it. This produces an upward lift. The shape of the wings determines how fast and high the plane can fly.

6   Wings may be attached at the top, middle or lower portion of the fuselage. These designs are referred to as **high-wing**, **mid-wing** and **low-wing**, respectively. The number of wings can also vary. Airplanes with a single set of wings are referred to as **monoplanes**, while those with two sets are called **biplanes**.

Monoplane (left) and Biplane (right)

7   Many high-wing airplanes have external **braces** or **wing struts**, which transmit the flight and landing loads through the struts to the main fuselage structure. Since the wing struts are usually attached approximately halfway out on the wing, this type of wing structure is called **semi-cantilever**. A few high-wing and most low-wing airplanes have a full **cantilever** wing designed to carry the loads without external struts.

8   The principal structural parts of the wing are **spars**, **ribs** and **stringers**. These are reinforced by trusses, **I-beams**, tubing or other devices, including the **skin**. The wing ribs determine the shape and thickness of the wing (airfoil). In most modern airplanes, the fuel tanks either are an integral part of the wing's structure or consist of **flexible containers** mounted inside of the wing.

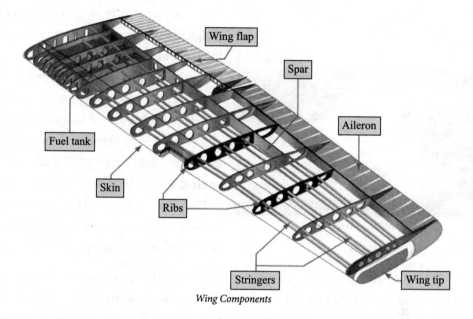

Wing Components

Empennage

9   The empennage includes the entire tail group and consists of the fixed surfaces such as the **vertical stabilizer** and the **horizontal stabilizer**. The movable surfaces include the **rudder**, the **elevator** and one or more **trim tabs**.

10   The rudder is attached to the back of the vertical stabilizer. During the flight, it is used to move the airplane's nose left and

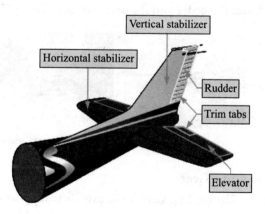

Empennage Components

right. The elevator, which is attached to the back of the horizontal stabilizer, is used to move the nose of the airplane up and down during flight. Trim tabs are small, movable portions of the **trailing edge** of the control surface. These movable trim tabs, which are controlled from the flight deck, reduce control pressures. Trim tabs may be installed on the ailerons, the rudder and/or the elevator.

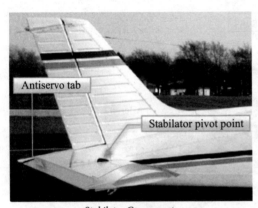

Stabilator Components

11   A second type of empennage design does not require an elevator. Instead, it incorporates a one-piece horizontal stabilizer that **pivots** from a central **hinge** point. This type of design is called a **stabilator** and is moved using the control wheel, just as the elevator is moved. For example, when a pilot pulls back on the **control wheel**, the stabilator pivots, so the trailing edge moves up. This increases the aerodynamic tail load and causes the nose of the airplane to move up.

12   The empennage is the rear part of the aircraft. In fighter jets, it may be constructed around the **exhaust nozzle**, as in some **three-engine airplanes** (with the third engine in the fuselage). In commercial aircraft, the empennage is built from the cabin pressure-cone and may contain the **Flight Data Recorder (black box), Cockpit Voice Recorder** and the **pressure out-flow valve**.

Three Types of Landing Gears

Landing Gear

13   The landing gear is the principal support of the airplane when **parked, taxiing**, taking off or landing. The most common type of the landing gear consists of wheels,

but airplanes can also be equipped with **floats** for water operations or **skis** for landing on snow.

14   The landing gear consists of three wheels—two main wheels and a third wheel positioned either at the front or rear of the airplane. Landing gear employing a rear-mounted wheel is called conventional landing gear. Airplanes with conventional landing gear are sometimes referred to as **tailwheel** airplanes. When the third wheel is located on the nose, it is called a **nosewheel**, and the design is referred to as a tricycle gear. A steerable nosewheel or tailwheel permits the airplane to be controlled throughout all operations while on the ground. Most aircraft are steered by moving the rudder pedals, whether nosewheel or tailwheel. Additionally, some aircraft are steered by **differential braking**.

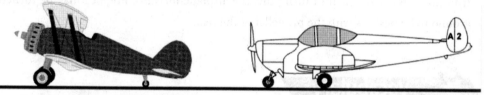

| Conventional Landing Gear (Tailwheel-type) | Tricycle Landing Gear (Nosewheel-type) |

15   The landing gear on an airplane is either fixed or **retractable**. Fixed gear is cheaper, easier to maintain and foolproof. **Aerodynamically**, a retractable gear is preferable, because with the wheels and struts placed inside the wing or fuselage, there is less interference with the airflow.

The Powerplant

16   The powerplant usually includes both the engine and the **propeller**. The primary function of the engine is to provide the power to turn the propeller. It also generates electrical power, provides a **vacuum** source

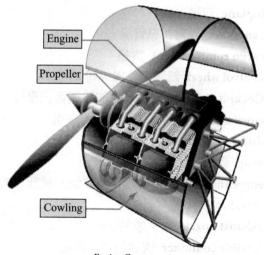

Engine Components

for some **flight instruments**, and in most **single-engine airplanes**, provides a source of heat for the pilot and passengers. The engine is covered by a **cowling** or a **nacelle**, which are both types of covered **housings**. The purpose of the cowling or nacelle is to streamline the flow of air around the engine and to help cool the engine by **ducting** air around the **cylinders**.

17   The propeller, mounted on the front of the engine, translates the rotating force of the engine into **thrust**, a forward acting force that helps move the airplane through the air. A propeller is a rotating airfoil that produces thrust through aerodynamic action. A high-pressure area is formed at the back of the propeller's airfoil, and low pressure is produced at the face of the propeller, similar to the way that lift is generated by an airfoil used as a lifting surface or wing. This **pressure differential** develops thrust from the propeller, which in turn pulls the airplane forward. Engines may be turned around to be pushers with the propeller at the rear.

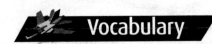 Vocabulary

Special Terms

airfoil 翼面

biplane 双翼飞机

cantilever 悬臂；悬臂梁

cargo compartment 货舱

control wheel 驾驶盘；操纵轮

Cockpit Voice Recorder 驾驶舱语音记录仪

cowling 整流罩；（发动机）防护罩

differential braking 差动刹车

drag 阻力

empennage 尾翼，机尾，尾翼组，尾部总成

elevator 升降舵

exhaust nozzle 排气喷管

flexible container 软油箱；软容器

Flight Data Recorder (black box) 飞行数据记录仪（黑匣子）

flight deck （飞机的）驾驶舱；飞行驾驶台；（航空母舰的）飞行甲板

flight instrument 飞行仪表

fuselage 机身

high-wing 上单翼（机翼在机身顶部）

horizontal stabilizer 水平安定面

I-beam 工字梁；工字钢

landing gear 起落架

lift 升力（作用于重于空气的航空器）；浮力（作用于轻于空气的航空器）

low-wing 下单翼（机翼在机身底部）

mid-wing 中单翼（机翼在机身中部）

monocoque （飞机的）硬壳式结构

monoplane 单翼飞机

nacelle 发动机短舱；机舱，吊舱

nosewheel （飞机的）前轮

rib 翼肋；肋；加强筋

passenger compartment 客舱

powerplant / power plant 动力装置；发电厂，发电站

pressure out-flow valve 压力放泄活门

pressure differential 压差

propeller 螺旋桨；推进器

rudder 方向舵

spar （飞机的）翼梁

semi-cantilever 半悬臂

semimonocoque 半硬壳式结构

single-engine airplane 单发动机飞机

skin 蒙皮

stabilator 全动式水平尾翼；安定升降舵

stringer 桁条；纵向加强条

taxi 滑行

tailwheel （飞机的）尾轮

three-engine airplane 三发动机飞机

thrust 推力

trailing edge 机翼后缘

trim tab 配平调整片

truss structure 桁架结构

vertical stabilizer 垂直安定面

wing strut 机翼斜支柱／撑杆

Words and Expressions

accommodate	[ə'kɒmədeɪt]	v.	为……提供空间；为……提供住宿（或膳宿、座位等）
aerodynamically	[ˌeərəudaɪ'næmɪkli]	ad.	空气动力学地
assembly	[ə'sembli]	n.	组件
brace	[breɪs]	n.	支架
bulky	['bʌlki]	a.	庞大的；笨重的
component	[kəm'pəunənt]	n.	组件；成分
compartment	[kəm'pɑːtmənt]	n.	舱，隔舱；隔间；水密舱
curve	[kɜːv]	n.	曲线；弯曲；曲面
cylinder	['sɪlɪndə]	n.	气缸，动作筒；圆柱，圆筒
duct	[dʌkt]	v.	用管道输送 n. 管道
float	[fləut]	n.	浮筒
hinge	[hɪndʒ]	n.	铰链；折叶 v. 装铰链，铰接
housing	['hauzɪŋ]	n.	套，罩
park	[pɑːk]	v.	停放（飞机、车辆）；滑进停机坪
pivot	['pɪvət]	v.	（使）在枢轴上旋转（或转动）n. 支点；枢轴
retractable	[rɪ'træktəbl]	a.	可收放的，可伸缩的
ski	[skiː]	n.	滑橇
streamline	['striːmlaɪn]	v.	使成流线型
sleek	[sliːk]	a.	线条流畅的；光滑的
tapered	['teɪpəd]	a.	锥形的
tubing	['tjuːbɪŋ]	n.	管子；管系，管路
vacuum	['vækjum]	n.	真空，真空状态
with respect to			关于；谈到

Exercises

Comprehension of the Text

I. Answer the following questions according to the text.

1. What are the major components of an airplane?

_____

2. What components does the fuselage of an aircraft contain?

_____

3. Why is a fuselage streamlined?

_____

4. How is the upward lift produced?

_____

5. What is the function of the external braces of the high-wing airplanes?

_____

6. What are the principal structural parts of the wing?

_____

7. How does the rudder function differently from the elevator during the flight?

_____

8. What is one of the advantages of a retractable landing gear?

_____

9. What is the function of the powerplant?

_____

10. Why is the engine covered by a cowling or a nacelle?

_____

Vocabulary Practice

II. Translate the principal structural units on an F-14 aircraft in the picture given below.

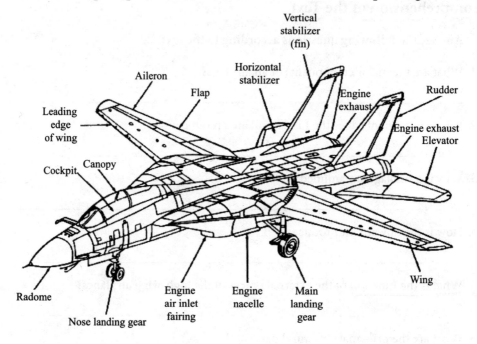

III. Complete each of the following sentences with a word from the box. Change the form if necessary.

accommodate	taxi	cockpit	streamline	pivot
compartment	curve	thrust	instrument	float

1. Flight _____, in the cockpit of an aircraft, provide the pilot with information about the flight situation of that aircraft, such as altitude, airspeed and direction.

2. Because her job had been the _____ of her life, retirement was very difficult.

3. An amphibious helicopter can be fitted with utility _____ in the same manner as a floatplane.

4. All the _____ in the boat are watertight.

5. It is said that J10B has super maneuverability due to its _____ -vectored engines that allow for sharp turns.

6. Boeing might have mocked up the 777 _____ just to see if all the switches could be reached from the pilot's seat.

7. These new cars all have a beautifully _____ design.

8. Most cruise ships are fitted with staterooms that provide lodging for two passengers, and then a fewer number that _____ three or four passengers.

9. The fish pushes water aside by the forward motion of its head and with a(n) _____ of its body and its flexible tail.

10. His friend started the engine and began to _____ onto the runway of the airport.

IV. Complete each of the following definitions with a word from the box.

vertical stabilizer	elevator	nacelle	trailing edge	cowling
stabilator	aileron	trim tab	landing gear	rudder

1. A(n) _____ is a hinged moveable part on the trailing edge of the vertical stabilizer for airplane yaw (left and right) control.

2. A(n) _____ is a hinged moveable part on the trailing edge of each wing for airplane roll (wing up and wing down) control.

3. A(n) _____ is the covering of a vehicle's engine, most often found on automobiles and aircraft.

4. The _____ is the structure that supports an aircraft on the ground and allows it to taxi, takeoff and land.

5. A(n) _____ is the horizontal component of an airplane's empennage extending on both sides of the fuselage or boom.

6. A(n) _____ is a small hinged movable part on the trailing edge of a control surface (aileron, rudder).

7. A(n) _____ is a vertical surface of the empennage for stability/control about the vertical axis.

8. A(n) _____ is a streamlined enclosure on the wing or fuselage for the engine.

9. A(n) _____ is a hinged moveable part on the trailing edge of the horizontal stabilizer for airplane pitch (nose up and nose down) control.

10. The _____ of an aerodynamic surface such as a wing is its rear edge, where the airflow separated by the leading edge rejoins.

V. Complete the following short passage with the words from the box. Change the form if necessary.

| streamlined | weapon | cockpit | weight | tube |
| fuselage | cargo | wing | drag | mission |

The *1*_____, or body of the airplane, is a long *2*_____ which holds all the pieces of an airplane together. It is hollow to reduce *3*_____. As with most other parts of the airplane, the shape of the fuselage is normally determined by the *4*_____ of the aircraft. A supersonic fighter plane has a very slender, *5*_____ fuselage to reduce the *6*_____ associated with high-speed flight. An airliner has a wider fuselage to carry the maximum number of passengers. On an airliner, the pilots sit in a *7*_____ at the front of the fuselage. Passengers and *8*_____ are carried in the rear of the fuselage and the fuel is usually stored in the *9*_____. For a fighter plane, the cockpit is normally on top of the fuselage, *10*_____ are carried on the wings, and the engines and fuel are placed at the rear of the fuselage.

Listening Practice

VI. Watch the video clip about the basic components of an airplane and fill in the blanks.

The empennage, derived from a French word having to do with feathering an arrow, is commonly referred to as the *1*_____ section of the aircraft. It consists of two important surfaces, the *2*_____ and *3*_____ stabilizers. These stabilizers are surfaces on the tail that help keep the airplane under control while flying through the air.

Beneath the fuselage sits the *4*_____, also known as the undercarriage. This structure is used to support the aircraft while on the ground. There are generally two different types of configurations: *5*_____ and *6*_____ gear. Tricycle gear is so named because wheel configuration resembles that of a child's tricycle. That is, it has one lead wheel near the plane's *7*_____ and two main wheels behind it, typically under the wings. Today, this is the more popular of the two types, because it allows for easier landings and improves *8*_____ while moving on the ground, also known as

*9*_____. Conventional gear on the other hand is the older style that was popular a few decades ago. Similar to before, two *10*_____ are typically situated under the wings, but the third wheel is located under the airplane's tail. This results in the tail of the plane being very close to the ground while the front of the airplane sits much higher. This obstructs the pilot's forward view because of the airplane's nose-high *11*_____. However, it does allow for larger engines and propeller to be installed on the aircraft. This setup is also the less stable of the two, making landings more difficult, especially in a *12*_____.

Finally, there is the powerplant, which in layman's terms is the engine. Airplanes can have one engine called a single-engine airplane or have multiple engines called *13*_____ airplanes. In most smaller general aviation aircraft, reciprocating engines are used like the ones found in cars. In many ways, however, airplane engines are simpler than car engines. The most basic of reciprocating engines on airplanes are not *14*_____, are not liquid-cooled and are not even fuel-injected. If you are unfamiliar with those concepts, don't worry. We'll cover the basics of those topics coming up.

With reciprocating engines also comes the requirement of a propeller. Just as there are different engine *15*_____, there are also different types of propellers. These propellers can range from the simplest two-bladed propeller made of a solid piece of wood to a complicated multi-bladed propeller with additional built-in features. These features can include the ability to shut office or even to change the blade angle during flight. The rotating of the blades is similar in purpose to a car's transmission. So there you have it. Those are the major components that make up an airplane.

Translating Practice

VII. Translate the following sentences into Chinese.

1. While wings produce most of the lift, the fuselage also produces a little. A bulky fuselage can also produce a lot of drag. For this reason, a fuselage is streamlined to decrease the drag.

_____

_____

2. As the wing moves, the air flowing over the top has farther to go and it moves faster than the air underneath the wing. So the air pressure above the wing is less than that below it. This produces an upward lift.

_____

_____

3. When a pilot pulls back on the control wheel, the stabilator pivots, so the trailing edge moves up. This increases the aerodynamic tail load and causes the nose of the airplane to move up.

_____

_____

4. Aerodynamically, a retractable gear is preferable because, with the wheels and struts placed inside the wing or fuselage, there is less interference with the airflow.

_____

_____

5. Most aircraft are steered by moving the rudder pedals, whether nosewheel or tailwheel. Additionally, some aircraft are steered by differential braking.

_____

_____

VIII. Translate the following paragraph into English.

   对于任何飞机而言，要飞行就必须能够提起飞机自重、燃油重量以及乘客和货物的重量。机翼能提供大部分升力使飞机在空中保持飞行。为了产生升力，必须推进飞机在空中飞行，而空气则以气动阻力的形式阻挡飞机运动。现代大型客机使用翼尖上的小翼来减少阻力。位于机翼下方的涡轮发动机也为飞机提供推力来克服阻力，推进飞机在空中向前飞行。

_____

_____

_____

_____

⊘ TEXT B

Types of Military Aircraft

1   A military aircraft is any **fixed-wing** aircraft or **rotary-wing aircraft** that is operated by a legal or **insurrectionary** armed service of any type. Military aircraft can be either combat or non-combat.

2   **Combat aircraft** are aircraft designed to destroy enemy equipment using their own **armaments**. Combat aircraft are normally developed and **procured** by military forces.

3   **Non-combat aircraft** are aircraft not designed for combat as their primary function but may carry weapons for self-defense. These mainly operate in support roles and may be developed by either military forces or civilian organizations.

Combat Aircraft

4   Combat aircraft or "warplanes", are divided broadly into **multirole fighters, bombers** and **attackers**, with several **variations** between them, including **fighter-bombers**, such as the MiG-23[1], **ground-attack aircraft**, such as the Soviet Ilyushin Il-2 Shturmovik[2]. Also included among combat aircraft are **long-range maritime patrol aircraft**, such as the

MiG-23

Hawker Siddeley Nimrod[3] and the S-3 Viking[4] that are often equipped to attack with **anti-ship missiles** and **anti-submarine weapons**.

---

1   **MiG-23:** 米格 -23 战斗机，第三代喷气式战斗机。
2   **Ilyushin Il-2 Shturmovik:** 伊柳申伊尔 2 型强击机，世界上制造数量最多的军用飞机。
3   **Hawker Siddeley Nimrod:** 霍克·西德利 "猎迷" 反潜 / 预警机，英国设计和制造的机型。
4   **S-3 Viking:** S-3 "北欧海盗" 反潜机。

Fighter Aircraft

5   The main role of fighter aircraft is destroying enemy aircraft in air-to-air combat, offensive or defensive. Many fighters are fast and highly **maneuverable**. **Escorting** bombers or other aircraft is also a common task. They are capable of carrying a variety of weapons, including machine guns, cannons, rockets and guided missiles. Many modern fighters can attack enemy fighters from a great distance even before the enemy sees them. Examples of **air superiority** fighters include the F-22 Raptor[1]. WWII fighters include the British Spitfire[2], the American P-51 Mustang[3] and German

F-22 Raptor

Bf-109[4]. An example of an **interceptor** (a fighter designed to take-off and quickly intercept and **shoot down** enemy planes) would be the MiG-25[5]. An example of a heavy fighter is the Messerschmitt Bf-110[6]. The term "fighter" is also applied to aircraft that have virtually no air-air capability, for example, the A-10[7] ground-attack aircraft operated by USAF "Fighters" squadrons.

Bomber Aircraft

6   Bomber aircraft are normally larger heavier and less maneuverable than fighter aircraft. They are capable of carrying large **payloads** of bombs. Bombers are used almost **exclusively** for ground attacks and not fast or **agile** enough to take on enemy fighters head-to-head. A few bombers have a single engine and require one pilot to operate, and others have two or more engines and require crews of two or more. A

---

1   **F-22 Raptor**: F-22 "猛禽" 战斗机，美国空军第五代单座双发全天候隐形战术战斗机。

2   **Spitfire**: 喷火式战斗机，英国及盟国在二战中和二战后使用的单座战斗机。

3   **P-51 Mustang**: P-51 "野马" 战斗机，英国空军和美国空军使用的单座单发战斗机。

4   **Bf-109**: Bf-109 战斗机，德国二战时期的战斗机，第一批真正的现代战斗机。

5   **MiG-25**: 米格 -25 战斗机，由苏联米高扬设计局设计，用作超音速截击机和侦察机。

6   **Messerschmitt Bf 110**: 梅塞施密特 Bf-110 战斗机，二战时纳粹德国研发的重型战斗机和歼击机。

7   **A-10**: 全称 A-10 Thunderbolt II，A-10 "雷电 II" 攻击机，20 世纪 70 年代美国空军用于近距空中支援的对地攻击机。

limited number of bombers, such as the B-2 Spirit[1], have **stealth** capabilities that keep them from being detected by the enemy radar. An example of a conventional modern bomber would be the B-52 Strato Fortress[2]. An example of a WWII bomber would be a B-17 Flying Fortress[3]. Bombers include **light bombers**, **medium bombers**, **heavy bombers**, **dive bombers** and **torpedo bombers**. The US Navy and Marines have traditionally referred to their light and medium bombers as "attack aircraft".

B-2 Spirit

Attack Aircraft

7   Attack aircraft can be used to provide support for friendly ground troops. Some are able to carry **conventional weapons** or **nuclear weapons** far behind enemy lines to strike **priority ground targets**. **Attack helicopters** attack enemy **armor** and provide close air support for ground troops. An example of historical ground-attack aircraft is the Soviet

AC-130

Ilyushin Il-2 Shturmovik. Several types of transport airplanes have been armed with **sideways** firing weapons as **gunships** for ground attack. These include the AC-130[4] and AC-47[5] aircraft.

8   In modern air forces, the distinction between bombers, fighter-bombers and attack aircraft has become **blurred**. Many attack aircraft, even ones that look like fighters, are optimized to drop bombs, with very little ability to engage in **aerial combat**. Indeed, the design qualities that make an effective low-level attack aircraft

---

1 **B-2 Spirit:** B-2 "幽灵" 隐形战略轰炸机。
2 **B-52 Strato Fortress:** B-52 "同温层堡垒" 轰炸机，远程亚音速喷气式战略轰炸机。
3 **B-17 Flying Fortress:** B-17 "飞行堡垒" 轰炸机，美国二战时期使用的四发重型轰炸机。
4 **AC-130:** AC-130 空中炮艇机，C-130 的对地攻击型飞机。
5 **AC-47:** AC-47 "幽灵" 空中炮艇机，美国空军在越战时期研发的飞机。

EF-111A Raven

make for a **distinctly** inferior air superiority fighter and vice versa. Perhaps the most meaningful distinction is that a bomber is generally a long-range aircraft capable of striking targets deep within enemy territory, whereas fighter bomber and attack aircraft are limited to "**theater**" missions in and around the immediate area of battlefield combat. Even that distinction is **muddied** by the availability of the aerial refueling, which greatly increases the potential **radius** of the combat operations.

Electronic Warfare Aircraft

9   Electronic warfare aircraft are military aircraft equipped for **Electronic Warfare (EW)**—i.e., **degrading** the effectiveness of the enemy's radar and radio systems.

P-8A Poseidon

Maritime Patrol Aircraft

10   Maritime patrol aircraft are fixed-wing military aircraft designed to operate for long durations over water in maritime patrol roles—in particular anti-submarine, anti-ship and **Search and Rescue (SAR)**.

Multirole Combat Aircraft

11   Many combat aircraft today have a multirole ability. Normally only applied to fixed-wing aircraft, this term signifies that the plane in question can be a fighter or a bomber, depending on what the mission calls for. An example of a multirole design is the F/A-18 Hornet. A WWII example would be the P-38

F-16 Fighting Falcon

Lightning[1]. Some fighter aircraft, such as the F-16 Fighting Falcon[2], are mostly used as "bomb trucks", despite being designed for aerial combat.

Non-Combat Aircraft

12   Non-combat roles of military aircraft include Search and Rescue, **reconnaissance**, observation/surveillance, **Airborne Early Warning and Control (AEW&C)**, transport, training and aerial refueling.

13   Many civil aircraft, both fixed-wing and rotary-wing, have been produced in separate models for military use, such as the civilian Douglas DC-3 airliner[3], which became the military Douglas C-47 Skytrain[4], British "Dakota" transport planes, and decades later, the USAF's AC-47 aerial gunships. Even the fabric-covered two-seat Piper J3 Cub[5] had a military version. **Gliders** and balloons have also been used as military aircraft; for example, balloons were used for observation during the American Civil War and WWI, and military gliders were used during WWII to deliver ground troops in **airborne assaults**.

AC-47

Military Transport Aircraft

14   Military transport (**logistics**) aircraft are primarily used to transport troops and **war supplies**. Cargo can be attached to **pallets**, which are easily loaded, secured for flight and quickly unloaded for delivery. Cargo may also be **discharged** from flying aircraft on

A KC-135R is refueling an F-15.

---

1   **P-38 Lightning:** P-38 "闪电" 战斗机，美国二战时期的活塞式战斗机。
2   **F-16 Fighting Falcon:** F-16 "战隼" 战斗机，美国空军的单发超音速多功能战斗机。
3   **Douglas DC-3 airliner:** 道格拉斯 DC-3 飞机，20 世纪 30 年代至 40 年代最重要的螺旋桨驱动运输机。
4   **Douglas C-47 Skytrain:** 道格拉斯 C-47 "空中列车" 运输机。
5   **Piper J3 Cub:** 派珀 J3 "幼兽" 飞机。

parachutes, eliminating the need for landing. Also included in this category are **aerial tankers** which can refuel other aircraft while in flight. An example of a transport aircraft is the C-17 Globemaster III[1]. A WWII example would be the C-47. An example of a tanker craft would be the KC-135 Stratotanker[2]. Helicopters and gliders can transport troops and supplies to areas where other aircraft would be unable to land.

15　Calling a military aircraft a "cargo plane" is incorrect, because military transport planes can also carry **parachuters** and other soldiers.

Airborne Early Warning and Control Aircraft

16　An Airborne Early Warning and Control (AEW&C) system is an **airborne radar system** designed to detect aircraft, ships and vehicles at long ranges, and control and command the **battle space** in an **air engagement** by directing fighter and attack aircraft

E-3 Sentry

strikes. AEW&C units are also used to carry out surveillance, including monitor over ground targets and frequently perform Command and Control, Battle Management (C2BM) functions similar to an Airport Traffic Controller giving military command over other forces. Used at a high altitude, the radars on the aircraft allow the operators to distinguish between **friendly and hostile aircraft** hundreds of miles away.

17　Airborne Early Warning and Control aircraft are used for both defensive and offensive air operations, and are to the **NATO** and the US Forces trained or integrated Air Forces what the **Command Information Center** (CIC) is to a Navy Warship[3], plus a highly mobile and powerful radar platform. The system is used offensively to direct fighters to their target locations and defensively to counter attacks by enemy

---

1　**C-17 Globemaster III:** C-17 "环球霸王 III" 运输机，20 世纪 80 年代至 90 年代研发的大型军用运输机。

2　**KC-135 Stratotanker:** KC-135 "同温层" 加油机，美国空军的首批喷气式加油机。

3　该句使用句型 "A is to B what X is to Y"，意思是 "A 之于 B 如同 X 之于 Y"。句中 what 为关系代词，相当于 that which，在从句中作表语 。该句型的语义功能是对两事物进行对比。如 "Air is to us what water is to fish." 译为 "空气之于我们，如同水之于鱼"。

forces, both air and ground. As useful is the advantage of command and control from a high altitude, the United States Navy operates AEW&C aircraft off its Supercarriers to **augment** and protect its carrier Command Information Centers.

MQ-4C Triton

18   AEW&C is also known by the older terms "**Airborne Early Warning**" (AEW) and "**Airborne Warning and Control System**" (AWACS) although AWACS is the name of a specific system currently used by the NATO and the USAF and is often used in error to describe similar systems.

Reconnaissance and Surveillance Aircraft

19   Reconnaissance aircraft are primarily used to gather intelligence. They are equipped with cameras and other **sensors**. These aircraft may be specially designed or modified from a basic fighter or bomber type. This role is increasingly being filled by satellites and **Unmanned Aerial Vehicles (UAVs)**.

20   Surveillance and observation aircraft use radar and other sensors for **battlefield surveillance**, airspace surveillance, maritime patrol and **artillery spotting**. They include modified civil aircraft designs, moored balloons and UAVs.

Experimental Aircraft

21   **Experimental aircraft** are designed in order to test advanced **aerodynamic**, structural, **avionic** or **propulsive** concepts. These are usually well instrumented, with performance data **telemetered** on radio-frequency **data links** to **ground stations** located at the **test ranges** where they are flown. An example of an experimental aircraft is the XB-70 Valkyrie[1].

XB-70 Valkyrie

---

1   **XB-70 Valkyrie:** B-70 "女武神"轰炸机，美国空军计划的深入渗透战略轰炸机的原型机；六发驱动，能以 3 马赫速度巡航数千海里。

Special Terms

aerial combat 空中战斗

aerial tanker 空中加油机

air engagement 空战

airborne assault 空降突击

Airborne Early Warning and Control (AEW&C) 空中预警与控制

Airborne Early Warning (AEW) 空中预警

airborne radar system 机载雷达系统

Airborne Warning and Control System (AWACS) 机载预警与控制系统

airspace surveillance 空域监视

air superiority 空中优势

anti-ship missile 反舰导弹

anti-submarine weapon 反潜武器

armor 装甲部队；（军舰、坦克等的）装甲；盔甲

artillery spotting 炮兵射击观测；火炮校射

attacker 攻击机；强击机

attack helicopter 攻击直升机，强击直升机

battlefield surveillance 战场监视

battle space 作战空间，战斗空间

bomber 轰炸机

Command and Control, Battle Management (C2BM) 指挥、控制和作战管理

combat aircraft 作战飞机

Command Information Center (CIC) 指挥情报中心；司令部情报中心

conventional weapon 常规武器

data link 数据链

dive bomber 俯冲轰炸机

Electronic Warfare (EW) 电子战

experimental aircraft 试验机

fighter-bomber 战斗轰炸机，歼轰机

fixed-wing aircraft 固定翼飞机

friendly and hostile aircraft 友机和敌机

glider 滑翔机

ground-attack aircraft 对地攻击机

ground station 地面站

gunship 空中炮艇机；武装运输机；武装直升机

heavy bomber 重型轰炸机

interceptor 截击机

light bomber 轻型轰炸机

long-range maritime patrol aircraft 远程海上巡逻飞机

medium bomber 中型轰炸机

multirole fighter 多功能战斗机；多用途战斗机

NATO (North Atlantic Treaty Organization) 北大西洋公约组织，简称"北约"

non-combat aircraft 非作战飞机

nuclear weapon 核武器

priority ground target 首要地面目标

rotary-wing aircraft 旋翼飞机

Search and Rescue (SAR) 搜救

sensor 传感器；探测装置

stealth 隐形，隐身

test range 试验靶场；试验区

torpedo bomber 鱼雷轰炸机

Unmanned Aerial Vehicle (UAV) 无人机

war supply 战争物资补给

Words and Expressions

aerodynamic	[ˌeərəʊdaɪˈnæmɪk]	a.	空气动力学的
agile	[ˈædʒaɪl]	a.	敏捷的，灵活的
armament	[ˈɑːməmənt]	n.	军事装备
augment	[ɔːgˈment]	v.	增加；增强；扩大
avionic	[ˌeɪviˈɒnɪk]	a.	航空电子学的
blur	[blɜː]	v.	（使）难以区分；（使）看不清
degrade	[dɪˈgreɪd]	v.	降低；削弱（尤指质量）
discharge	[ˈdɪstʃɑːdʒ]	v.	卸货；释放
escort	[ˈeskɔːt]	v./n.	护送；护航，护卫
exclusively	[ɪkˈskluːsɪvli]	ad.	专门；仅仅
distinctly	[dɪˈstɪŋktli]	ad.	显然地；特定地
insurrectionary	[ˌɪnsəˈrekʃnri]	a.	叛乱的；起义的
logistics	[ləˈdʒɪstɪks]	n.	后勤；物流
maneuverable	[məˈnuːvərəbl]	a.	可机动的；可操纵的
muddy	[ˈmʌdi]	v.	使混乱；使混浊
pallet	[ˈpælət]	n.	货盘，集装托板；空投装货底座
parachute	[ˈpærəʃuːt]	n.	降落伞
parachuter	[ˈpærəʃuːtə]	n.	伞兵；跳伞员
payload	[ˈpeɪləʊd]	n.	有效载荷；商业载重；弹头
procure	[prəˈkjʊə]	v.	取得；获得
propulsive	[prəˈpʌlsɪv]	a.	推进的；推动力的
radius	[ˈreɪdɪəs]	n.	半径；半径距离
reconnaissance	[rɪˈkɒnɪsns]	n.	侦察
sideways	[ˈsaɪdweɪz]	a.	一边（或一侧）的；旁边的 ad. 一边（或一侧）向前地
telemeter	[ˈtelimiːtə]	v.	遥测；用遥测发射器传送 n. 遥测装置
theater	[ˈθɪetə]	n.	战区；剧场
variation	[ˌveərɪˈeɪʃn]	n.	变体；变种；变化
make for			有利于；支持
shoot down			打下，击落

 Exercises

Comprehension of the Text

I. **The following table shows the types and functions of the military aircraft. Fill in the blanks according to the text.**

Category	Type	Function
Combat aircraft	fighter aircraft	_____ enemy aircraft in _____ combat, offensive or defensive
	bomber aircraft	carry large _____
	attack aircraft	provide _____ for friendly ground troops; carry _____ or _____ weapons to _____
	electronic warfare aircraft	_____ the effectiveness of _____ and radio systems
	maritime patrol aircraft	operate for _____ in maritime patrol roles— in particular _____, _____ and _____
	multirole combat aircraft	can be a _____ or a _____, depending on _____
Non-combat aircraft	military transport aircraft	transport _____ and _____
	AEW&C aircraft	be used for both _____ and _____
	reconnaissance & surveillance aircraft	be equipped with _____ and other _____; used to _____
	experiment aircraft	test _____, _____, _____, or _____ concepts

Vocabulary Practice

II. **Match the meanings in Column B with the special terms in Column A and translate the terms into Chinese.**

Column A	Column B
1. Unmanned Aerial Vehicle _____	a. a bomber aircraft that dives directly at its targets in order to provide greater accuracy for the bomb it drops
2. dive bomber _____	b. a light aircraft that flies without an engine
3. Airborne Early Warning and Control _____	c. any action involving the use of the electromagnetic spectrum or directed energy to control the spectrum, attack an enemy or impede enemy assaults
4. glider _____	d. a room in a warship or AWACS aircraft that functions as a tactical center and provides processed information for command and control of the near battlespace or area operations
5. conventional weapons _____	e. an aircraft without a human pilot on board
6. torpedo bomber _____	f. weapons that are in relatively wide use and not weapons of mass destruction (e.g., nuclear, biological, and chemical weapons)
7. Electronic Warfare _____	g. a military aircraft designed primarily to attack ships with aerial torpedoes
8. aerial refueling _____	h. bomber aircraft capable of delivering the largest payload of air-to-ground weaponry (usually bombs)
9. Command Information Center _____	i. the process of transferring aviation fuel from one military aircraft (the tanker) to another (the receiver) during flight
10. heavy bomber _____	j. a technology which detects enemy aircraft and missiles and then controls interception by friendly fighters

III. **Complete each of the following sentences with a word from the box. Change the form if necessary.**

cannon	escort	superiority	degrade	parachute
augment	theater	payload	armor	intercept

1. Two squadrons of fighters were sent to _____ the bombers.

2. The frontal _____ on this tank is 150mm thick.

3. The object of the airstrikes was to _____ the country's offensive capability.

4. This is the sort of weapon that would be used in an infantry squad to _____ the fire-power of the individual soldiers.

5. From the beginning of May, the gradual arrival of these troops gave the Versailles forces a decided _____.

6. They were firing a(n) _____ over the water and were trying to make my body come up the top of the water.

7. Strategic mobility implies the ability of forces to move rapidly between _____.

8. The group _____ behind enemy lines.

9. These _____ ships can discover and attack the submarine rapidly.

10. The _____ of this aircraft includes laser-guided bombs and heat-seeking missiles.

Translating Practice

IV. **Translate the following sentences into Chinese.**

1. Also included among combat aircraft are long-range maritime patrol aircraft, such as the Hawker Siddeley Nimrod and the S-3 Viking that are often equipped to attack with anti-ship missiles and anti-submarine weapons.

_____

_____

2. The term "fighter" is also applied to aircraft that have virtually no air-air capability, for example, the A-10 ground-attack aircraft operated by USAF "Fighters" squadrons.

_____

_____

3. Normally only applied to fixed-wing aircraft, this term signifies that the plane in question can be a fighter or a bomber, depending on what the mission calls for.

_____

_____

4. Used at a high altitude, the radars on the aircraft allow the operators to distinguish between friendly and hostile aircraft hundreds of miles away.

_____

_____

5. Airborne Early Warning and Control aircraft are used for both defensive and offensive air operations, and are to the NATO and the US Forces trained or integrated Air Forces what the Command Information Center (CIC) is to a Navy Warship, plus a highly mobile and powerful radar platform.

_____

_____

V. Translate the following paragraph into English.

　　C-5 运输机有一个五人空勤组，包括驾驶员、副驾驶员、领航员、空勤机械师和装卸长（loadmaster）。空勤机械师的座位在驾驶舱内，他负责发动机、燃料系统和机上许多其他机械系统与电子系统的运转。装卸长对货物的装载、固定和卸载负责；如果有乘客的话，他也要对乘客负责。

_____

_____

_____

_____

_____

_____

 TEXT C

Aircraft Flight Control Surfaces

1   Aircraft flight control surfaces allow a pilot to adjust and control the aircraft's flight attitude. The development of an effective set of **flight controls** (飞行操纵系统) was a critical advance in the development of aircraft. Early efforts at fixed-wing aircraft design succeeded in generating sufficient lift to get the aircraft off the ground, but once aloft, the aircraft proved uncontrollable, often with disastrous results. The development of the effective flight controls is what allowed stable flight. This text describes the control surfaces used on a fixed-wing aircraft of the conventional design. Other fixed-wing aircraft configurations may use different control surfaces, but the basic principles remain. The controls (stick and rudder) for rotary-wing aircraft (helicopter or auto-gyro) accomplish the same motions about the three axes of rotation, but manipulate the rotating flight controls (**main rotor disk and tail rotor disk**) (主旋翼桨盘和尾桨桨盘) in a completely different manner.

Ailerons

2   On the trailing edge of the wing are two sets of movable surfaces. Those farthest from the center of the airplane are called ailerons.

3   The ailerons move when you turn the control wheel or move the **control stick** (操纵杆) side by side. They move in opposite directions, one going up while the other going down.

4   The ailerons are hinged on the wings and move downward to push the air down and make the wings tilt up. This moves the plane to the side and helps it turn during the flight. After landing, the **spoilers** (扰流板) are used like air brakes to reduce any remaining lift and slow down the airplane.

5   Ailerons are moving surfaces usually placed near the tips of the wings. The function of an aileron is simple, and by moving upwards or downwards, the aileron modifies the angle of attack of that section of the wing, sinking or lifting it. This

change in the aerodynamic is due to the modification of relative curve of the airfoil. Note that ailerons are complementary, so if one moves, the other will move on the other direction in the same proportion. This improves the effect as one wing is lifted and the other is sunk. Ailerons control the X-axis or roll movement of the aircraft.

6   Ailerons are controlled by the pilot from the cockpit, with the lateral axis of the **joystick** (操纵杆). To make coordinated turns, the movement must be combined with the rudder in the same direction. In some planes (delta-wing airplanes), ailerons are just divided elevators, being possible to use the same surface as aileron or elevator.

Rudder

7   The vertical stabilizer functions with the same principle as a wing does, but being symmetrical. It is a main control surface of the airplanes (fixed-wing aircraft). Obviously, it has a vertical position, usually in the tail of the aircraft. There can be multiple vertical stabilizers (in large aircraft usually).

8   The vertical stabilizer has a moving part which is called rudder. This acts as an aileron does in the wing. When it is moved to one or the other side, it produces a pressure difference over the stabilizer since its movement is equal to change the angle of attack of this "wing".

9   The rudder controls the Y-axis or **yaw** (偏航) of the plane and is controlled from the cockpit with the pedals. In a coordinated turn, rudder and ailerons must be coordinated, but you can use rudder only to "slide" the aircraft.

Elevator

10   The horizontal stabilizer is the main control surface of the aircraft, mainly of the airplanes (fixed-wing aircraft). It functions as a wing does, creating a second point of lift along the fuselage which provides stability to the aircraft in the Z-axis. Its function is not to provide more lift but to control the **pitch** (俯仰) of the aircraft (by modifying the angle of attack of the wing). This is thanks to a moving part or parts called elevators, which act like an aileron, and are controlled by the **longitudinal axis** (纵轴) of the joystick or wheel.

11　　Obviously, the horizontal stabilizer has a horizontal position, usually in the tail of the aircraft. It can be on the top of the vertical stabilizer (**T-tail aircraft**) (T型尾翼飞机) or divided into two parts crossing the vertical stabilizer. Some horizontal stabilizers have no elevators but are a whole elevator (mainly in gliders since it has better aerodynamic performance). In **Canard-configuration planes** (鸭式布局飞机), the horizontal stabilizer is positioned not in the tail but in the nose of the aircraft. (Noting that its movement to reduce or increase pitch will be inverted from the one it does when it's placed in the tail.)

12　　Sometimes, elevators are mixed with rudders in the same control surface, creating **V-tail aircraft** (V型尾翼飞机). It can also be combined with ailerons, mainly in delta-wing planes.

Flaps (襟翼)

13　　The hinged control surfaces are used to steer and control the airplane. The flaps and ailerons are connected to the backside of the wings. The flaps slide back and down to increase the surface of the wing area. They also tilt down to increase the curve of the wing. The **slats** (缝翼) move out from the front of the wings to make the wing space larger. This helps to increase the lifting force of the wing at slower speeds like takeoff and landing.

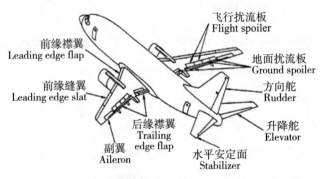

Flight Control Surfaces

14　　Flaps are hinged surfaces mounted on the trailing edges of the wings of a fixed-wing aircraft to reduce the speed at which an aircraft can be safely flown and to increase the angle of descent for landing. They shorten takeoff and landing distances. Flaps do this by lowering the **stall** (失速) speed and increasing the drag.

15   Extending flaps increases the **camber** (曲度) or **curvature** (曲率) of the wing, raising the maximum lift coefficient—or the lift that a wing can generate. This allows the aircraft to generate as much lift as possible but at a lower speed, reducing the stalling speed of the aircraft, or the minimum speed at which the aircraft will maintain flight. Extending flaps increases drag which can be beneficial during approach and landing because it slows the aircraft. On some aircraft, a useful side effect of flap deployment is a decrease in aircraft pitch angle which improves the pilot's view of the runway over the nose of the aircraft during landing; however, the flaps may also cause pitch up, depending on the type of flap and the location of the wing.

16   There are many different types of flaps in use, with the specific choice depending on the size, speed and complexity of the aircraft on which they are to be used, as well as the era in which the aircraft was designed. **Plain flaps** (简单襟翼), **Slotted flaps** (开缝襟翼), and **Fowler flaps** (富勒襟翼) are the most common. **Kruger flaps** (克鲁格襟翼) are positioned on the **leading edge of the wings** (机翼前缘) and are used on many jet airliners.

 Exercises

Comprehension of the Text

Decide whether the following statements are true (T) or false (F) according to the text.

( ) *1.* Effective flight controls make aircraft fly stable.

( ) *2.* Ailerons move in the same direction with the same angle of attack.

( ) *3.* The rudder controls the Z-axis of the plane.

( ) *4.* The horizontal stabilizer can create a second point of lift along the fuselage which provides stability to the aircraft in the Z-axis.

( ) *5.* The flaps and ailerons are connected to the front side of the wings.

( ) *6.* Extending flaps increases drag which can be harmful during approach and landing, because it slows the aircraft.

UNIT PROJECT

Mind Mapping

Work in groups and draw two mind maps respectively according to the following topics.

1. major components of an airplane and their main functions
2. different types of military aircraft

Oral Practice

Work in groups and find more information on one of the popular types of the military aircraft. And one student from each group will make a 3-minute oral presentation to introduce the important roles, features and some performance data of this type of aircraft on the basis of the group work. You may refer to Text B of this unit and the relevant information from the Internet.

Writing Practice

Based on the group work above, write a composition with at least 150 words on the topic of "My Favorite Aircraft". You may refer to the questions below.

1. What is your favorite type of aircraft?
2. Why do you love it? (List some impressive functions it possesses.)
3. What does this type of aircraft require of a pilot?

Unit 5
Airspace and Air Traffic Control

⊘ Warming Up

Task 1 Watch the video clip about airways and fill in the blanks.

For cars, we have highways, signs and GPS navigation to tell us where to go. But you can't see anything like that in the sky. So why don't planes get lost?

Well, actually there are kind of highways in the sky, too. They're called *1*_____. They are a bit bigger than highways, about 19 kilometers wide. And they connect all the airports. The airways even have *2*_____ and markers called *3*_____. They all have a *4*_____ name, like Didos or Neviv, or more fun ones like Leaky, Boats, Siink in Australia, and Spicy, Barbq, Ribbs in America.

The pilots can see the highways and waypoints with a GPS system. They even have GPS *5*_____. But instead of telling us where to go, the *6*_____ flies them there. Much cooler!

That gives the pilots time to check the *7*_____ or talk to *8*_____ control. Between airports, aerial control centers support the pilots in the sky. There are about 400 around the world. They know all the *9*_____ of all the airplanes and make sure they don't fly at the same *10*_____ or fly too close to each other.

That way, airplanes fly safe and always find their way!

Task 2 Discuss the following questions in groups.

1. Do you know what airspace is?

2. How much do you know about the ATC?

3. Is there any connection between ATC and the classification of airspace?

 # TEXT A

Airspace Classification

1   **Airspace** is commonly defined by the outline of the geographical area below it, and is considered to extend upward indefinitely, but it may also be considered as the limited space occupied by a formation of aircraft or the space used in an **aerial maneuver**.

2   Airspace is classified based on the activities **therein** which must be **confined** because of their nature. The two categories of airspace are: **regulatory** (Class A, B, C, D and E airspace areas, **restricted areas and prohibited areas**) and non-regulatory (**military operations areas**, **warning areas**, **alert areas** and **controlled firing areas**). Within these two categories, there are four types: controlled, uncontrolled, special use and other airspace.

3   The categories and types of airspace are **dictated** by the complexity or **density** of the aircraft movements, the nature of the operations conducted within the airspace, the level of safety required, and the national and public interest. It is important that pilots should be familiar with the operational requirements for each of the various types or classes of airspace.

Controlled Airspace

4   **Controlled airspace** is a **generic** term that covers different classifications of airspace of defined dimensions within which **Air Traffic Control (ATC)** service is provided in accordance with the airspace classifications. Controlled airspace exists where it is deemed necessary that ATC has some form of **positive control** over aircraft flying in that airspace. Controlled airspace consists of Class A, Class B, Class C, Class D and Class E.

Class A[1] Airspace

5   Class A airspace is generally the airspace from 18,000 feet Mean Sea Level (MSL) up to and including **Flight Level (FL)** 600, including the airspace **overlying** the waters within 12 **Nautical Miles (NM)** of the coast of the 48 **contiguous** states and Alaska. **Unless otherwise authorized**, all operations in Class A airspace are conducted under Instrument Flight Rules (IFR).

Class A Airspace

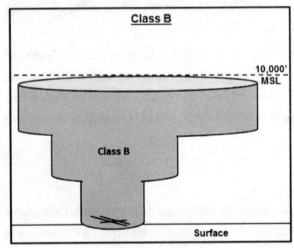

Class B Airspace

Class B Airspace

6   Class B airspace is generally the airspace from the surface to 10,000 feet MSL surrounding the nation's busiest airports **in terms of** airport operations or passenger **enplanements**. The configuration of each Class B airspace area is individually **tailored**, consisting of a surface area and two or more layers (Some Class B airspace areas resemble upside-down wedding cakes.), and is designed to contain all published instrument procedures once an aircraft enters the airspace. **ATC clearance** is required for all aircraft to operate in the area, and all aircraft that are so cleared receive separation services within the airspace.

---

1   **Class A:** A 类空域。在空域划分中，A 类、B 类、C 类、D 类、E 类和 G 类空域分别读作 Class Alpha、Class Bravo、Class Charlie、Class Delta、Class Echo 和 Class Golf，其中"Class"在陆空通话中可省略。

Class C Airspace

7   Class C airspace is generally the airspace from the surface to 4,000 feet above the **airport elevation** surrounding those airports that have an operational control tower, are serviced by a **radar approach control**, and have a certain number of IFR operations or passenger enplanements. Although the configuration of each Class C area is individually tailored, the airspace usually consists of a surface area with a five NM radius, an outer circle with a ten NM radius that extends from 1,200 feet to 4,000 feet above the airport elevation, and an outer area. Each aircraft must establish **two-way radio communications** with the ATC facility providing air traffic services **prior to** entering the airspace, and **thereafter** maintain those communications while within the airspace.

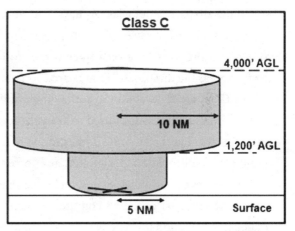

Class C Airspace

Class D Airspace

8   Class D airspace is generally the airspace from the surface to 2,500 feet above the airport elevation surrounding those airports that have an operational control tower. The configuration of each Class D airspace area is individually tailored and when instrument procedures are published, the airspace is normally designed to contain the procedures. **Arrival** extensions

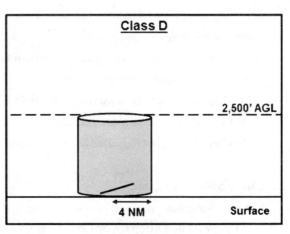

Class D Airspace

for **Instrument Approach Procedures (IAPs)** may be Class D or Class E airspace. Unless otherwise authorized, each aircraft must establish two-way radio communications with the ATC facility providing air traffic services prior to entering the airspace, and thereafter maintain those communications while in the airspace.

Class E Airspace

9   If the airspace is not Class A, B, C or D, and is controlled airspace, then it is Class E airspace. Class E airspace extends upward from either the surface or a designated altitude to the overlying or **adjacent** controlled airspace. When designated as a surface area, the airspace is **configured** to contain all instrument procedures. Also in this Class are federal **airways**, the airspace beginning at either 700 or 1,200 feet Above Ground Level (AGL) used to **transition** to and from the **terminal** or **en route** environment, and the en route domestic and **offshore** airspace areas designated below 18,000 feet MSL. Unless designated at a lower altitude, Class E airspace begins at 14,500 MSL over the United States, including that airspace overlying the waters within 12 NM of the coast of the 48 contiguous states and Alaska, up to but not including 18,000 feet MSL, and the airspace above FL 600.

Hierarchy of the Overlapping Airspace Designations

10   When **overlapping** airspace designations apply to the same airspace, the operating rules associated with the more **restrictive** airspace designation apply.

For the purpose of clarification:

(1) Class A airspace is more restrictive than Class B, C, D, E or G airspace;

(2) Class B airspace is more restrictive than Class C, D, E or G airspace;

(3) Class C airspace is more restrictive than Class D, E or G airspace;

(4) Class D airspace is more restrictive than Class E or G airspace; and

(5) Class E is more restrictive than Class G airspace.

Uncontrolled Airspace
Class G Airspace

11   **Uncontrolled airspace** or Class G airspace is the portion of the airspace that has not been designated as Class A, B, C, D or E. In other words, uncontrolled airspace

is the one in which ATC does not **exert** any executive authority, although it may act in an **advisory** manner. It is therefore designated the uncontrolled airspace. Class G airspace extends from the surface to the base of the overlying Class E airspace. Although ATC has no authority or responsibility to control air traffic, pilots should remember that there are Visual Flight Rules (VFR) minimums which apply to Class G airspace.

Special Use Airspace

12 **Special use airspace** or **Special Area of Operation (SAO)** is the designation for airspace in which certain activities must be confined, or where limitations may be imposed on aircraft operations that are not part of those activities. Certain special use airspace areas can create limitations on the mixed-use of airspace. The special use airspace **depicted** on instrument charts includes the area name or number, the effective altitude, time and weather conditions of the operation, the **controlling agency**, and the chart panel location. On **National Aeronautical Charting Group (NACG) en route charts**, this information is available on one of the end panels. Special use airspace usually consists of prohibited areas, restricted areas, warning areas, Military Operation Areas (MOA), alert areas and Controlled Firing Areas (CFA).

Other Airspace Areas

13 "Other airspace areas" is a general term referring to the majority of the remaining airspace. It includes: **Temporary Flight Restrictions (TFR), Wildlife and Recreational Area, Air Defense Identification Zone (ADIZ), Airport Advisory/ Information Services Area, Military Training Routes (MTR), Parachute Jump Aircraft Operations Area, Published VFR Routes, Terminal Radar Service Area (TRSA)**, and so on.

14 Airspace may be further **subdivided into** a variety of areas and zones, including those where there are either restrictions on flying activities or complete **prohibition** of flying activities.

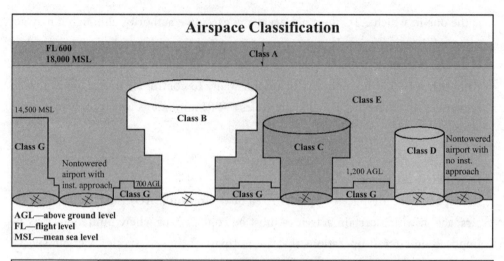

Airspace Classification

FL 600
18,000 MSL

Class A

Class E

14,500 MSL

Class B

Class G

Nontowered
airport with
inst. approach

700 AGL

Class G

Class C

Class G

1,200 AGL

Class G

Class D

Class G

Nontowered
airport with
no inst.
approach

AGL—above ground level
FL—flight level
MSL—mean sea level

Airspace	Class A	Class B	Class C	Class D	Class E	Class G
Entry Requirements	ATC clearance	ATC clearance	Prior two-way communications	Prior two-way communications	Prior two-way communications*	Prior two-way communications*
Minimum Pilot Qualifications	Instrument Rating	Private or Student certification. Local restrictions apply	Student certificate	Student certificate	Student certificate	Student certificate
Two-Way Radio Communications	Yes	Yes	Yes	Yes	Yes, under IFR flight plan*	Yes*
Special VFR Allowed	No	Yes	Yes	Yes	Yes	N/A
VFR Visibility Minimum	N/A	3 statute miles	3 statute miles	3 statute miles	3 statute miles**	1 statute mile†
VFR Minimum Distance from Clouds	N/A	Clear of clouds	500'=below, 1,000'=above, 2,000'=horizontal	500'=below, 1,000'=above, 2,000'=horizontal	500'=below,** 1,000'=above, 2,000'=horizontal	Clear of clouds†
VFR Aircraft Separation	N/A	All	IFR aircraft	Runway Operations	None	None
Traffic Advisories	Yes	Yes	Yes	Workload permitting	Workload permitting	Workload permitting
Airport Application	N/A	• Radar • Instrument Approaches • Weather • Control Tower • High Density	• Radar • Instrument Approaches • Weather • Control Tower	• Instrument Approaches • Weather • Control Tower	• Instrument Approaches • Weather	• Control Tower

*Exception: temporary tower or control tower present
**Only true below 10,000 feet.
†Only true during day at or below 1,200 feet AGL (see 14 CFR Part 91).

Airspace Classification

Special Terms

aerial maneuver 空中机动动作

airspace 空域

airport elevation 机场标高

Air Defense Identification Zone (ADIZ) 防空识别区

Air Traffic Control (ATC) 空中交通管制

ATC clearance 航行调度许可证，放行许可

Airport Advisory/Information Services Area 机场咨询 / 问讯服务区

airway 航路，航线

alert area 警戒区

arrival 到达；进场

controlled airspace 管制空域

controlling agency 管制机构

Controlled Firing Area (CFA) 射击控制区

en route / enroute 在途中；航线飞行

en route chart 航线图

Flight Level (FL) 飞行高度层

Instrument Approach Procedure (IAP) 仪表进近程序

Military Operations Area (MOA) 军事活动区

Military Training Route (MTR) 军事训练飞行航线，军事训练航路区

National Aeronautical Charting Group (NACG) 国家航图组

Nautical Mile (NM) 海里

Parachute Jump Aircraft Operations Area 飞机跳伞作业区

positive control （空中交通的）全面管制；绝对控制

prohibited area 禁航区

published VFR routes 已公布的目视飞行航线

radar approach control 雷达进近控制

restricted area 限航区

Special Area of Operation (SAO) 特殊作战区域，特殊作战空域

special use airspace 专用空域；禁区空域

Terminal Radar Service Area (TRSA) 航站雷达服务区

Temporary Flight Restriction (TFR) 临时性飞行限制（区）

two-way radio communication 双向无线电通信

uncontrolled airspace 非管制空域

warning area 危险区；警告区

Wildlife and Recreational Area 野生动物和娱乐区

Words and Expressions

adjacent	[ə'dʒeɪsnt]	a.	邻近的；毗连的
advisory	[əd'vaɪzəri]	a.	建议的；咨询的，顾问的
confine	[kən'faɪn]	v.	限制；监禁，禁闭
configure	[kən'fɪgə]	v.	设定；以（特定形式、结构）装配，安装
contiguous	[kən'tɪnjuəs]	a.	邻近的；连续的；接触的
depict	[dɪ'pɪkt]	v.	描述；描绘
dictate	[dɪk'teɪt]	v.	规定；命令，要求
density	['densəti]	n.	密度
enplanement	[en'pleɪnmənt]	n.	登机的旅客，乘客数
exert	[ɪg'zɜːt]	v.	发挥；施以影响
generic	[dʒə'nerɪk]	a.	一般的；通用的
hierarchy	['haɪərɑːki]	n.	层次体系；等级制度（尤指社会或组织）；统治集团
offshore	[ˌɒf'ʃɔː]	a.	近海的；海上的；离岸的
overlap	[ˌəʊvə'læp]	v.	交叠，（使）部分重叠
overlie	[ˌəʊvə'laɪ]	v.	置于……上面；叠加
prohibition	[ˌprəʊɪ'bɪʃn]	n.	禁止；禁令
regulatory	['regjələtəri]	a.	管理的；监管的
restrictive	[rɪ'strɪktɪv]	a.	限制（性）的；约束的
tailor	['teɪlə]	v.	专门制作
terminal	['tɜːmɪnl]	n.	航空站；候机楼区；终点站
thereafter	[ˌðeər'ɑːftə]	ad.	在……之后
therein	[ˌðeər'ɪn]	ad.	在其中；在那里

transition	[træn'zɪʃən]	v. 过渡；转变
impose...on...		把……强加于……
in terms of		就……来说；根据；在……方面
prior to		在……之前
subdivide...into...		把……再分 / 细分成……
unless otherwise authorized		除非另有规定

Exercises

Comprehension of the Text

I. Complete the following table with the information from the text.

Airspace	_____	Class A, _____ , _____ , _____ , _____ airspace
	Uncontrolled airspace	_____ airspace
	_____	Prohibited area, _____ , _____ , _____ , _____ , _____
	Other airspace areas	_____ , _____ , _____ , _____ , _____ , _____ , _____

II. Answer the following questions according to the text.

1. What is the definition of airspace?

_____

2. What are the two categories of airspace or airspace areas?

_____

3. What does Class A airspace cover?

_____

4. What are the characteristics of Class B airspace?

_____

5. What is required of an airplane before entering Class C airspace and Class D airspace?

_____

6. What is the definition of Class E airspace?

_____

7. What is the difference between controlled airspace and uncontrolled airspace?

_____

8. What should pilots remember when entering Class G airspace?

_____

9. What is the definition of special use airspace?

_____

10. What information about special use airspace is included on the instrument charts?

_____

Vocabulary Practice

III. Match the meanings in Column B with the special terms in Column A and translate the terms into Chinese.

Column A	Column B
1. restricted area _____	a. a service operated by appropriate authority to promote the safe, orderly and expeditious flow of air traffic
2. warning area _____	b. the level of the sea midway between mean low water and mean high water
3. Air Traffic Control _____	c. airspace established outside Class A airspace to separate or segregate certain non-hazardous military activities from IFR traffic and to identify for VFR traffic where these activities are conducted
4. mean sea level _____	d. an area containing hazards to any aircraft not participating in the activities being conducted in the area
5. flight level	e. rules governing a specific type of aviation where flight may be conducted with reference to the flight instruments alone

Column A	Column B
6. Instrument Flight Rules _____	f. the airspace above a specified geographical area in which the control and ready recognition of aircraft is required
7. airport elevation _____	g. rules governing the procedures for conducting flight under visual conditions
8. air defense identification zone _____	h. the airspace within which the flight of aircraft is subject to restriction while not wholly prohibited
9. military operations area _____	i. a level of constant atmospheric pressure related to a reference datum of 29.92 inches of mercury
10. Visual Flight Rules _____	j. the highest point of an airport's usable runways measured in feet from mean sea level

IV. Complete each of the following sentences with a word from the box. Change the form if necessary.

dictate	executive	configuration	elevation	radius
designate	prohibition	transition	terminal	hierarchy

1. The administration found that Iraqis were unwilling to allow the US to _____ their new rulers.

2. Fighters remaining in service at the time of change were _____ "F-51".

3. The only solution to the problem of nuclear weapons in the interests of all the people is complete _____.

4. At an airport, there is transport within the _____ as well as outside.

5. We were all within the lethal blast _____ of even a small car bomb.

6. A military department such as the Department of the Navy or Department of the Army should be distinguished from a(n) _____ department.

7. _____ training refers to the training given to a pilot or other crew members as he moves from the operation of one type of aircraft to another.

8. Rank such as corporal, sergeant or lieutenant refers to an official title, indicating a serviceman's position in the _____.

9. While the missile shield is never a threat to Russia, the new _____ will reduce Moscow's concern.

10. Target _____ refers to the angular altitude of a radar target.

V. Give the full names of the following abbreviations.

1. MOA _____   *2.* CFA _____

3. ATC _____   *4.* MSL _____

5. FL _____   *6.* NM _____

7. IFR _____   *8.* IAP _____

9. VFR _____   *10.* SAO _____

11. AGL _____   *12.* TFR _____

13. TRSA _____   *14.* ADIZ _____

15. MTR _____

VI. Complete the following short passage with the words or expressions from the box. Change the form if necessary.

monitor	air traffic controller	instruction	instrument	weather
service	Air Traffic Control	defense	flight plan	vision

The movement of aircraft through the various airspace divisions is much like players moving through a "zone" *1*_____ that a basketball or football team might use. As an aircraft travels through a given airspace division, it is *2*_____ by the one or more *3*_____ responsible for that division. They monitor this plane and give *4*_____ to the pilot. Some pilots of small aircraft fly by only *5*_____. These pilots are not required by the FAA to file *6*_____ and, except for FSS and local towers, are not *7*_____ by the mainstream *8*_____ system. Pilots of large commercial flights use *9*_____ to fly, so they can fly in all sorts of *10*_____.

Translating Practice

VII. Translate the following sentences into Chinese.

1. Airspace is commonly defined by the outline of the geographical area below it, and is considered to extend upward indefinitely, but it may also be considered as the limited space occupied by a formation of aircraft or the space used in an aerial maneuver.

2. The categories and types of airspace are dictated by the complexity or density of the aircraft movements, the nature of the operations conducted within the airspace, the level of safety required, and the national and public interest.

3. Controlled airspace is a generic term that covers different classifications of airspace of defined dimensions within which Air Traffic Control (ATC) service is provided in accordance with the airspace classifications.

4. Unless otherwise authorized, each aircraft must establish two-way radio communications with the ATC facility providing air traffic services prior to entering the airspace, and thereafter maintain those communications while in the airspace.

5. Special use airspace or Special Area of Operation (SAO) is the designation for airspace in which certain activities must be confined, or where limitations may be imposed on aircraft operations that are not part of those activities.

VIII. Translate the following paragraph into English.

空域的分类是为了确保空域的安全、有序和充分利用，满足不同空域用户的需求并达到空管资源的最优配置。自 1993 年 9 月 16 日，美国开始选择性地引入国际民航组织的空域分类标准，将美国的空域分为 A、B、C、D、E 和 G 类空域。

_____

_____

_____

_____

_____

◎ TEXT B

Air Traffic Control

Introduction

1   Just as on a busy highway, the tremendous **volume** of aircraft flying in the sky today requires traffic management. Someone has to be in control of where all those aircraft are flying, at what altitude and speed, and by what route. The task falls to the various air traffic control agencies located in nearly every country around the world. Air traffic control is a vital component for the safety and economy of the nations of the world. Without a system to keep things moving safely, people and goods cannot be transported efficiently in a **timely** manner.

2   In November 2000, the top 20 airports in the United States handled over 316,000 takeoffs and landings (**US Bureau of Transportation Statistics** Website). Smaller busy airports often surround these big airports **situated** in heavy air-traffic areas. The **round-the-clock** coordination required to keep this system working is crucial. **Air traffic controllers** are the people who do the job. They are highly-trained individuals who have to take yearly **refresher training**, as well as monthly computer-based instruction and evaluations of their use of proper **phraseology**.

3   There are different types of air traffic controllers who communicate with pilots, from the time that the pilot calls for a **clearance**, through taxi, takeoff, **cruise**, arrival, landing and taxiing to parking. Some controllers work in the tall **towers** that you've seen at airports; others stare at a radar screen miles from any airport. Some serve more than one role, for example, when a **tower controller** acts as a **ground controller**.

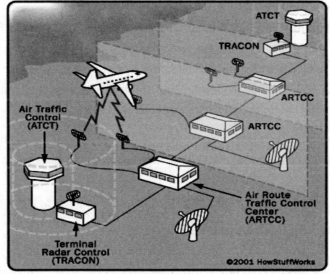

The Air Traffic Control System

Call Signs

4   How do the controllers **keep track of** who's **on the radio**? All aircraft use a call sign. Call signs are composed of the registration letters and numbers painted on the side of the plane for civilian aircraft, **airline flight numbers** for airliners, and often a combination of a **branch name** and a number for military flights. Most countries use only letters for call signs, but the US uses a combination of letters and numbers for many call signs. A few examples are:

5   "N700MS" is an aircraft that has the civilian registration "N700MS". The call sign of it is spoken as "November seven zero zero Mike Sierra". November, in this instance, is the letter with which all US aircraft registrations begin. "World Travel 455" is the call sign for Flight 455 flown by World Travel Airlines. You generally say this as, "World Travel four fifty-five" or "World Travel four five five". "Navy 44F" is the call sign for

a military flight. This is spoken as "Navy four four Foxtrot". However, there are many **variations** of military call signs, depending on the **branch of service**, **squadron designation** and what type of aircraft is being flown. You can search the Web for "military call signs" to see some of the real-world military call signs in use today.

Transponder (Squawk) Codes

6   In addition to the call sign, an aircraft can be identified on radar by a **"squawk"** code. Most modern aircraft, from the little guys to the big planes, are equipped with a radio called a **transponder**. The pilot can dial a series of four numbers (the **transponder code**, or **squawk code**) into the transponder. The transponder code identifies the aircraft on the ATC radar screen.

7   The standard real-world squawk code for VFR flight is 1200. If the flight is IFR (and in some instances while VFR), the controller will provide a squawk code to the pilot.

The Language of the Air Traffic Control

8   Pilots, air traffic controllers, and **Ground Controlled Approach (GCA)** operators use a special kind of English. This special English is used all over the world. A French pilot landing in Bangkok[1] uses this language, and so does a Japanese pilot taking off from Frankfurt[2]. In this language, letters of the **alphabet** are not usually spoken by their usual names, but by words. For example, A is spoken as Alfa and R is spoken as Romeo. Air Force people are so familiar with these words and they sometimes use them on the telephone, too, if the spelling is necessary. For example, Captain Turner might spell his name "Tango Uniform Romeo November Echo Romeo".

9   The language of Air Traffic Control has its own grammar, too, as well as a very special vocabulary. For example, a pilot calling an Air Route Traffic Control Center to tell them that he has just arrived over the center may say, "Air Force one niner

---

1   **Bangkok:** 泰国首都曼谷。

2   **Frankfurt:** 德国城市法兰克福。

niner zero six, El Paso[1] four five, one niner thousand. I. F. R., Randolph, **Clear-Air Turbulence (CAT)**. Over."

10   What he meant was, "I am calling the Air Route Traffic Control Center at El Paso. My aircraft number is 19906. I arrived here at 7:45 cruising at 19,000 feet altitude. I will land at Randolph Air Force Base[2]. The air is very rough at the moment. That is all I have to say; I am ready to listen to you."

Special Terms

airline flight number 航班号

air traffic controller 空中交通管制员

branch name 兵种名称

branch of service 兵种

Clear-Air Turbulence (CAT) 晴空湍流

clearance （飞行起降的）许可；准许

cruise 巡航；航行

Ground Controlled Approach (GCA) 地面控制进近

ground controller 地面管制员

refresher training 复训

squadron designation 飞行中队番号

squawk （口语）（应答机）发送信号；将敌我识别器转到"正常"位置（通话代语）

squawk code 应答机编码

tower controller 塔台管制员

transponder 应答机，应答器；脉冲转发器

transponder code 应答机编码

US Bureau of Transportation Statistics 美国交通统计局

---

1   **El Paso:** 美国得克萨斯州最西端的边境城市埃尔帕索。

2   **Randolph Air Force Base:** 伦道夫空军基地，美国空军教育和培训司令部所在地。

Words and Expressions

alphabet	['ælfəbet]	n.	字母表，字母系统；入门，初级
phraseology	[ˌfreɪzi'ɒlədʒi]	n.	用词，措辞
round-the-clock	[ˌraʊndðə'klɒk]	a.	24 小时不间断的，昼夜连续的
situate	['sɪtʃueɪt]	v.	使位于；使处于……地位
timely	['taɪmli]	a.	及时的；适时的
tower	['taʊə]	n.	塔台；塔状建筑
variation	[ˌveəri'eɪʃn]	n.	变体；变化；变异
volume	['vɒljum]	n.	量；音量；体积
fall to			（任务）由……负责；落到……的肩上
keep track of			追踪，跟踪
on the radio			无线电联络

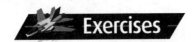

Exercises

Comprehension of the Text

I. **Answer the following questions according to the text.**

1. Why is air traffic control a vital component for the safety and economy of the nations of the world?

_____

2. Are there different types of air traffic controllers? What are they?

_____

3. What should a qualified air traffic controller do to fulfill his job well?

_____

4. What are call signs composed of?

_____

5. What is the composition of call signs adopted by the US?

_____

6. How should the call sign of "N700MS" be spoken?

_____

7. What factors might lead to many variations of military call signs?

_____

8. In addition to call signs, how can an aircraft be identified on the ATC radar screen?

_____

9. What is the standard real-world squawk code for VFR flight? How will the controller do with the squawk code if the flight is IFR?

_____

10. What are the special characteristics of the English language used by air traffic controllers, pilot and GCA operators?

_____

Vocabulary Practice

II. Complete each of the following definitions with a special term from the box.

tower controller	refresher training	transponder	clear-air turbulence
ground controller	call sign	GCA	TRACON

1. A _____ is a sign used as a signal by aircraft to identify themselves to friendly forces.
2. _____ is a radar approach system operated from the ground by the air traffic personnel, transmitting instructions to the pilot by radio.
3. A _____ is the turbulence or gustiness in unclouded air, as distinguished from the storm turbulence.
4. A _____ is an air traffic controller who controls aircraft within the immediate vicinity of the airport and uses visual observation from the airport tower.
5. A _____ is an electronic device that receives a challenging signal and automatically transmits a response.
6. A _____ is an air traffic controller who gives instructions to the pilot by radio using a radar approach system on the ground.
7. _____ refers to training, such as military training given a person after he has been inactive for a considerable period of time, to refresh his skills and knowledge and bring him up to date in any given field.

8. Also within each zone are portions of airspace, about 50 miles (80.5 km) in diameter, called _____ airspaces. It handles departing and approaching aircraft within its space.

Listening Practice

III. Watch the video clip about air traffic control and fill in the blanks.

In our busy skies, controlling each flight from departure to arrival is integral to maintaining our excellent safety records. "Flight is controlled by a controller from the time it pushes off the gate, to the time it gets to its destination and parks at the gate, and the door is open. The reason for that is for *1*_____. There are so many planes in the *2*_____. They need to be separated, and need to be controlled. "

It's a complex world. Simply *3*_____ each flight from the gate to the runway may involve several steps. "The pilot will call for clearance either be it electronic means or *4*_____, he receives his clearance from departure to destination. The airplane will then push off the gate, and talk to the *5*_____ in Dulles, who will take him to the appropriate runway, and put him where he needs to be in reference to other aircraft or in line for his sequence for reference whether any other factors are affecting their flying. The *6*_____ will then take the aircraft and he is the one that actually issues a *7*_____ to the aircraft to get him airborne."

After a flight takes off, the tower controller tells the pilot to contact *8*_____, a part of another air traffic entity known as TRACON. TRACONs typically handles those departures and *9*_____ for instrument flights within a designated area, which usually includes both large and small airports.

"Once the air traffic control towers successfully hand the flights off to us, the TRACONs, it's our job to get you through all the other aircraft in the local area, and up to cruising altitude on the way to your destination."

"We work with aircraft that are transiting from the airports into the inner structure, so we have all of the *10*_____ and descending from roughly 23,000 feet down to the surface."

As each flight moves beyond the terminal *11*_____, it is passed onto a regional air route traffic control center, where the flight is carefully directed to its destination, there are 20 regional *12*_____ covering the continental United States. In every center, they have *13*_____, they have areas. The sector is the smallest part of a center, and then there is the area which would be a larger portion of the center but with different sectors within that area.

The FAA is working vigorously with the air transportation industry to keep *14*_____ as *15*_____ as it can be. So the US air traffic system of tomorrow will continue to be the best in the world.

Translating Practice

IV. Translate the following sentences into Chinese.

1. Air traffic control is a vital component for the safety and economy of the nations of the world. Without a system to keep things moving safely, people and goods cannot be transported efficiently in a timely manner.

_____

_____

2. They are highly-trained individuals who have to take yearly refresher training, as well as monthly computer-based instruction and evaluations of their use of proper phraseology.

_____

_____

3. There are different types of air traffic controllers who communicate with pilots, from the time that the pilot calls for a clearance, through taxi, takeoff, cruise, arrival, landing and taxiing to parking.

_____

_____

4. Call signs are composed of the registration letters and numbers painted on the side of the plane for civilian aircraft, airline flight numbers for airliners, and often a combination of a branch name and a number for military flights.

_____

_____

5. However, there are many variations of military call signs, depending on the branch of service, squadron designation and what type of aircraft is being flown. You can search the Web for "military call signs" to see some of the real-world military call signs in use today.

_____

_____

V. Translate the following paragraph into English.

除了保障空中交通安全之外，空中交通管制部门还担负着多项任务，例如，协调各部门对空域的使用，为国土防空系统提供空中目标识别情报，预报外来航空器入侵和本国飞机擅自飞入禁区信息等。

_____

_____

_____

_____

🧭 TEXT C

Air Traffic Control Services

1   Air Traffic Control (ATC) is a service provided by ground-based controllers who direct aircraft on the ground and through controlled airspace, and can provide advisory services to aircraft in non-controlled airspace. The primary purpose of ATC worldwide is to prevent collisions, organize and **expedite** (加快) the flow of traffic, and provide information and other support for pilots. In some countries, ATC plays a security or defensive role, or is operated by the military.

2   To prevent collisions, ATC enforces traffic separation rules, which ensure that each aircraft maintains a minimum amount of empty space around it at all times. Many aircraft also have **collision avoidance systems** (防撞系统), which provide

additional safety by warning pilots when other aircraft get too close.

3   In many countries, ATC provides services to all private, military and commercial aircraft operating within its airspace. Depending on the type of flight and the class of airspace, ATC may issue instructions that pilots are required to obey or advisories (known as flight information in some countries) that pilots may, **at their discretion** (由他们决定), disregard. Generally, the pilot in command is the final authority for the safe operation of the aircraft and may, in an emergency, **deviate** (违背) ATC instructions to the extent required to maintain safe operation of their aircraft. In many instances, a pilot is required to have contact with ATC, but even when not required, a pilot finds it helpful to request their services.

Primary Radar / Primary Surveillance Radar (PSR) (一次监视雷达)

4   Radar is a device which provides information on **range** (距离), **azimuth** (方位角), and/or elevation of objects in the path of the **transmitted pulses** (发射脉冲). It measures the time interval between transmission and reception of **radio pulses** (无线电脉冲) and correlates the **angular orientation** (角定向) of the radiated **antenna** (天线) beam or beams in azimuth and/or elevation. Range is determined by measuring the time it takes for the radio wave to go out to the object and then return to the receiving antenna. The direction of a detected object from a radar site is determined by the position of the rotating antenna when the reflected portion of the radio wave is received.

5   Modern radar is very reliable and there are seldom **outages** (运行中断). This is due to reliable maintenance and improved equipment. There are, however, some limitations which may affect ATC services and prevent a controller from issuing advisories concerning aircraft which are not under his or her control and cannot be seen on radar.

ATC Radar Beacon System (ATCRBS) (空中交通管制雷达信标系统)

6   The ATC Radar Beacon System (ATCRBS) is often referred to as "**Secondary Surveillance Radar (SSR)** (二次监视雷达)." This system consists of three components and helps in **alleviating** (减少；减轻) some of the limitations associated

with primary radar. The three components are **interrogator** (询问机), transponder and **radarscope** (雷达示波器). The advantages of ATCRBS are the **reinforcement** (增强) of radar targets, the rapid target identification and a unique display of selected codes.

Transponder (应答机)

7   The transponder is the airborne portion of the secondary surveillance radar system and a system with which a pilot should be familiar. The ATCRBS cannot display the secondary information unless an aircraft is equipped with a transponder. A transponder is also required to operate in certain controlled airspace.

8   A transponder code consists of four numbers from 0 to 7 (4,096 possible codes). There are some standard codes, or the ATC may issue a four-digit code to an aircraft. When a controller requests a code or function on the transponder, the word "squawk" may be used.

Automatic Dependent Surveillance–Broadcast (ADS–B) (广播式自动相关监视)

9   Automatic Dependent Surveillance–Broadcast (ADS–B) is a surveillance technology being deployed throughout the NAS to facilitate improvements needed to increase the capacity and efficiency of the NAS while maintaining safety. ADS–B supports these improvements by providing a higher update rate and enhances accuracy of surveillance information over the current radar-based surveillance system. In addition, ADS-B enables the expansion of the ATC surveillance services into areas where none existed previously. The ADS–B ground system also provides **Traffic Information Services–Broadcast (TIS–B)** (广播式交通信息服务) and **Flight Information Services–Broadcast (FIS–B)** (广播式飞行信息服务) for the use on appropriately equipped aircraft, enhancing the user's **Situational Awareness (SA)** (态势感知) and improving the overall safety of the NAS.

10   The ADS–B system is composed of aircraft avionics and ground infrastructure. Onboard avionics determine the position of the aircraft by using the GPS and

transmit its position, along with additional information about the aircraft, to ground stations for use by ATC and nearby ADS–B equipped aircraft.

Radar Traffic Advisories (雷达交通咨询)

11   Radar equipped ATC facilities provide radar assistance to aircraft on instrument flight plans and VFR aircraft provided the aircraft can communicate with the facility and are within radar coverage. This basic service includes safety alerts, traffic advisories, limited **vectoring** (引导) when requested and **sequencing** (排序) at locations where this procedure has been established. ATC issues traffic advisories based on observed radar targets. The traffic is referenced by azimuth from the aircraft in terms of the 12-hour clock. Also, distance in nautical miles, the direction in which the target is moving, and the type and altitude of the aircraft, if known, are given. An example would be: "Traffic 10 o'clock 5 miles eastbound, Cessna[1] 152, 3,000 feet". The pilot should note that the traffic position is based on the aircraft track, and that the wind correction can affect the clock position at which a pilot locates traffic. This service is not intended to relieve the pilot of the responsibility to see and avoid other aircraft.

12   In addition to basic radar service, **Terminal Radar Service Area (TRSA)** (航站雷达服务区) has been implemented at certain terminal locations. TRSAs are depicted on the **sectional aeronautical charts** (分区航图) and listed in the **Airport/Facility Directory (A/FD)** (机场/设施手册). The purpose of this service is to provide separation between all participating VFR aircraft and all IFR aircraft operating within the TRSA. Class C service provides approved separation between IFR and VFR aircraft, and sequencing of VFR aircraft to the primary airport. Class B service provides approved separation of aircraft based on IFR, VFR, and/or weight, and sequencing of VFR arrivals to the primary airport(s).

---

1 **Cessna:** 赛斯纳飞行器公司。该公司以制造小型通用飞机为主，其产品线从小型双座单引擎飞机到商用喷气机。

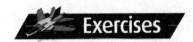

Exercises

Comprehension of the Text

Decide whether the following statements are true (T) or false (F) according to the Text.

( ) *1.* ATC service is not provided in uncontrolled airspace.

( ) *2.* Traffic separation rules enforced by ATC are the only measures to prevent the collisions of the aircraft.

( ) *3.* In many cases, a pilot is required to have contact with ATC. When not required to do so, the pilot cannot seek assistance from ATC.

( ) *4.* The reliability of modern radar is attributed to reliable maintenance and improved equipment.

( ) *5.* ATCRBS demonstrates some advantages, such as the reinforcement of radar targets, rapid target identification and a unique display of selected codes.

( ) *6.* ATCRBS can still display the secondary information even if an aircraft is not equipped with a transponder.

( ) *7.* ADS−B is a surveillance technology being deployed throughout the NAS to facilitate improvements needed to increase the capacity and efficiency of the NAS while maintaining safety.

( ) *8.* The position of the aircraft is decided by the onboard avionics equipped with GPS.

( ) *9.* Radar equipped ATC facilities provide radar assistance to aircraft on instrument flight plans and VFR aircraft under all circumstances.

( ) *10.* TRSA is implemented at certain terminal locations, providing separation between all participating VFR aircraft and all IFR aircraft operating within the TRSA.

⊘ UNIT PROJECT

 Mind Mapping

Work in groups and draw a mind map to depict airspace classification and the operational requirements for each of the various classes of airspace.

 Oral Practice

Work in groups and discuss the requirements and the conditions about different classes of airspace on the chart of Page 130 so as to have a deeper understanding of the airspace classification. And one student from each group will make a 3-minute oral presentation to introduce one class of airspace in detail including its definition, function, requirements and limitations on the basis of the group discussion. You may refer to Text A of this unit and the relevant information from the Internet.

Writing Practice

Based on the group discussion above, write a composition with at least 150 words to introduce one of the major classes of airspace. You may refer to the outline below.

1. the definition
2. the types of flight it allows and the services it can provide
3. the restrictions and limitations when operating in that class of airspace

Unit 6
Basic Flight Procedures

⊘ Warming Up

Task 1 Watch the video clip about how a plane gets ready for takeoff and fill in the blanks.

How does an airplane get in the sky? Well, there are big catapults at every airport shooting planes into the sky. No! The plane has to do it all by itself. First, the pilot and co-pilot plan the best *1*_____. They look at the *2*_____, how many people and bags are on the flight, and calculate how much *3*_____ they need. On average, a plane needs about twelve liters per kilometer. They also bring extra fuel in case there's a lot of wind, or they have to fly to a different airport nearby. Better safe than sorry. Then they check the plane. The pilots check the *4*_____ and the systems on the *5*_____. Check! Next, they drive to the runway. That's called *6*_____. Sometimes that takes a few minutes. Sometimes it takes more than half an hour. There, they hit the *7*_____ and make their wings bigger. Yep. They can do that with *8*_____ on the back and *9*_____ on the front. It's easier to lift up. Then they power up the *10*_____, let go of the brakes. And wow, once they're going fast enough, the pilots lift up the nose and off he goes! Bon voyage!

Task 2 Discuss the following questions in groups.

1. If you were scheduled to carry out a flight mission tomorrow, what would you do tonight as a pilot?

2. On the basis of the flight training you've received, which phase of flight is more challenging, takeoff or landing?

3. Can you briefly describe the basic flight procedures?

⊘ TEXT A

Basic Flight Procedures

1   A normal aircraft flight would include several parts of flight including **taxiing**, takeoff, climb, cruise, **descent** and **landing**.

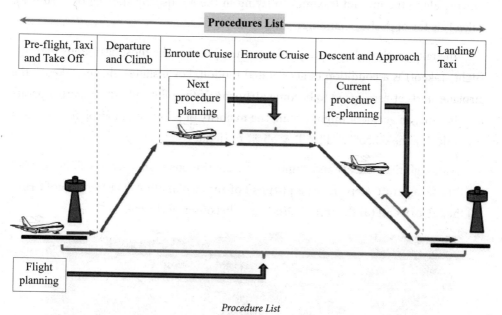

Procedure List

Taxiing

2   Taxiing, also sometimes written "taxying", is the controlled movement of an aircraft under its own power while on the ground, in contrast to **towing** or **push-back** where the aircraft is moved by a **tug**. The aircraft usually moves on wheels, but the term also includes aircraft with skis or floats (for water-based travel). An airplane uses **taxiways** to taxi from one place on an airport to another, for example, when moving from a terminal to the **runway**. The term "taxiing" is not used for the **accelerating** run along a runway before takeoff or the **decelerating** run immediately after landing.

3   When taxiing, aircraft travel slowly. This ensures that they can be stopped quickly and do not risk wheel damage on larger aircraft if they accidentally turn off the paved

surface. Taxi speeds are typically from 5 to 20 knots (9 to 37 km/h; 6 to 23 mph). **Rotor downwash** limits helicopter **hover-taxiing** near parked light aircraft. The use of **engine thrust** near terminals is restricted due to the possibility of **jet blast** damage.

Takeoff

4   Takeoff is the phase of flight in which an aircraft goes through a **transition** from moving along the ground (taxiing) to flying in the air, usually starting on a runway. Takeoff is the opposite of landing.

5   The takeoff, though relatively simple, often presents the most hazardous part of a flight. Takeoff is a condition of accelerated motion. For instance, during takeoff, the airplane starts at zero speed to become **airborne**. If the pilot did not properly operate the airplane, an accident might occur. The majority of pilot-caused airplane accidents occur during the takeoff and landing phase of flight.

6   Although the "takeoff and climb" is one continuous maneuver, it will be divided into three separate steps for the purpose of the explanation: (1) the **takeoff roll**, (2) the **lift-off**, and (3) the **initial climb** after becoming airborne.

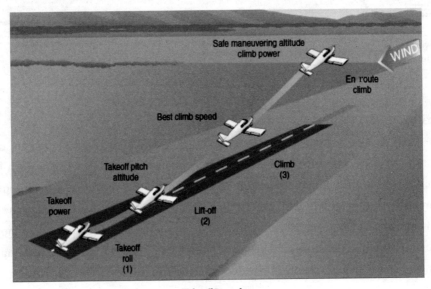

Takeoff Procedure

- **Takeoff roll (Ground roll)**—the portion of the takeoff procedure during which the airplane is accelerated from a **standstill** to an airspeed that provides sufficient lift for it to become airborne.
- **Lift-off (Rotation)**—the act of becoming airborne as a result of the wings lifting the airplane off the ground or the pilot rotating the nose up, increasing the angle of attack to start a climb.
- **Initial climb**—begins when the airplane leaves the ground and a **pitch attitude** has been established to climb away from the takeoff area. Normally, it is considered complete when the airplane has reached a safe maneuvering altitude, or an **en route climb** has been established.

Climb

7   In aviation, the term "climb" refers both to the actual operation of increasing the altitude of an aircraft and to the logical phase of a typical flight (often called the climb phase or **climb-out**) following takeoff and preceding the cruise, during which an increase in altitude to a **predetermined** level is **effected**.

8   A climb is carried out by increasing the lift of airfoils (wings) supporting the aircraft until their lifting force exceeds the weight of the aircraft. Once this occurs, the aircraft will climb to a higher altitude until the lifting force and weight are again in balance. The increase in lift may be accomplished by increasing the angle of attack of the wings, by increasing the thrust of the engines to increase speed (thereby increasing lift), by increasing the surface area or shape of the wings to produce greater lift or by some combination of these techniques. In most cases, engine thrust and angle of attack are **simultaneously** increased to produce a climb.

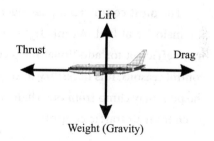

Forces acting on the airplane in flight

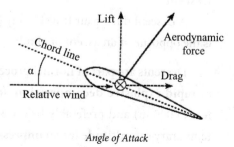

Angle of Attack

9   Because lift **diminishes** with decreasing **air density**, a climb, once initiated, will end by itself when the diminishing lift with increasing altitude drops to a point that equals the gravity of the aircraft. At that point, the aircraft will return to **level flight** at a constant altitude.

10   However, during a constant rate climb at a reasonably steady angle, the lift force is generally less than the gravity with the engine operating. This is due to the upward fraction of the **thrust vector**. This in turn causes the **load factor** to be slightly less than 1. It is only during the **radial** (the constant increase in pitch) or vertical acceleration that the lift vector is larger than the **gravity vector**.

Cruise

11   Cruise is the level portion of aircraft travel in which flight is the most fuel-efficient. It occurs between **ascent** and descent phases and is usually the majority of a journey. Technically, cruise consists of heading changes only at a constant airspeed and altitude. It ends as the aircraft approaches the destination where the descent phase of flight **commences** in preparation for landing.

12   For most commercial passenger aircraft, the cruising phase of flight consumes the majority of fuel. As this **lightens** the aircraft **considerably**, higher altitudes are more efficient for additional fuel economy. However, for operational and air traffic control reasons, it is necessary to stay at the cleared flight level. On **long haul flights**, the pilot may climb from one flight level to a higher one as clearance is requested and given from air traffic control.

Descent

13   A descent during air travel is any portion where an aircraft decreases altitude and is the opposite of an ascent or climb.

14   Descents are part of normal procedures, but also occur during emergencies, such as **rapid explosive decompression**, forcing an **emergency descent** to below 10,000 feet (3,000 m) and preferably below 8,000 feet (2,400 m), respectively the maximum temporary **safe altitude** for an **unpressurized** aircraft and the **maximum safe altitude** for an extended duration.

15   Intentional descents might be undertaken to land, avoid other air traffic or poor flight conditions (**turbulence, icing conditions** or bad weather), come across clouds (particularly under visual flight rules), see something lower, enter warmer air, or take advantage of the wind direction of a different altitude.

16   Normal descents take place at a constant airspeed and constant **angle of descent** (3-degree **final approach** at most airports). The pilot controls the angle of descent by varying engine power and **pitch angle** (lowering the nose) to keep the airspeed constant. **Unpowered descents** (such as **engine failure**) are steeper than **powered descents**, but flown similarly as a glider. If the nose is too high for the chosen power, the airspeed will decrease until eventually the aircraft stalls or loses lift.

Landing

17   Landing is the last part of a flight, where a flying animal, aircraft or spacecraft returns to the ground. Aircraft usually land at an airport on a firm runway or helicopter **landing pad**, generally constructed of **asphalt** concrete, concrete, **gravel** or grass. Landing occurs after the descent. Landing is the opposite of takeoff. Both takeoff and landing are made **into the wind**.

18   A **flare** is performed by rotating the wings where the **rate of descent** will be reduced often by adopting a **nose-up attitude**. During the final approach, the aircraft should be descending towards the **aiming point**. Maybe two or three seconds before it, the aircraft is "flared", so that the aircraft's attitude is smoothly changed, from the **nose-down attitude** of the approach to a nose-high attitude for landing.

19   The basic landing sequence is varied, but according to the **prevailing** conditions, it usually has four parts: (1) joining the **circuit pattern**; (2) approach; (3) transition; (4) **touchdown**.

20   In joining the circuit pattern, the aircraft is decelerated from **cruise speed** to **circuit speed**. Meanwhile, the following tasks should be accomplished:
   (1) The airfield is visually checked for **serviceability**;
   (2) **Surface wind** direction is **ascertained**;
   (3) Other traffic is established;

(4) Landing direction and approach are planned;

(5) **Pre-landing cockpit checks** are carried out.

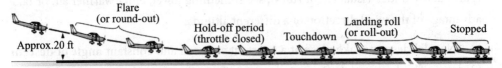

Approx.20 ft | Flare (or round-out) | Hold-off period (throttle closed) | Touchdown | Landing roll (or roll-out) | Stopped

From Landing Flare to Full Stop

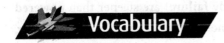

Special Terms

ascent 上升，爬高

aiming point 标定点，瞄准点

air density 空气密度

airborne 飞行的；空中的；机载的

angle of descent 下降角

circuit speed 起落航线飞行速度

circuit pattern 起落航线

climb-out 起始上升（起飞后）；转入稳定上升状态

cruise speed 巡航速度

descent 下降

downwash 下洗流，气流下洗

emergency descent 紧急下降

en route climb 航线飞行爬升

engine failure 发动机故障，发动机失效

engine thrust 发动机推力

final approach 第五边进近，最终进近

flare （飞机着陆前）拉平；起飞离地后一段平飞

gravity vector 重力矢量

ground roll 着陆滑跑；起飞滑跑

hover-taxi 空中滑行

icing condition 积冰条件

initial climb 起始爬升，（离地后）上升起始阶段

jet blast 飞机喷射流

landing 着陆

landing pad 降落场，着陆缓冲垫

level flight 水平飞行

lift-off 离地升空

load factor 负载系数，载荷因数

long haul flight 长途飞行

maximum safe altitude 最大安全高度

nose-down/nose-low attitude 低头姿态，机头低的姿态

nose-up/nose-high attitude 抬头姿态，机头高的姿态

pitch angle 俯仰角

pitch attitude 俯仰姿态

powered/powered-on descent 带油门下降

pre-landing cockpit check 着陆前座舱检查

push-back 推出

rapid explosive decompression 快速爆发性减压

rate of descent 下降率

rotation 起飞抬前轮

rotor downwash 旋翼下洗流

runway 跑道

safe altitude 安全高度

serviceability 适用性；可用性

surface wind 地面风

takeoff roll 起飞滑跑

taxiing/taxi 滑行

taxiway 滑行道

thrust vector 推力矢量

touchdown （着陆）接地

transition 过渡

tug 拖车；拖船

turbulence 湍流，急流
unpowered descent 无动力下降

New Words and Expressions

accelerate	[ək'seləreɪt]	v.	加速
ascertain	[ˌæsə'teɪn]	v.	确定；查明
asphalt	['æsfælt]	n.	沥青
commence	[kə'mens]	v.	开始
considerably	[kən'sɪdərəbli]	ad.	大幅度地；相当大地
decelerate	[ˌdiː'seləreɪt]	v.	减速
diminish	[dɪ'mɪnɪʃ]	v.	减少；减弱
effect	[ɪ'fekt]	v.	实现，达成
gravel	['grævl]	n.	砾石，沙砾
lighten	['laɪtn]	v.	减轻；减少（工作量等）
prevailing	[prɪ'veɪlɪŋ]	a.	盛行的，流行的；通行的
predetermine	[ˌpriːdɪ'tɜːmɪn]	v.	预设；事先安排
radial	['reɪdiəl]	a.	径向的
simultaneously	[ˌsɪml'teɪniəsli]	ad.	同时地，同时发生地
standstill	['stæn(d)stɪl]	n.	静止；停顿
tow	[təʊ]	v.	拖，拉
unpressurized	[ʌn'preʃəraɪzd]	a.	未增压的
vector	['vektə]	n.	向量，矢量
into the wind			迎风，逆风，顶风

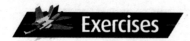 Exercises

Comprehension of the Text

I. **Answer the following questions according to the text.**

1. What does a normal aircraft flight include?

2. Why do aircraft travel slowly when taxiing?

_____

3. Why does the takeoff often present the most hazardous part of a flight?

_____

4. What is the purpose of a takeoff roll?

_____

5. How is a climb usually achieved?

_____

6. How to accomplish an increase in the lift?

_____

7. When will a climb end by itself? And what will happen to the aircraft at that point?

_____

8. What should be done when rapid explosive decompression occurs?

_____

9. What might be the reasons for intentional descents?

_____

10. Why is a flare performed two or three seconds before the final approach?

_____

Vocabulary Practice

II. **Match the meanings in Column B with the special terms in Column A and translate the terms into Chinese.**

Column A	Column B
1. pitch _____	a. the change in the direction of air deflected by the aerodynamic action of an airfoil, wing or helicopter rotor blade in motion, as part of the process of producing lift
2. angle of attack _____	b. the angle of the wing chord in relation to the free stream airflow as it moves forward through the air
3. downwash _____	c. the rotation of an airplane around its lateral axis

Column A	Column B
4. rotate _____	d. a maneuver conducted during the takeoff ground roll
5. transition _____	e. the nose-up landing posture normal for most land-based aircraft
6. flare _____	f. the loss of internal aircraft air pressure
7. circuit pattern _____	g. to change from one phase of flight to another
8. stall _____	h. a flight condition during which lift is destroyed due to low airplane speed or attitude
9. decompression _____	i. the point at which an aircraft first makes contact with the runway
10. touchdown _____	j. a standard path followed by aircraft when taking off or landing while maintaining visual contact with the airfield

III. Complete each of the following sentences with a word from the box. Change the form if necessary.

air density	angle of attack	Air Traffic Control	landing flare	pushback
jet blast	terminal	airspeed	tug	runway

1. _____, like air pressure, decreases with increasing altitude. It also changes with the variation in temperature or humidity.

2. An air _____ is a building at an airport where passengers transfer between ground transportation and the facilities that allow them to board and disembark from aircraft.

3. A(n) _____ is a "defined rectangular area on a land prepared for the landing and takeoff of aircraft". It may be a man-made surface (often asphalt, concrete or a mixture of both) or a natural surface (grass, dirt, gravel, ice or salt).

4. In aviation, _____ is an airport procedure during which an aircraft is pushed backwards away from an airport gate by an external power. They are carried out by special, low-profile vehicles called _____.

5. _____ is the phenomenon of rapid air movement produced by the jet engines of aircraft, particularly on or before takeoff.

6. _____ is a service provided by ground-based controllers who direct aircraft on the ground and through controlled airspace, and can provide advisory services to aircraft in non-controlled airspace.

7. In aerodynamics, _____ specifies the angle between the chord line of the wing of a fixed-wing aircraft and the vector representing the relative motion between the aircraft and the atmosphere.

8. The _____ is a maneuver or stage of the landing of an aircraft, in which the nose of the plane is raised, slowing the descent rate, and the proper attitude is set for the touchdown.

9. _____ is the speed of an aircraft relative to the air.

IV. **Complete the following short passage with the words from the box. Change the form if necessary.**

retract	throttle	airspeed	airborne	nose
level	climbing	takeoff	cruising speed	drag

Climbing

After 1_____, the next step is to 2_____ the landing gear—it creates unnecessary 3_____, and once you're 4_____, it's important that you reduce drag in order to build up speed.

Keep your 5_____ on its full setting, and pitch the 6_____ slightly upward until it's at about a 20° angle. If you start to lose 7_____ or if the stall warning appears onscreen, dip the nose down until you're again flying 8_____. Then, resume climbing at a gentler angle.

As long as no approaching aircraft are in your flight path, you can maintain this 9_____ position until you reach the desired altitude.

Once you decide you're ready to level out, reduce the throttle until you slow down to the desired 10_____. Make slight adjustments to the throttle setting until you're flying at a constant speed and altitude.

- Retracting landing gear

- Maintaining full throttle
- Pitching upward at a 20° angle
- Leveling out
- Reducing throttle to the desired airspeed
- Making slight throttle adjustments until you have a constant speed and altitude

Listening Practice

V. Watch the video clip about how planes land sideways in high winds and fill in the blanks.

Narrator: It's not always a smooth and pleasant landing for airplanes. *1*_____ strong winds can affect the position of how planes land on the runway, making it look like the plane is literally landing *2*_____. Here's how planes land sideways in high winds. Landings like this actually have a name, *3*_____. The name comes from the way that crabs walk sideways across the beach. That's kind of what the airplane looks like when it's landing this way. Crabbing is usually needed because of high *4*_____.

Expert: The wind can either be blowing *5*_____ down the runway or 90 degrees to the runway or somewhere in between. And usually, it's somewhere in between there.

Narrator: That's Les Westbrooks. He teaches aeronautical science at Embry-Riddle Aeronautical University and is a retired airline pilot.

Expert: Landing in a crosswind situation requires a couple of different *6*_____. When we're at altitude, the aircraft just flies in a crab, and we just go across, kinda sideways. Once we get down to the ground, we can't land with the aircraft in a crab, because that's gonna put a lot of *7*_____ on the outside of the landing gear, and could actually cause the landing gear to collapse if we put too much stress on it.

Narrator: Whenever there is a crosswind, there's a lot of *8*_____, so it's not like that the pilots are flying through a slight summer breeze. Of course, the ultimate goal is for the aircraft to land straight, where the *9*_____ of the plane is in alignment with the stripe that's down the runway. Those crosswinds sure make it challenging!

Expert: There is an *10*_____ to that. You know, it's a force vector, so the direction and the intensity that it's coming at will determine how much *11*_____ we have to put into the aircraft's flight controls.

Narrator: So, exactly how do the aircraft land in these conditions?

Expert: So, at the last minute, we want to move the nose of the aircraft *12*_____ the runway, but as soon as we do that, the aircraft's gonna start blowing off to the side of the runway with the wind. So in order to counteract that, we'd lower the wing, the *13*_____ wing. We lower the wing and straighten the nose out, and a perfect crosswind landing will be when the upwind wheel *14*_____ first, the aircraft is straight down the runway, and then the second wheel will come down after that.

Narrator: Finally, the plane is on the runway and heading to the *15*_____.

Translating Practice

VI. Translate the following sentences into Chinese.

1. Taxiing, also sometimes written "taxying", is the controlled movement of an aircraft under its own power while on the ground, in contrast to towing or push-back where the aircraft is moved by a tug.

_____

_____

2. Although the "takeoff and climb" is one continuous maneuver, it will be divided into three separate steps for the purpose of the explanation: (1) the takeoff roll, (2) the lift-off, and (3) the initial climb after becoming airborne.

_____

_____

3. In aviation, the term "climb" refers both to the actual operation of increasing the altitude of an aircraft and to the logical phase of a typical flight following takeoff and preceding the cruise, during which an increase in altitude to a predetermined level is effected.

_____

_____

4. Because lift diminishes with decreasing air density, a climb, once initiated, will end by itself when the diminishing lift with increasing altitude drops to a point that equals the gravity of the aircraft.

_____

_____

5. During the final approach, the aircraft should be descending towards the aiming point. Maybe two or three seconds before it, the aircraft is "flared", so that the aircraft's attitude is smoothly changed, from the nose-down attitude of the approach to a nose-high attitude for landing.

_____

_____

VII. Translate the following paragraph into English .

失速是指失去升力。失速是由于飞机的速度已低于维持升力所需要的空速。没有升力，飞机会向地面坠落，而且飞行控制面会失效，就像一艘没有风驱动的帆船。失速常常在急转弯、陡爬升、斤斗或起飞和降落的过程中发生。

_____

_____

_____

_____

_____

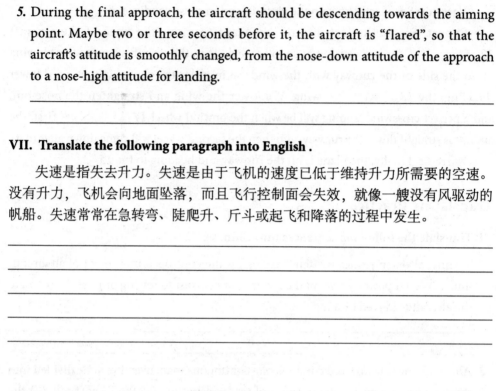 TEXT B

A Plane in Flight

1   Lieutenant (Lt.) Anderson taxied his plane onto the end of the runway, turned its nose toward the far end of the runway and stopped. Then he waited for the air traffic controller in the tower to give him the signal to takeoff. There were several planes around the base on training missions, so he had to wait a few minutes until the air was **clear of traffic**.

2   After a moment, he heard a click on his radio and then the words he was waiting for, "Six seven seven eight, **cleared to take off**." He answered with the number of his aircraft, "six seven seven eight," and increased the runway, gradually gaining speed. A

few seconds later, the plane lifted into the air and he **retracted the landing gear**. He climbed, then **banked** and turned toward the west, and continued his climb.

3   When he reached his **cruising altitude**, he reduced the power and cruised at 300 knots, flying straight and level, and enjoying the view. It was a beautiful day. There were only a few clouds below him and there was no traffic to worry about.

4   Two hours later, although he was still fifty miles away, he could see the base that he was going to. He waited until he was a little closer and then called on his radio for instructions.

5   He was told to approach from the south. Using the ailerons, he banked the plane to the left. At the same time, he used the elevators to raise the nose. Because the plane was in a bank, the elevators caused the nose to point both to the left and upward. But Lt. Anderson did not want to climb as he turned, so he used the rudder to hold the nose down and to turn it toward the left. These actions were not performed separately; they were all done smoothly at the same time. The plane turned and flew south.

6   When he was in the proper location, Lt. Anderson was instructed by radio to begin his descent and to watch for traffic. He couldn't see any other planes, but he knew the air traffic controller could see them, either with his eyes or with radar. As he flew closer to the base, he saw that one aircraft was on its final approach and that another was descending ahead of him. He called the tower for landing instruction.

7   A few minutes later, he **lowered the landing gear** and started his final approach. The plane's nose was pointed down, and the end of the runway was rapidly coming nearer. For Lt. Anderson, the landing was always the most exciting part of a flight. It was also the part that required the most skill. Perhaps that is why he enjoyed it so much. He was proud of his landings.

8   As his plane approached the concrete of the runway. Lt. Anderson pulled the nose up slightly and the plane touched down gently, first on its main gear and then on its nose gear. He pushed his toes forward on the pedals to apply the **brakes** and **slow** the plane **down**.

9　　Near the other end of the runway, he pressed harder on the brake for the right wheel, making the plane turn to the right on the taxiway. Unlike most aircraft that can be steered on the ground with the rudder pedals, his aircraft only used the brakes. The flight was over. Lt. Anderson called the tower for the instruction on where to park his plane.

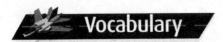

Special Terms

bank 带坡度转弯；（飞行）倾斜，坡度；压坡度

brake 刹车装置；减速装置

clear of traffic 活动解除，无其他飞行（指先前发布的飞行情况已不存在）

cleared to take off / cleared for takeoff 准许起飞

cruising altitude 巡航高度

lieutenant (Lt.) （陆军／空军）中尉；（海军）上尉

lower the landing gear 放起落架

retract the landing gear 收起落架

slow…down 为……减速

Comprehension of the Text

I. Rearrange the following steps according to the text.

1. extend the landing gear and start the final approach

2. taxi the plane onto the end of the runway, turn the nose toward the far end of the runway, stop and wait for the signal to take off

3. answer with the number of the aircraft and speed up on the runway

4. push the brake pedal to slow down the plane and use the brake to turn to the right on the taxiway

5. reach cruising altitude, reduce the power and cruise at 300 knots, fly straight and level

6. hold nose down and turn the plane to fly to the south, ready for approach from the south

7. when in the proper location, begin to descend with the instruction on the radio and call for landing instruction

8. see the base and call on the radio for approach instructions

9. the plane touch the concrete of the runway gently on the landing gear

10. fly in the air, retract the landing gear, climb, bank, turn to the west, and continue climbing

11. call for the instruction on where to park the plane

12. receive the signal "clear to take off" on the radio

Vocabulary Practice

II. Complete each of the following sentences with a word or an expression from the box. Change the form if necessary.

cruising altitude	cleared for takeoff	park	taxiway	steer
lieutenant	retractable landing gear	brake	pedal	bank

1. A typical takeoff clearance may state, for example, "Speedbird 123 RNAV to MPASS, Runway 26L, _____."

2. In the Air Force, a first _____ may be a flight commander or the section's officer in charge with varied supervisory responsibilities.

3. _____ stow in fuselage or wing compartments while in flight. Once in these wheel wells, gears are out of the slipstream and do not cause parasite drag.

4. A fundamental aircraft motion is a banking turn. This maneuver is used to change the aircraft heading. The turn is initiated by using the ailerons or spoilers to roll, or _____, the aircraft to one side.

5. Typically, _____ refers to the highest altitude reached during a flight and sustained between the ascent of takeoff and the descent of landing, which is around 35,000 feet.

6. A _____ is a path for aircraft at an airport connecting runways with aprons, hangars, terminals and other facilities.

7. Air _____ are used when the aircraft needs to reduce its airspeed, while spoilers are only able to be opened when the airplane is approaching the runway and about to touch down.

8. Differential braking is a very popular technique to _____ a plane that doesn't have a tiller.

9. In every modern aircraft, pushing on the right _____ will make the nose of the aircraft yaw to the right.

10. Whenever an aircraft is positioned in a _____ stand, it must be secured by chocks at wheel positions in accordance with the landing gear configuration of the aircraft type.

Translating Practice

III. Translate the following sentences into Chinese.

1. There were several planes around the base on training missions, so he had to wait a few minutes until the air was clear of traffic.

_____

_____

2. A few seconds later, the plane lifted into the air and he retracted the landing gear. He climbed, then banked and turned toward the west, and continued his climb.

_____

_____

3. He was told to approach from the south. Using the ailerons, he banked the plane to the left. At the same time, he used the elevators to raise the nose.

_____

_____

4. When he was in the proper location, Lt. Anderson was instructed by radio to begin his descent and to watch for traffic.

_____

_____

5. A few minutes later, he lowered the landing gear and started his final approach. The plane's nose was pointed down, and the end of the runway was rapidly coming nearer.

_____

_____

🧭 TEXT C

Aerobatic Maneuvers

1   Aerobatic maneuvers are flight paths putting aircraft in unusual attitudes, in air shows, dogfights or competition aerobatics. Aerobatics can be performed by a single aircraft or in formation with several others. Nearly all aircraft are capable of performing aerobatic maneuvers of some kind, although it may not be legal or safe to do so in certain aircraft.

2   Aerobatics consists of five basic maneuvers: **lines (both horizontal and vertical)** (水平飞行和垂直飞行), **loops** (斤斗), rolls, **spins** (螺旋) and **hammerheads** (跃升下坠倒转). Most aerobatic figures are the composites of these basic maneuvers with rolls superimposed.

Aerobatic Maneuver

3   A loop is performed when the pilot pulls the plane up into the vertical and continues going around until he is heading back in the same direction, like making a 360-degree turn, except it's in the vertical instead of the horizontal. The pilot will be inverted (upside down) at the top of the loop. A loop

can also be performed by going inverted and making the same maneuver but diving towards the ground. It can be visualized as making a loop of ribbon, hence its name is given.

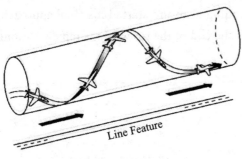

Aerobatics—Barrel Roll

4   A roll is simply rotating the plane about its roll axis, using the ailerons. It can be done in the increments of 360 degrees (i.e., four short 90 degrees rolls bringing the aircraft back to its upright position).

5   A spin is more complex, involving intentionally stalling a single wing, causing the plane to descend spiraling around its **yaw axis** (偏航轴) in a **corkscrew** (螺旋)motion.

6   A hammerhead (also known as a stall turn) is performed by pulling the aircraft up until its pointing straight up (much like the beginning of a loop), but the pilot continues to fly straight up until the airspeed has dropped to a certain critical point. He then uses the rudder to rotate the aircraft around its yaw axis until it has turned 360 degrees and is pointing straight down facing the direction that he came from. The aircraft gains speed, and the pilot continues back exactly the way that he came. It is also known as a "**tailslide**" (尾冲), from the yawing turn, which is different from the typical method of turning an aircraft in the **pitch axis** (俯仰轴).

Dogfight

7   Dogfight or dog fight is a form of engagement between fighter aircraft; in particular, the combat of maneuver at short range, where each side is aware of the other's presence. Dogfight first appeared during World War I, shortly after the invention of the airplane. Until at least 1992, it was a component in every major war, despite there are some beliefs that the increasingly greater speeds and longer range weapons made dogfighting obsolete after World War Ⅱ. Modern terminology for air-to-air combat is **Air Combat Maneuvering (ACM)** (空战机动), which refers to

the tactical situations requiring the use of individual **Basic Fighter Maneuvers (BFM)** (基本空战机动) to attack or evade one or more opponents. This differs from aerial warfare, which deals with the strategy involved in planning and executing various missions.

8　　The term dogfight has been used for centuries to describe a **melee** (空中混战) which is a fierce battle between two or more opponents. The term gained popularity during World War II, although its origin in air combat can be traced to the latter years of World War I. The first written reference to the modern-day usage of the word comes from *Fly Papers*, Written by A. E. Illingworth in 1919, "The battle develops into a 'dogfight', small groups of machines engaging each other in a fight to the death." The term **fighter ace** (战斗机 "王牌" 飞行员) generally applies to any pilot who eliminates five opponent aircraft in the air (or, in Germany during World War I, ten aircraft), although not necessarily in a dogfight.

9　　Since World War II, there have been many cases of air-to-air combat. Even in the jet age, modern air-to-air combat can develop into dogfights. A fighter can evade a missile by abrupt **maximum-performance turns** (最大性能转弯) and employing **countermeasures** (干扰)—such as chaff and flares, provided they can detect the missile via a **Radar Warning Receiver** (**RWR**) (雷达报警接收器) or visually. If **Beyond-Visual-Range (BVR)** (超视距) missiles can be defeated, pilots can press the attack and arrive at the **Within-Visual-Range (WVR)** (视距内的) arena very quickly. This will typically result in a high-speed neutral pass or **merge** (交会) from which the opposing pilots must decide to turn and continue the fight with their opponent or continue straight and "**bug-out**" (撤出战区). The turning fight that develops can be commonly called a dogfight or air combat maneuvering.

10　　Superiority in a dogfight can depend on a pilot's experience and skill, and the agility of his fighter when flown at minimum airspeeds approaching loss of control (causing a danger of stalling). The winner typically plays to the strengths of his own aircraft while forcing his adversary to fly at a design disadvantage. Dogfights are generally the contests fought at low airspeeds, while maintaining enough energy for violent acrobatic maneuvering, as pilots attempt to remain within airspeeds with a maximum turn rate and minimum turn radius: the so-called "**corner speed** (角

点速度)" that often lies between 300 and 400 knots, depending on the aircraft's design. Therefore, a dogfight has nothing to do with the supersonic speed, but much to do with the engine power that makes the supersonic flight possible. The super maneuverable F-22 Raptor can stand on its steerable **nozzles** (喷管) at less than 100 knots airspeed, yet quickly maneuver to bring its M-61 Vulcan cannon or Aim-9 sidewinder missiles to bear on a nearby evasive target, while an F-15 Eagle is more likely to use its thrust to maintain its relatively high corner speed, working to counter the drag caused by **tight turns** (急转弯).

11   Today, modern advances in the Unmanned Aerial Vehicle have thrown into question the continuing relevance of dogfight. A computer-chip can be subject to far greater G-forces than a human pilot even with a G-suit. Yet air superiority fighter planes continue to be developed by multiple nations.

Exercises

Comprehension of the Text

Answer the following questions according to the text.

1. What are aerobatic maneuvers?

_____

2. What are the five basic maneuvers of aerobatics?

_____

3. How does a pilot perform a loop?

_____

4. What does a roll refer to?

_____

5. Why is a spin more complex?

_____

6. How is a hammerhead usually performed?

_____

7. What does dogfight refer to?

_____

8. What determines the superiority in a dogfight?

_____

9. What is the "corner speed"?

_____

10. Do you think Unmanned Aerial Vehicles are challenging the continuing relevance of the dogfight? Why?

_____

⊘ UNIT PROJECT

 Mind Mapping

Work in groups and draw two mind maps respectively according to the following topics.

1. basic flight procedures
2. basic aerobatic maneuvers

 Oral Practice

Work in groups and discuss the characteristic of each flight procedure. And one student from each group will make a 3-minute oral presentation about the most impressive phase of flight on the basis of the group discussion. You may recall your previous flight experience, refer to Text A or surf the Internet to find more specific information about the topic.

Writing Practice

Based on the group discussion above, write a composition with at least 150 words on the topic of "The Most Impressive Phase of Flight in My Eyes". You may refer to the questions below.

1.   What is the most impressive phase of flight in your eyes?
2.   Why do you enjoy it?
3.   What are the basic steps that you have to follow in this phase of flight?

Unit 7
Flight Services and Ground Services

⊘ Warming Up

Task 1 Watch the video clip about the airport and fill in the blanks.

Every airport has an air traffic control tower. They're like the traffic cops you sometimes see at *1*_____. But instead of cars, they *2*_____ those huge airplanes, everyone on the ground and every other airplane in the area. Yeah, air traffic control is no walk in the park. The tower welcomes the airplane and tells it when and where it can *3*_____.

Then it instructs everyone on the ground. A super *4*_____ as strong as a tank drags the plane to the gate. Those cute cars collect the *5*_____. And the stairs, well, they are stairs. Every car is specially made to help the plane.

Now inside the airport, you passengers are being prepped. In bigger airports, their bags are moved with a special kind of luggage *6*_____ hidden behind the walls and floors of the airport.

And the cabin crew helps everyone on board. The airport also has *7*_____ where airplanes can be *8*_____ so they're ready for a new trip.

Task 2 Discuss the following questions in groups.

1. How much do you know about flight services? Give an example.

2. How much do you know about ground services? Give an example.

3. Are flight services or ground services necessary for the pilots? Why or why not?

 TEXT A

Flight Services

1   No one has ever made an accurate count of the number of people who work on the ground to assure the safety and success of a single air mission. There must be at least several hundred. What **Air Force personnel** call "**flight services**" are like **ground services**; the jobs are all performed on the ground. They differ from the ground services in only one way: they assist the **aircrew** during the actual flight of the aircraft.

2   These services begin, however, before the plane leaves the **ramp** to takeoff. The first place the pilot goes to before a flight is **Flight Operations**, which he usually calls "**Ops**". Other names for it are **Base Operations** or **Bps**. The pilot tells the personnel in this office where he is going and, unless he knows which plane he will fly, asks for a plane. Then he goes to the **flight planning room**. If he needs maps (maps for pilots are often called **charts**), he can get them there. He writes a **flight plan** that indicates when he will take off, what route he will take and when he expects to arrive.

Sample Flight Plan

3   He decides how high he will fly, how fast, what airways he will use and many other facts about his flight. Of course, he needs information about the wind, the air temperature and other **meteorological** information. The weather information **is made available to** him at Base Operations. He uses this information to decide whether it will be an IFR or a VFR flight and to **fill out** his flight plan.

4   The pilot gives this information to the personnel at Flight Operations. This is called "**filing** a flight plan". After the plane takes off, the pilot's flight plan is sent to the air base at which he plans to land. If it is an IFR flight plan, Base Operations also sends the flight plan to the Air Route Traffic Control Centers along his route.

5   When he is ready to start, the pilot must call the tower (on his radio) and talk to

the ground controller, who will give him instructions and permission to taxi to the runway. When he reaches the end of the runway, he must call the tower again, but this time he talks to the air traffic controller, who gives him permission and instructions for his takeoff.

6   Thus, before the aircraft leaves the ground, the pilot has received help from several people: Ops, the **meteorologist** and two people who work in the air traffic control tower. There are others, too, but we will not describe them here.

Air Traffic Controllers

7   During his flight, the pilot is helped by more people on the ground. He uses the **radio beacons**[1] to help him **navigate**. Most of these beacons are automatic: there is no one there. However, **maintenance** personnel must go to each beacon from time to time to inspect and, if necessary, repair them. (Pilots rarely call these stations "beacons". They usually call them by their technical names.)

8   The personnel at each Air Route Traffic Control Center along the pilot's flight path expect the plane to fly over at a particular time. (Remember that each Center receives the pilot's flight plan from Ops.) As the aircraft flies over the Center, the pilot calls them on his radio to let them know the number of his aircraft, the time he arrived at his present location, his altitude, where he is going and other information. Sometimes, he will also tell them about the weather at his altitude so they can pass on the information to other planes.

9   Sometimes a flight begins in good weather but ends in bad weather, so the pilot should fly VFR for the first part of the flight and IFR for the last part. For example,

---

1   **radio beacon:** 无线电导航设备。一些常见的无线电导航设备有：
    NDB（Non-Directional Beacon）无方向性信标，全向信标，导航台；
    VOR（VHF Omnidirectional Range）甚高频全向无线电信标，简称为"伏尔"；
    DME（Distance Measuring Equipment）测距装置；
    TACAN（Tactical Air Control and Navigation System）战术空中导航设备，塔康导航设备；
    VORTAC 是 VOR/DME 和 TACAN 的统称，用于近距导航的甚高频全向无线电信标导航系统；
    LORAN（Long-Range Navigation System）罗兰远距导航系统，此系统适用于广阔海面；
    OMEGA 奥米加导航系统，此系统适用于洲际导航。

it may be VFR until the final approach, but the air base at which the pilot wants to land may be covered by low clouds. The pilot can then call the tower for a Ground Controlled Approach(GCA). The GCA operator uses a special kind of radar that shows him exactly where the plane is as it descends. The GCA operator talks to the pilot constantly during a GCA and guides him directly to the end of the runway for the landing.

 Vocabulary

Special Terms

aircrew 空勤人员，空勤组
Air Force personnel 空军人员
Base Operations (Bps) 基地调度室
chart / aeronautical chart 航图，航空地图
Flight Operations (Ops) 飞行调度室
flight plan 飞行计划
flight planning room 飞行计划室
flight service 飞行保障勤务
ground service 地面勤务
radio beacon 无线电信标

New Words and Expressions

beacon	['biːkən]	*n.*	信标
file	[faɪl]	*v.*	提交（申请等）；把（文件等）归档
maintenance	['meɪntənəns]	*n.*	维修，维护
meteorological	[ˌmitiərə'lɒdʒɪkl]	*a.*	气象的
meteorologist	[ˌmitiə'rɒlədʒɪst]	*n.*	气象学家；气象工作者
navigate	['nævɪgeɪt]	*v.*	领航，导航；航行
ramp	[ræmp]	*n.*	停机坪；斜坡，坡道
be available to			可被……获得 / 利用
fill out			填写

 **Exercises**

Comprehension of the Text

I. Answer the following questions according to the text.

1. What is the difference between flight services and ground services?

_____

2. What is the first place the pilot goes to before a flight? Why does he go there?

_____

3. What is "filing a flight plan"?

_____

4. If the flight plan is an IFR flight plan, where will the Bps send the flight plan to?

_____

5. Whose help does a pilot receive before the aircraft leaves the ground?

_____

6. Whose help will the pilot get during his flight?

_____

7. What devices can help pilots navigate during their flight?

_____

8. What information will the pilot give to the personnel at the Air Route Traffic Control Center as the aircraft flies over the Center?

_____

9. What if the flight begins in good weather but ends in bad weather?

_____

10. How does the GCA operator guide the pilot's landing?

_____

Vocabulary Practice

II. Match the meanings in Column B with the special terms in Column A and translate the terms into Chinese.

Column A	Column B
1. flight service _____	a. the last leg of a landing pattern or the last heading flown by an aircraft before touchdown, during which the aircraft is lined up with the runway and is held to a fairly constant speed and rate of descent
2. flight plan _____	b. a transmitter at a known location, which transmits a continuous or periodic radio signal with limited information content (for example, its identification or location) on a specified radio frequency
3. Air Route Traffic Control Center _____	c. specified information relating to the intended flight of an aircraft that is filed orally or in writing with an FSS or an ATC facility
4. final approach _____	d. an organization within the Military Air Transport Service established to promote the safe and efficient extended flight operation of military aircraft within the US
5. radio beacon _____	e. a facility established to provide air traffic control services to aircraft operating on IFR flight plans within controlled airspace and principally during the en-route phase of flight

III. Complete each of the following sentences with a word or an expression from the box. Change the form if necessary.

navigate	aircrew	ramp	automatic	ground service
runway	chart	file	meteorological	maintenance

1. Some types of aerial camera mounts are _____ controlled to aid in taking aerial photographs.

2. Cleared area refers to the graded or otherwise prepared area at either side or end of the _____ from which trees, boulders or other objects have been removed.

3. The _____ group is responsible for fixing aircraft or other equipment.

4. Radio beacons are used by pilots to _____ during flight.

5. It makes much sense to _____ a flight plan before the aircraft leaves the ground.

6. In related news, the American _____ Society released its official statement on climate change.

7. Allied _____ who flew on such missions believed that they fought for a just cause.

8. The aircraft was searched while parking on the _____.

9. Layout _____ shows the various physical facilities of an installation and indicates the interrelationship of the facilities.

10. The performance test and fault diagnosis for airborne equipment is an important facet of aircraft maintenance in _____.

IV. Complete the following short passage with the words from the box. Change the form if necessary.

traffic advisory	service	flight plan	briefing	weather
air traffic controller	radio	clearance	emergency	VFR

The precise *1*_____ provided by FSS vary by countries, but typically, they may include providing preflight *2*_____ including weather and notices to airmen; filing, opening and closing *3*_____; monitoring navigational aids; collecting and disseminating pilot reports and airport surface *4*_____ observations; offering *5*_____ to aircraft on the ground or in flight; relaying instructions or *6*_____ from air traffic control; providing weather advisories to the aircraft inflight; initiating search and rescue on missing *7*_____ aircraft in *8*_____. In many countries, flight service stations also operate at mandatory frequency airports to help coordinate the traffic in the absence of *9*_____. In most cases, it is possible to reach flight service stations by *10*_____ in flight or by telephone on the ground.

Listening Practice

V. Watch the video clip about the ATC clearance and fill in the blanks.

In order to fly in controlled airspace when the weather is below VFR minimums, you must file an IFR flight plan and receive an ATC clearance.

An ATC clearance is your authorization to proceed to your destination while maintaining the rules established for *1*_____. In order for ATC to provide the proper aircraft *2*_____, you must not deviate from the clearance, unless you are experiencing an *3*_____ or receive a mandate clearance. Therefore, if it's apparent that the clearance will in some way jeopardize the safety of your flight, you should request an amendment. For example, let's see that you receive this instruction before you take off...*Climb and maintain 15,000.*

Your aircraft, however, is not equipped with supplemental oxygen, making the proposed flight at 15,000 feet unsafe and illegal in a non-pressurized aircraft. In this case, you need to request an *4*_____ to your altitude prior to departure.

Sometimes the clearance you received is different from the one you requested. For this reason, pay close attention when copying it and note any changes from your *5*_____. You should not attempt to copy the information when you are in the process of *6*_____ or performing other flight duties. If ATC advises you that your clearance is ready to copy, you should ask the controller to *7*_____.

4312 clearance, Cincinnati Ground Warrior 312 standby.

Cincinnati Ground Warrior 312, ready to copy.

Warrior 81312 is cleared to the Greater Pittsburgh Airport. Lunken 1 Departure. Appleton transition then as filed. Maintain 2,500, expect 10,000, 10 minutes after departure. Contact the departure control on 124.5. Squawk 5415.

Roger. Warrior 81312 is cleared to the Greater Pittsburgh Airport. Lunken 1 Departure. Appleton transition then as filed.

Although a complete *8*_____ isn't required, you are expected to read back the altitude assignments and any instructions requiring verification. You should also repeat the clearance if you feel the need for *9*_____, especially if it's different from the one you are anticipating.

To assist you in copying clearances, they are always given in a particular order,

beginning with the aircraft *10*_____, then the *11*_____, *12*_____, *13*_____, *14*_____, *15*_____ if appropriate, any special information, and frequency and transponder code.

Translating Practice

VI. Translate the following sentences into Chinese.

1. What Air Force personnel call "flight services" are like ground services; the jobs are all performed on the ground. They differ from the ground services in only one way: they assist the aircrew during the actual flight of the aircraft.

_____

_____

2. The weather information is made available to him at Base Operations. He uses this information to decide whether it will be an IFR or a VFR flight and to fill out his flight plan.

_____

_____

3. After the plane takes off, the pilot's flight plan is sent to the air base at which he plans to land. If it is an IFR flight plan, Base Operations also sends the flight plan to the Air Route Traffic Control Centers along his route.

_____

_____

4. During his flight, the pilot is helped by more people on the ground. He uses the radio beacons to help him navigate. Most of these beacons are automatic: there is no one there.

_____

_____

5. The GCA operator uses a special kind of radar that shows him exactly where the plane is as it descends. The GCA operator talks to the pilot constantly during a GCA and guides him directly to the end of the runway for the landing.

_____

_____

VII. Translate the following paragraph into English.

飞行勤务站属于空中交通设施，可直接与飞行员交流、发布飞行前简令、处理飞行计划、提供飞行咨询、实施搜救以及在紧急情况下向飞机提供援助。飞行勤务站也可以转播航空调度许可、处理航空通告以及提供最新的飞行气象和航空信息。

_____

_____

_____

_____

_____

🧭 TEXT B

Ground Services

1   In the early days of aviation, a single **mechanic** could learn to do all the maintenance required on a plane. Aircraft were simpler then, so a man who understood engines and was a good **electrician**, **carpenter** and **metalworker** could do all the necessary jobs.

2   Modern **jet aircraft** are much more complicated. Even if one man could learn all the **specialties**, he could not possibly find the time to do all the jobs. Therefore, a great many **specialists** are required to keep the aircraft flying safely. The lives of the aircrew depend on the specialists' work and so does the defense of the nation.

3   You will find these men on the flight line, in the **hangars** and in the repair shops, working under the direction and advice of the crew chief. They have many titles.

4   The **jet engine** mechanic must know how to remove a jet engine from an aircraft and **take** it **apart**. He checks its parts for **wear** and cracks, and if he finds them, he must remove the damaged or faulty parts and replace them. Then he must be able to

Engine Mechanic

Avionics Instrument Systems Specialist

put the engine back together again and replace it in the plane, with all the proper connections of wires, fuel and **oil tubes** and so on.

5   Another specialist, the **airframe** mechanic, is responsible for the maintenance of the fuselage, the wings, the tail and the landing gear, all of which form the airframe. When necessary, he or she repairs the ailerons, rudder and elevators, too.

6   There are several kinds of avionics specialists. The avionics instrument systems specialist is responsible for the **accuracy** of the instruments on the pilot's instrument panel and those instruments used by the **navigator**. All of these instruments must work perfectly, since it is vital that the aircrew know their altitude, airspeed, direction and the condition of the air in which they fly.

7   The avionics communications specialist is another member of the **ground crew**. His job involves the maintenance of the plane's radios. If the problem is serious, he usually takes the entire radio out and replaces it with a new one. He then takes the bad radio to his maintenance shop and repairs it there.

8   Other avionics specialists maintain special navigation equipment and some repair computers. The electronic warfare systems specialist has a particularly interesting job. To understand it, you must remember what radar is. Radar equipment uses **radio waves** to "see" aircraft that are many miles away or are hidden in clouds. Modern bombers and fighters have avionics equipment that can "feel" the enemy's radar waves and, in addition, send out other waves to confuse or **blind** the enemy's radar. This is called electronic warfare, and the specialist who is responsible for the maintenance of this kind of equipment is the electronic warfare systems specialist.

9   There is a "mechanical member" of the aircrew called the **automatic pilot**, which is also called the automatic flight control system. One member of the ground crew is responsible for the maintenance of this critical system that automatically controls the flight of the aircraft. You will remember that when the pilot takes his hands and feet off the controls to rest or to perform other duties, he depends on this system to fly the plane. At such a time, his life and the lives of all other persons on the plane depend upon the automatic pilot and upon the member of the ground crew who must maintain it. Thus, it might be said that the only man on the ground crew who is ever responsible for flying the plane is the automatic flight control systems specialist.

10   Another important member of the ground crew is the **Petroleum, Oil and Lubricants(POL)** specialist. A plane, just like an automobile, cannot run without fuel and oil. However, putting jet fuel in a bomber is not as simple as putting gasoline in an automobile. The fuel specialist, who is one type of POL specialist, must

POL Specialist

also know how to test several kinds of fuel and maintain the equipment that stores, carries and **pumps** the fuel. The fuel specialist has other duties, too. For example, he is responsible for the oxygen that the aircrews breath at **high altitudes**. (Except in informal conversations, the term POL, is not used in NATO countries other than the United States.)

11   In conversation, the long titles of ground crew personnel are rarely used. Usually, all avionic specialists are simply called avionics specs (pronounced "specks").

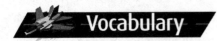

Special Terms

airframe （飞机）机体；（导弹）弹体

automatic pilot 自动驾驶仪

ground crew 地勤

hangar 机库

high altitude 高空

jet aircraft 喷气式飞机

jet engine 喷气发动机

navigator 领航员；领航仪，导航仪

oil tube 滑油管

Petroleum, Oil and Lubricants (POL) 油料

radio waves 无线电波

specialist 专业技师；专业兵

Words and Expressions

accuracy	['ækjərəsi]	*n.*	精度
blind	[blaɪnd]	*v.*	使失明；使眼花
carpenter	['kɑːpəntə]	*n.*	木匠，木工
electrician	[ɪˌlek'trɪʃn]	*n.*	电工，电气技师
mechanic	[mə'kænɪk]	*n.*	机械师
metalworker	['metlwɜːkə]	*n.*	金工工人；工具制造师
pump	[pʌmp]	*v.*	用泵抽吸或抽运（液体、气体等）*n.* 泵
specialty	['speʃlti]	*n.*	专业
wear	[weə]	*n.*	磨损；磨坏
take…apart			将……拆开；分解

 Exercises

Comprehension of the Text

I. Complete the following table with the information from the text.

Ground Crew		Duties
Jet engine specialists		
		Be responsible for the maintenance of the fuselage, the wings, the tail and the landing gear, and repair the ailerons, rudder and elevators too when necessary.
Avionics specialists	Avionics instrument systems specialists	
		Be responsible for the maintenance of the plane's radio.
	Electronic warfare systems specialists	
	Other avionics specialists	
Automatic flight control systems specialist		
		Test several kinds of fuel and maintain the equipment that stores, carries and pumps the fuel; be responsible for the oxygen that the aircrew breathe at high altitudes.

Vocabulary Practice

II. Complete each of the following definitions with a special term from the box. Change the form if necessary.

jet aircraft	electronic warfare	automatic pilot	avionics	airframe
radio wave	ground crew	jet engine	navigator	navigation

1. _____ is a general term for all electronic systems on an aircraft or an acronym designating the field of aviation electronics.

2. A(n) _____ refers to a person who plots and directs the movement of an aircraft or a ship from within the aircraft or ship.

3. The _____ refers to a team of engine mechanics and other technicians who maintain, service or handle aircraft on the ground.

4. _____ refers to the military action involving the use of electromagnetic and directed energy to control the electromagnetic spectrum or attack the enemy.

5. _____ is a system which automatically controls and guides the flight of an airplane.

6. A(n) _____ refers to an aircraft, especially a fixed-wing aircraft, powered with one or more jet engines.

7. _____ refer to electromagnetic waves used in radio or radar.

8. _____ refers to the art of determining the geographical position and maintaining the desired direction of an aircraft relative to the earth's surface.

9. A(n) _____ is a species of reaction engine, namely, an engine that takes in air from outside for using as a fuel oxidizer and projects a jet of hot gases backward to create thrust, the gases being derived from combustion within the engine.

10. _____ is defined as the structure of an aircraft, rocket vehicle or missile without the power plant.

Listening Practice

III. Watch the video clip about space-based ADS-B over the North Atlantic and fill in the blanks.

The North Atlantic is the world's busiest oceanic airspace, but there's no radar here, which means no *1*_____ coverage. Aircraft positions are updated every 14 minutes, so flights are planned hours in advance on what's known as the *2*_____ Track Structure (OTS).

Aircraft have to stick to very *3*_____ routes, speeds and altitudes that aren't always efficient. As things get even busier, this isn't sustainable. That's why NATS is jointly leading a revolution in air traffic management. We're introducing *4*_____ surveillance over the North Atlantic for the very first time.

This innovative and transformational surveillance technology is called space-based ADS-B. With ADS-B, aircraft are monitored by 66 orbiting *5*_____ to provide near real-time updates of their progress.

The benefits will improve the performance of the airline industry in many ways. If an aircraft changes level or route without *6*_____ from air traffic control, we'll know about it in seconds rather than minutes, so controllers can quickly intervene to keep aircraft safe *7*_____ apart.

With ADS-B in place, the airspace will be safer, flights will be more efficient and our service will be more *8*_____. Distances between aircraft can be safely reduced to increase flexibility and airspace capacity.

Now aircraft can fly at their most cost-effective speed, can take more efficient routes using less airline fuel. And this means lower CO_2 *9*_____ for everyone and lower costs for airlines. Using ADS-B gives us access to valuable data that will make flying safer, increase airspace capacity, minimize costs and reduce *10*_____ impact.

Here at NATS, we're proud to be part of the team making global aircraft surveillance a reality for the first time in history. And the North Atlantic is just the start of that journey.

Translating Practice

IV. Translate the following sentences into Chinese.

1. Therefore, a great many specialists are required to keep the aircraft flying safely. The lives of the aircrew depend on the specialists' work and so does the defense of the nation.

_____

_____

2. Another specialist, the airframe mechanic, is responsible for the maintenance of the fuselage, the wings, the tail and the landing gear, all of which form the airframe. When necessary, he or she repairs the ailerons, rudder and elevators, too.

_____

_____

3. The avionics instrument systems specialist is responsible for the accuracy of the instruments on the pilot's instrument panel and those instruments used by the navigator.

---

4. Modern bombers and fighters have avionics equipment that can "feel" the enemy's radar waves and, in addition, send out other waves to confuse or blind the enemy's radar.

---

5. Thus, it might be said that the only man on the ground crew who is ever responsible for flying the plane is the automatic flight control systems specialist.

V. Translate the following paragraph into English.

机场地勤服务是各级航空站的一项重要服务，与航空站的运作息息相关且不可或缺。所有民用、商用及军用飞行器都需要接受地勤的服务，从飞机进入停机坪那一刻起，到离开停机坪进入滑行道为止，停泊期间的所有后勤服务皆为机场地勤人员的工作范围。

 TEXT C

Preflight Check

1   Once, when Lieutenant Anderson was a student and learned to fly a plane, he forgot to inspect the nose gear during his preflight check. He started the engine and began to taxi the plane from its place on the ramp. When he turned the plane toward the taxiway, he felt that something was wrong: the air pressure in the tires was too low. He had to stop, turn off the engine and wait for help. It was very embarrassing. He wished he could have returned the plane to its parking place, but the aircraft cannot back up.

2   Since then, he has always made a complete preflight check of his plane. He always uses his preflight **checklist** (检查单) to remind him of each part to inspect.

3   So this morning he had his checklist in his hand as he inspected the plane. He began near the nose of the aircraft, looking into the **air intake** (空气进气道) to be sure that there was nothing inside it. There was. He reached in and pulled out a piece of newspaper that the wind had

Preflight Check

blown into the intake during the night. That was unusual and seemed unimportant, but it could have caused a serious problem. The paper could have prevented air from reaching the engine, or it could have gotten into the engine and caused some damage. He folded the piece of paper and put it in the pocket of his jacket.

4   Lt. Anderson bent down to examine the nose gear. Then he stood and walked along the **front edge** (前缘) of the right wing, examining it as he went along. He stopped at the tip of the wing to check the glass cover on the green **navigation light** (航行灯). Then he turned again toward the fuselage, walking behind the wing. He

stopped, looked at his checklist, and inspected the right aileron, the surface of the wing and its other parts.

5   A moment later, he bent down to check the right main gear. It was okay, so he moved along the fuselage toward the tail, stopping a few times to read the checklist and inspect parts of the fuselage.

6   At the tail of the plane, he looked up at the navigation light on the top of the vertical stabilizer. He also checked for small cracks in the **aluminum** (铝) "skin" of the vertical and horizontal stabilizers and tried the **hinges** (铰链) of the rudder and the elevators. They worked smoothly. He noticed a very small **dent** (凹痕) in the aluminum on the left side of the vertical stabilizer, but he decided it was not important. Nevertheless, he wrote a note to himself as a reminder to report it.

7   He then inspected the left wing and its aileron, the left main gear, the red navigation light at the end of the wing and several other parts of the aircraft, both outside and inside. When he reached the end of the checklist, he was satisfied that the plane was in good condition and ready to fly.

8   Anderson turned away from the plane and walked toward Base Operations to discard the piece of newspaper and look at the weather reports. He too, would be ready to fly in a few minutes. He whistled an old song as he walked.

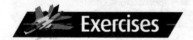 Exercises

Comprehension of the Text

Answer the following questions according to the text.

1. What happened when Lt. Anderson once forgot to check the nose gear in his preflight check? What did he learn from this experience?

_____

2. What did Anderson find while checking the air intake and what problem could the newspaper in the air intake result in?

_____

3. How did he deal with the problem in the air intake?

_____

4. What did Lt. Anderson examine during the preflight check?

_____

5. What did Lt. Anderson find on the left side of the vertical stabilizer? How did he deal with it?

_____

⊘ UNIT PROJECT

Mind Mapping

Work in groups and draw a mind map to depict the duties of different ground personnel.

Oral Practice

Work in groups and discuss the importance of flight services and ground services. And one student from each group will make a 3-minute oral presentation about either the importance of flight services or the importance of ground services by giving examples. You may refer to the texts of this unit and the relevant information from the Internet.

Writing Practice

Based on the discussion above, write a composition with at least 150 words on the topic of "The Importance of Flight Services / Ground Services". You may refer to the questions below.

1. What do flight services / ground services usually consist of?

2. Can you give some examples to illustrate the importance of flight services / ground services?

3. Are there any suggestions to improve the current flight services / ground services?

Unit 8
Carrier-based
Aircraft Operations

⊘ Warming Up

Task 1 Watch the video clip about China's second aircraft carrier and fill in the blanks.

Why does China want a homemade aircraft carrier? China did not develop an aircraft carrier until the late 2000s. The country's first carrier was the "Liaoning", which was renovated from the Ukrainian vessel Varyag. It is classified as a *1*_____ ship intended to allow the Chinese navy to *2*_____ and practice. It does not play the same roles as a *3*_____ ready aircraft carrier. But times are changing and now China is *4*_____ its first indigenous aircraft carrier. Constructed from 2014, this ship, likely called "Shandong", will be China's first aircraft carrier for *5*_____. The steam-turbines-powered "Shandong" has similar *6*_____ with the "Liaoning". Yes, it is much smaller than America's Nimitz-class carriers, but outshines India's and Japan's carriers. The carrier will carry between 30 to 40 helicopters, J-15 *7*___·_____, and over a hundred long-range anti-air and surface attack missiles. The "Shandong" will travel with a combat-ready *8*_____, likely an arsenal of drones and submarines more heavily armed than current Chinese attack boats. The "Shandong" is scheduled to hit the water in mid-2017, and its focus will remain on *9*_____ rather than offense. While the US maintains an unnecessary naval *10*_____ in the waters, in particular in the South China Sea, China needs a complete fleet for coastal defense.

Task 2 Pre-reading Activities.

Work in groups and label the picture on the next page, using the words and expressions in the box.

bow	bridge	deck	elevator
flight deck	hangar bay	hull	island
port	starboard	stern	waterline

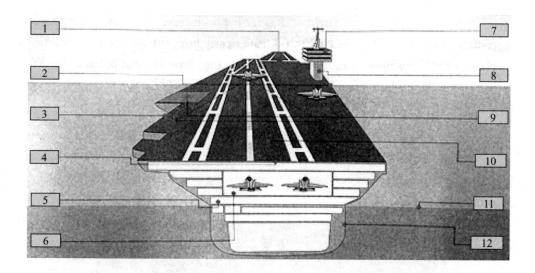

⊘ TEXT A

Taking Off from an Aircraft Carrier

Tom Harris

1   An aircraft carrier **flight deck** is one of the most **exhilarating** and dangerous work environments in the world (not to mention one of the loudest). The deck may look like an ordinary land runway, but it works very differently, due to its smaller size. When the crew is **in full swing**,

An A-6E Intruder launches from the USS George Washington.

planes are landing and taking off at a **furious** rate in a limited space. One careless moment, a fighter jet engine could **suck** somebody in or blast somebody off the edge of the deck into the ocean.

2   But as dangerous as the flight deck is for the deck crew[1], they have it pretty easy compared to the pilots. The flight deck isn't nearly long enough for most military planes to make ordinary landings or takeoffs, so they have to head out and come in with some extraordinary machine assistance.

3   If you've learned how airplanes work, you know that an airplane has to get a lot of air moving over its wings to generate lift. To make takeoff a little easier, carriers can get additional airflow over the flight deck by **speeding** through the ocean, into the wind, in the direction of takeoff. This air moving over the wings lowers the plane's **minimum takeoff speed**.

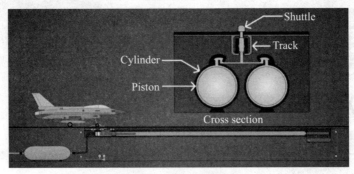

Working Principle of the Carrier's Catapults

4   Getting air moving over the deck is important, but the primary takeoff assistance comes from the carrier's four **catapults**, which get the planes up to high speeds in a very short distance. Each catapult consists of two **pistons** that sit inside two parallel

Catapult Hookup

cylinders, each about as long as a football field, positioned under the deck. Each piston has a metal **lug** on the tip, which **protrudes** through a narrow gap along the top of each cylinder. The two lugs extend through rubber **flanges**, which seal the cylinders, and through a gap in the flight deck, where they attach to a small **shuttle**.

---

1 句中 as...as 引导让步状语从句，所以该句也可理解为 "dangerous as the flight deck is for the deck crew"，中文意思是 "尽管飞行甲板对于甲板工作人员来说是危险的"。

5   To prepare for a takeoff, the flight deck crew moves the plane into position at the rear of the catapult and attaches the towbar on the plane's nose gear (front wheels) to a slot in the shuttle. The crew positions another bar, the holdback, between the back of the wheel and the shuttle. (In F-14 and F/A-18 fighter jets, the holdback is built into the nose gear; in other planes, it's a separate piece.)

6   While all of this is going on, the flight crew raises the **Jet Blast Deflector (JBD)** behind the plane (**aft** of the plane, in this case). When the JBD, towbar and holdback are all in position, and all the final checks have been made, the **catapult officer** (also known as the "**shooter**") gets the catapults ready from the **catapult control pod**, which is a small, **encased control station** with a **transparent dome** that protrudes above the flight deck.

catapult control pod

Steam rises from the catapult as an F/A-18C Hornet prepares to launch from the USS George Washington.

Jet Blase Deflector(JBD)

An F-14 Tomcat positioned in front of the jet blast deflector on USS Nimitz's catapult number 1.

7   When the plane is ready to go, the catapult officer opens valves to fill the catapult cylinders with high-pressure steam from the ship's **reactors**. This steam provides the necessary force to propel the pistons at high speed, **slinging** the plane forward to generate the necessary lift for takeoff. Initially, the pistons are locked into place, so the cylinders simply build up pressure. The catapult officer carefully monitors the pressure level, so it's just right for the particular plane and deck conditions. If the pressure is too low, the plane won't get moving fast enough to take off, and the catapult will throw it into the ocean. If there's too much pressure, the sudden **jerk** could break the nose gear right off.

8   When the cylinders are charged to the appropriate pressure level, the pilot blasts the plane's engines. The holdback keeps the plane on the shuttle, while the engines

generate considerable thrust. The catapult officer releases the pistons, then the force causes the holdbacks to release, and the steam pressure **slams** the shuttle and plane forward. At the end of the catapult, the towbar **pops out of** the shuttle, releasing the plane. This totally steam-driven system can **rocket** a 45,000-pound plane from 0 to 165 miles per hour (a 20,000-kg plane from 0 to 266 kph) in two seconds!

9   If everything goes well, the speeding plane has generated enough lift to take off. If not, the pilots **activate** their **ejector seats** to escape before the plane goes **hurdling** into the ocean ahead of the ship. (This hardly ever happens, but the risk is always there.)

10   Taking off is extremely difficult, but the real trick is coming back in. In Text B, we'll take a look at the standard carrier landing or recovery procedure.

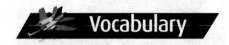

Vocabulary

Special Terms

aft 在/从机尾

catapult 弹射器

catapult control pod 弹射器控制舱

catapult officer 弹射官

control station 控制站；引导站

ejector seat 弹射座椅

flight deck 飞行甲板；驾驶舱

holdback 牵制杆；制动杆

Jet Blast Deflector (JBD) 发动机喷焰挡板；喷焰偏转器

minimum takeoff speed 最小起飞速度

reactor 反应堆

shooter 弹射官，放飞助理

shuttle 滑梭，滑块

towbar / launch bar 拖曳杆，弹射杆；牵引杆

Words and Expressions

activate	['æktɪveɪt]	v.	激活；启动，触发
dome	[dəʊm]	n.	穹顶；圆屋顶
encased	[ɪn'keɪst]	a.	密闭的；密封的
exhilarating	[ɪg'zɪləreɪtɪŋ]	a.	使人兴奋的，令人激动的
flange	[flændʒ]	n.	凸缘；安装盘；法兰盘
furious	['fjʊəriəs]	a.	高速的；狂怒的；激烈的
hurdle	['hɜːdl]	v.	（奔跑中）跨越
jerk	[dʒɜːk]	n.	急拉；猛推
lug	[lʌg]	n.	凸块；凸缘
piston	['pɪstn]	n.	活塞
protrude	[prə'truːd]	v.	突出；伸出
rocket	['rɒkɪt]	v.	（非正式）迅速地移动；飙升，骤增；发射火箭
slam	[slæm]	v.	用力一放；使劲一推；猛劲一摔
sling	[slɪŋ]	v.	投，掷，抛 n. 吊索
speed	[spiːd]	v.	加速，急行
suck	[sʌk]	v./n.	吮吸；咂；啜
transparent	[træns'pærənt]	a.	透明的；显而易见的
in full swing			热烈进行中；热火朝天
pop out of			突然从⋯⋯伸出

 Exercises

Comprehension of the Text

I. **Answer the following questions according to the text.**

   1. Why is an aircraft carrier flight deck one of the most exhilarating and dangerous work environments in the world?

   _____

   2. What should carriers do to make takeoff a little easier?

   _____

3. Where does the primary takeoff assistance come from?

_____

4. What is the carrier's catapult composed of?

_____

5. In order to prepare for a takeoff, what should the flight crew undertake?

_____

6. What's the catapult officer's responsibility?

_____

7. Why does the catapult officer open valves when the plane is ready to go?

_____

8. What would happen if the high-pressure steam filled in the catapult cylinders were not right for the particular plane and deck conditions?

_____

9. What will a pilot do if the plane has not generated enough lift to take off?

_____

10. Can you briefly describe the procedures of the catapult launch?

_____

Vocabulary Practice

II. Translate the following special terms into Chinese according to the cutaway view and top view of an aircraft carrier.

engine room _____   catapult control station _____

waterline _____   optical landing system _____

main hangar deck _____   jet blast deflector _____

gallery deck _____   island _____

bridge _____   arresting wire _____

flag bridge _____   elevator _____

primary flight control _____   weapons elevator _____

catapult _____   barricade _____

launcher _____   antenna mast _____

CIWS _____

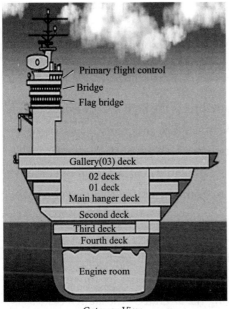

Cutaway View

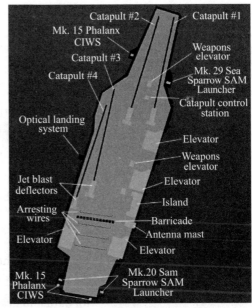

Top View

III. Match the meanings in Column B with the special terms in Column A and translate the terms into Chinese.

Column A	Column B
1. catapult _____	a. a seat that allows a pilot to be thrown out of an aircraft in an emergency
2. towbar _____	b. a device used to launch aircraft from ships, most commonly used on aircraft carriers, as a form of assisted takeoff
3. holdback _____	c. a small encased control station with a transparent dome above the flight deck
4. recovery _____	d. the person who is responsible for making a final check of catapult settings and giving the signal to launch
5. shuttle _____	e. in, near or towards the back of a ship or an aircraft

Column A	Column B
6. Jet Blast Deflector _____	f. a device generally used to restrain an aircraft prior to catapulting
7. aft _____	g. a safety device that redirects the high energy exhaust from a jet engine to prevent damage and injury
8. catapult officer _____	h. the phase of a mission which involves the return of an aircraft to a land base or platform afloat in air operations
9. catapult control pod _____	i. a rigid metal bar or frame used for towing vehicles or aircraft
10. ejector seat _____	j. a device attached to the catapult gear under the flight deck and used for assisting takeoff by moving rapidly forward and dragging the aircraft by the launch bar

IV. Complete each of the following sentences with a word from the box. Change the form if necessary.

airflow	protrude	exhilarate	blast	transparent
cylinder	hurdle	parallel	valve	suck

1. In commercial aircraft, the empennage is built from the cabin pressure-cone and may contain the Flight Data Recorder (the black box), Cockpit Voice Recorder and the pressure out-flow _____.

2. He said Japan had sought to portray itself as a(n) _____ and responsible partner, rebuilding military-to-military links with the US.

3. The more severe the icing, the higher the stall speed. This is not only because the smooth _____ over the wings becomes increasingly more difficult, but also because of the added weight of the accumulated ice.

4. Something like a fin _____ from the water.

5. Upwind leg is a flight path _____ to the landing runway in the direction of landing.

6. The pollution-control team is at the scene and is due to start _____ up oil any time now.

7. Life onboard an aircraft carrier is undeniably difficult and exhausting, but it can also be _____, especially for the men and women up on the flight deck, flying and bringing in planes on a tiny patch of runway.

8. He _____ the fence and ran off down the street.

9. The purpose of the cowling or nacelle is to streamline the flow of the air around the engine and to help cool the engine by ducting air around the _____.

10. The use of engine thrust near terminals is restricted due to the possibility of jet _____ damage.

V. **Complete the following short passage with the words or expressions from the box. Change the form if necessary.**

wind	holdback	rear		flight deck	knot
launch bar	catapult firing	nose landing gear		accelerate	catapult shuttle

Catapult hookup is accomplished by placing the aircraft *1*_____, which is attached to the front of the aircraft's *2*_____, into the *3*_____, which is attached to the catapult gear under the *4*_____. An additional bar, the *5*_____, is connected from the *6*_____ of the nose landing gear to the carrier deck. Its fitting keeps the aircraft from moving forward prior to *7*_____. Once the catapult fires, the holdback breaks free as the shuttle moves rapidly forward, dragging the aircraft by the launch bar. The aircraft *8*_____ from zero (relative to the carrier deck) to approximately 150 *9*_____ in about 2 seconds. There is typically *10*_____ (natural or ship motion generated) over the flight deck, giving the aircraft additional lift.

Listening Practice

VI. **Watch the video clip about the first sea trials of China's second aircraft carrier and fill in the blanks.**

China's second aircraft carrier, Type 001A, will conduct its first sea trials in the

Bohai Sea and the Yellow Sea areas this week. The first sea trials of China's second aircraft carrier built at the Dalian Shipyard is likely to take place in the Bohai Sea and the Yellow Sea to test its *1*_____ and design. Sun Xiaoping, a military expert and TV commentator, told *Global Times* Sunday. China had launched its second aircraft carrier in April 2017 after it *2*_____ the first carrier the "Liaoning", a refitted Soviet Union-made vessel in 2012. Last Friday, Liaoning Maritime Safety Administration issued three *3*_____, saying that as military operations would be conducted from April 20th to 28th in parts of the Bohai Sea and Yellow Sea, no vessels would be allowed to enter the areas, according to a notice on its website. Online pictures showed that scaffold around the type 001A carrier had been removed, and *4*_____ radar had been installed, the *Science and Technology Daily* reported on April 10th. Military expert Xiu Weigang told news site "people.com.cn" on April 11th that China's first *5*_____ aircraft carrier is likely to finish sea trials in the second half of this year, which means that it may be delivered to the PLA navy at that time.

The "Liaoning" has conducted 3 cross-sea *6*_____ in 2013, 2016 and 2017. Xiu said it was no surprise that *7*_____ may start soon as China had accumulated much experience with its first aircraft carrier. Technical staff and other shipbuilders had been working overtime to ready the new vessel in the past year. Sun predicted the carrier could be ready for combat in two years after sea trials, as well as tests on its radar, *8*_____ and shipboard flights. "In just two years, China will have two aircraft carriers with *9*_____, which will greatly improve China's blue water *10*_____ as well as effectively safeguard national interests," Sun added.

Translating Practice

VII. Translate the following sentences into Chinese.

1. To make takeoff a little easier, carriers can get additional airflow over the flight deck by speeding through the ocean, into the wind, in the direction of takeoff. This air moving over the wings lowers the plane's minimum takeoff speed.

_____

_____

2. Getting air moving over the deck is important, but the primary takeoff assistance comes from the carrier's four catapults, which get the planes up to high speeds in a very short distance.

   _____

   _____

3. To prepare for a takeoff, the flight deck crew moves the plane into position at the rear of the catapult and attaches the towbar on the plane's nose gear (front wheels) to a slot in the shuttle. The crew positions another bar, the holdback, between the back of the wheel and the shuttle.

   _____

   _____

4. When the JBD, towbar and holdback are all in position, and all the final checks have been made, the catapult officer gets the catapults ready from the catapult control pod, which is a small, encased control station with a transparent dome that protrudes above the flight deck.

   _____

   _____

5. When the plane is ready to go, the catapult officer opens valves to fill the catapult cylinders with high-pressure steam from the ship's reactors. This steam provides the necessary force to propel the pistons at high speed, slinging the plane forward to generate the necessary lift for takeoff.

   _____

   _____

VIII. Translate the following paragraph into English.

起飞前约 45 分钟，机组人员进行起飞前绕机检查并登上飞机。起飞前约 30 分钟，起动发动机并进行飞行前检查。起飞前约 15 分钟，准备好的飞机从停靠位置滑行至指定位置或直接滑行至弹射器后。母舰迎向自然风。当飞机滑行至弹射器上时，机翼展开，发动机排气管后一个大的喷气偏流挡板从飞行甲板上升起。

在最后勾上弹射器前，最终检验员（检查官）对飞机做最后的外部检查，军械师
负责装载武器。

_____

_____

_____

_____

_____

🧭 TEXT B

Landing on an Aircraft Carrier

Tom Harris

An ES-3A Shadow comes in for a landing aboard the USS George Washington.

1   Landing on a flight deck is one of the most difficult things that a navy pilot will ever do. The flight deck only has about 500 feet (about 150 meters) of runway space for landing planes, which isn't nearly enough for the heavy, high-speed jets on US carriers.

2   To land on the flight deck, each plane needs a tailhook, which is exactly what it sounds like—an extended hook attached to the plane's tail. The pilot's goal is to **snag** the tailhook on one of the four **arresting wires**, which are **sturdy** cables **woven** from high-tensile steel wire.

3   The arresting wires are stretched across the deck and are attached on both ends to hydraulic cylinders below deck. If the tailhook snags an arresting wire, it pulls the wire out and the hydraulic cylinder system absorbs the energy to bring the plane to a

stop. The arresting wire system can stop a 54,000-pound aircraft travelling 150 miles per hour in only two seconds, in a 315-foot landing area (a 24,500-kg aircraft travelling at 241 kph in a 96-meter landing area).

4   There are four parallel arresting wires, spaced about 50 feet (15 meters) apart, to expand the target area for the pilot. Pilots are aiming for the third wire, as it's the safest and most effective target. They never shoot for the first wire, because it's dangerously close to the edge of the deck. If they come in too low on the first wire, they could easily crash into the stern of the ship. It's acceptable to snag the second or fourth wire, but for a pilot to move up through the ranks, he or she has to be able to catch the third wire consistently.

5   To pull off this incredible trick, the pilot needs to approach the deck at exactly the right angle. The landing procedure starts when the various returning planes "**stack up**" in a huge **oval** flying pattern near the carrier. **The Carrier Air Traffic Control Center (CATCC)** below deck decides the landing order of the waiting planes based on their various fuel levels. (A plane that's about to run out of fuel comes down before one that can keep flying for a while.) When it's time for a

This is the tailhook of a KA-6D Intruder aircraft, about to catch an arresting wire on the USS Dwight D. Eisenhower.

An F/A-18C Hornet catches an arresting wire on the USS Nimitz.

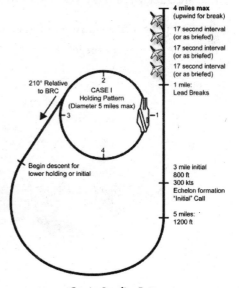

Carrier Landing Pattern

LSO at Work

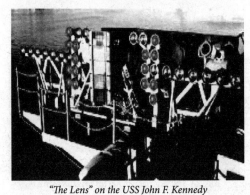

"The Lens" on the USS John F. Kennedy

plane to land, the pilot breaks free of this landing pattern and heads toward the stern of the ship.

6   Landing Signal Officers (LSO) help guide the plane in, through radio communication as well as a collection of lights on the deck. If the plane is **off course**, the LSOs can use radio commands or **illuminate** other lights to correct it or "wave it off" (send it around for another attempt).

7   In addition to the LSOs, pilots look to the **Fresnel Lens Optical Landing System (FLOLS)**, commonly referred to as the Lens, for landing guidance. The Lens consists of a series of lights and Fresnel lenses mounted to a **gyroscopically** stabilized platform. The lenses focus the light into narrow beams that are directed into the sky at various angles.

8   The pilot will see different lights depending on the plane's **angle of approach**. If the plane is right **on target**, the pilot will see an **amber** light, dubbed the "meatball",

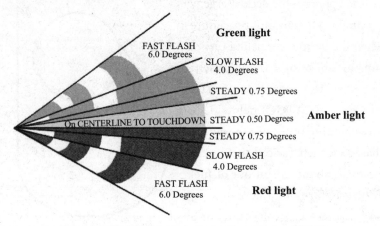

A Diagram Illustrating the "Long-Range Lineup System (LRLS)"

in line with a row of green lights. If the amber light appears above the green lights, the plane is coming in too high; if the amber light appears below the green lights, the plane is coming in too low. If the plane is coming in way too low, the pilot will see red lights.

9　　As soon as the plane hits the deck, the pilot will push the engines to full power, instead of slowing down, to bring the plane to a stop. This may seem **counterintuitive**, but if the tailhook doesn't catch any of the arresting wires, the plane needs to be moving fast enough to take off again and come around for another pass. The landing runway is tilted at a 14-degree angle to

*An S-3A Viking aircraft lands on the USS Abraham Lincoln with the help of the crash **barricade**.*

the rest of the ship, so bolters like this can take off from the side of the ship instead of **plowing into** the planes on the other end of the deck.

10　　As soon as an aircraft lands, it's pulled out of the **landing strip** and **chained down** on the side of the flight deck. **Inactive** aircraft are always tightly secured to keep them from sliding around as the deck rocks back and forth.

11　　The flight-deck crew has to be prepared for a wide range of unexpected events, including the **raging** aircraft fires. During takeoff or recovery operations, they have plenty of safety equipment **at the ready**. Among other things, the flight deck has a small fire truck, and nozzles leading to water tanks and **Aqueous Film-Forming Foam(AFFF)**, an Advanced **Fire-Extinguishing Material**. (There are also nozzles for jet fuel and a number of other useful liquids.)

12　　Flight-deck personnel also face the risk of being blown overboard by a jet engine. Safety nets around the side of the flight deck offer some protection, but for extra safety, personnel are also equipped with float coats, the **self-inflating** jackets with flashing **distress lights** activated by contact with water. Flight-deck personnel also wear **heavy-duty** helmets, called "**cranials**", which protect their heads and their hearing.

Vocabulary

Special Terms

angle of approach / approach angle 进近角，着陆下滑角

Aqueous Film-Forming Foam (AFFF) 水成膜泡沫灭火剂

arresting wire 拦阻索

barricade 拦机网，防冲网；路障

Carrier Air Traffic Control Center (CATCC) 航母空中交通管制中心

distress light 遇险信号灯

fire-extinguishing material 灭火材料

Fresnel Lens Optical Landing System (FLOLS) "菲涅尔"透镜光学助降系统

gyroscopically 使用陀螺仪地

landing strip / airstrip 简易着陆场；简易跑道；可着陆区

Long Range Lineup System (LRLS) 远距对准系统

off course 偏离航线

on target 到达目标上空；已捕获目标；命中目标

overboard 从船上落水

stack up 飞机作分层盘旋等待

Words and Expressions

amber	['æmbə]	a.	琥珀色的
counterintuitive	[ˌkaʊntəin'tjuːɪtɪv]	a.	反常的
cranial	['kreɪnɪəl]	a.	颅的；颅侧的
illuminate	[ɪ'luːmɪneɪt]	v.	照明；照射
inactive	[ɪn'æktɪv]	a.	不活动的，不活跃的
heavy-duty	[hevi 'djuːtɪ]	a.	重型的；耐用的
oval	['əʊvl]	a.	椭圆形的
rage	[reɪdʒ]	v.	猛烈地继续；激烈进行；发怒
self-inflating	[self ɪn'fleɪtɪŋ]	a.	自行充气式的
snag	[snæg]	v.	钩住；抓住
sturdy	['stɜːdi]	a.	结实的；坚固的

tensile	['tensaɪl]	a.	张力的；拉力的
weave	[wiːv]	v.	编，织；（用……）编成
at the ready			处在准备状态，准备立即行动
chain down			拴住
plow into			撞上；全力冲进
pull off			赢得，做成某事；在路边停车

Exercises

Comprehension of the Text

I. Answer the following questions according to the text.

1. Why is landing on a flight deck one of the most difficult things for a navy pilot?

_____

2. How does the arresting wire system stop a 54,000-pound aircraft travelling 150 miles per hour in only two seconds?

_____

3. How many arresting wires are there on the carrier? Which arresting wire are the pilots aiming for when landing on the carrier?

_____

4. Why do pilots never shoot for the first wire?

_____

5. What's the responsibility of the Carrier Air Traffic Control Center?

_____

6. What's the duty of LSOs?

_____

7. In addition to the LSOs, what system do pilots use for landing guidance?

_____

8. How does the Fresnel Lens Optical Landing System guide pilots to the flight deck successfully?

_____

9. When landing, what will pilots do as soon as the plane hits the deck? Why?

_____

10. Why is the landing runway tilted at a 14-degree angle to the rest of the ship?

_____

Vocabulary Practice

II. Complete each of the following definitions with a special term from the box.

tailhook	Landing Signal Officer	Carrier Air Traffic Control Center
arresting wire	Long Range Lineup System	Fresnel Lens Optical Landing System

1. A(n) _____ is a Naval Aviator specially trained to facilitate the "safe and expeditious recovery" of the naval aircraft aboard aircraft carriers.

2. A(n) _____ is a device attached to the empennage (rear) of some military fixed-wing aircraft and used to achieve rapid deceleration during routine landings aboard aircraft carrier flight decks at sea.

3. A (n) _____ is a mechanical system stretched across the deck and used to rapidly decelerate an aircraft as it lands.

4. _____ is a landing system that uses eye-safe lasers, projected aft of the ship, to give pilots a visual indication of their lineup with relation to the centerline.

5. _____ is a light system that is designed to provide a "glideslope" for aviators approaching a carrier.

6. _____ is a zone in the carrier that is established primarily to provide air traffic service to aircraft operating.

Translating Practice

III. Translate the following sentences into Chinese.

1. To land on the flight deck, each plane needs a tailhook, which is exactly what it sounds like—an extended hook attached to the plane's tail. The pilot's goal is to snag the tailhook on one of the four arresting wires, which are sturdy cables woven from high-tensile steel wire.

_____

_____

2. The arresting wires are stretched across the deck and are attached on both ends to hydraulic cylinders below deck. If the tailhook snags an arresting wire, it pulls the wire out and the hydraulic cylinder system absorbs the energy to bring the plane to a stop.

_____

_____

3. Landing Signals Officers (LSO) help guide the plane in, through radio communication as well as a collection of lights on the deck. If the plane is off course, the LSOs can use radio commands or illuminate other lights to correct it or "wave it off".

_____

_____

4. The Lens consists of a series of lights and Fresnel lenses mounted to a gyroscopically stabilized platform. The lenses focus the light into narrow beams that are directed into the sky at various angles.

_____

_____

5. As soon as an aircraft lands, it's pulled out of the landing strip and chained down on the side of the flight deck. Inactive aircraft are always tightly secured to keep them from sliding around as the deck rocks back and forth.

_____

_____

 TEXT C

The Island

Tom Harris

1   An aircraft carrier's "island" is the command center for flight-deck operations, as well as the ship as a whole. The island is about 150 feet (46 m) tall, but it's only 20 feet (6 m) wide at the base, so it won't take up too much space on the flight deck. The top of the island, well above the height of any aircraft on the flight deck, is spread out to provide more room.

2   The top of the island is outfitted with an array of radar and communications **antennas** (天线), which keep tabs on surrounding ships and aircraft, intercept and jam enemy radar signals, target enemy aircraft and missiles, and pick up satellite phone and TV signals, among other things. Below that is the **Primary Flight Control** (主飞行控制室) or Pri-Fly. In the Pri-Fly, the **air officer** (航空部门长) and **air officer assistant** (known as the "Air Boss" and the "Mini Boss") direct all aircraft activities on the flight deck and within a 5-mile (8-km) radius.

The Island on the USS Abraham Lincoln

3   The Air Boss and Mini Boss, both experienced aviators, have an array of computers and communications equipment to keep tabs on everything, but they get a lot of information just by looking out their windows, six stories above the flight deck. When an approaching plane gets within three-quarters of a mile (1.2 km), the Landing Signals Officers take over control to direct the landing procedure. At the same level as the Pri-Fly, crew and visitors can walk out onto the vulture's row[1], a balcony platform with a great view of the entire flight deck.

---

1   **vulture's row:** 航母舰岛外围的走廊，是全舰最佳的"观景台"，又译为"秃鹫走廊"。

4　　The next level down is the bridge, the ship's command center. The commanding officer (the captain) usually controls this ship from a stately leather chair surrounded by computer screens. The commanding officer directs the **helmsman** (操舵兵), who actually steers the carrier, the **lee helmsman** (副操舵兵), who directs the engine room to control the

The Lee Helmsman (left) and Helmsman on the USS Theodore Roosevelt

speed of the ship, the **Quartermaster of the Watch** (值更航海军士), who keeps track of the navigation information, and a number of **lookouts** (向外观察；对空观察) and support personnel. When the commanding officer is not on the bridge, he puts an **Officer of the Deck** (值更官) in charge of operations.

5　　Interestingly enough, many carrier commanding officers are former Navy airplane pilots, so they have a personal understanding of flight-deck operations. As long as they're in command of a carrier, however, they're prohibited from climbing into the cockpit to fly a plane themselves.

6　　Just like the Pri-Fly, the bridge is outfitted with an array of high-end monitors, including GPS receivers and many radar screens. But the commanding officer and his team still rely heavily on their own eyes to keep tabs on activities around the ship.

7　　The level below the bridge is the **flag bridge** (司令官舰桥), the command center for the **admiral** (舰队司令) in charge of the entire carrier group. Below that, there are various operational centers, including the **flight deck control and launch operations room** (飞行甲板控制与弹射操作室). In this tight and windowless space, the **aircraft handling officer** (舰载机调配官) (also called the handler or

Crew members on the USS George Washington circle around the "Ouija Board".

mangler) and his or her crew keep track of all the aircraft on the flight deck and in the hangar. The handler's primary tracking tool is the **Ouija Board** (通灵板，即飞行甲板模拟板), a two-level transparent plastic table with etched outlines of the flight deck and hangar deck. Each aircraft is represented by a scale aircraft cut-out on the table. When a real plane moves from point to point, the handler moves the model plane accordingly. When the plane is out of service for it needs repair work, the handler turns it over.

An Air Traffic Controller Onboard the USS Kitty Hawk

An antisubmarine warfare specialist on the USS Carl Vinson monitors activities in the Persian Gulf.

8   There are a number of additional control centers below deck, including the Carrier Air Traffic Control Center (CATCC), which takes up several rooms on the **gallery deck** (顶楼甲板) (immediately below the flight deck). Like a land-based air traffic control center, the CATCC is filled with all sorts of radio and radar equipment, which are used by the controllers to keep track of the aircraft in the area (in this case, mainly the aircraft outside Air Boss's supervision).

9   The CATCC is next to the **Combat Direction Center (CDC)** (作战指挥中心), the ship's battle command center. The CDC's primary responsibility is to process incoming information on enemy threats, in order to keep the commanding officer fully informed.

 **Exercises**

Comprehension of the Text

Decide whether the following statements are true (T) or false (F) according to the text.

(   ) *1.* An array of radar and communications antennas can target enemy aircraft and missiles, and pick up satellite phone and TV signals.

( ) *2.* In the Primary Flight Control, it's the air officer that directs all aircraft activities on the flight deck.

( ) *3.* In the bridge, the commanding officer controls the ship. When he is not on the bridge, he puts the Quartermaster of the Watch in charge of operations.

( ) *4.* Many carrier commanding officers are former Navy airplane pilots, so sometimes they're allowed to climb into the cockpit to fly a plane themselves.

( ) *5.* The flag bridge serves as the command center for the admiral in charge of the entire carrier group.

( ) *6.* In the air traffic control center, the aircraft handling officer and his or her crew keep track of all the aircraft on the flight deck.

( ) *7.* The controllers in the CATCC are responsible for keeping track of aircraft in the area.

( ) *8.* The Combat Direction Center functions as a tactical center and provides processed information for command and control of the near battle space or area of operation.

⊘ UNIT PROJECT

Mind Mapping

Work in groups and draw two mind maps respectively to depict the following processes of carrier-based aircraft operations.

1. taking off from an aircraft carrier
2. landing on an aircraft carrier

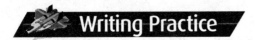

Oral Practice

Work in groups and discuss the great challenges that a carrier-based pilot has to face and whether you are going to meet these challenges or not. And one student from each group will make a 3-minute oral presentation according to the discussion. You may refer to the texts of this unit and the relevant information from the Internet.

Writing Practice

Based on the discussion above, write a composition with at least 150 words on the topic of "Dancing on the Edge of the Blade". You may refer to the questions below.

1. What does "Dancing on the Edge of the Blade" mean to a carrier-based pilot?
2. What great challenges might a carrier-based pilot face?
3. Are you going to meet these challenges? Why or why not?

Unit 9
Helicopter
Operations

🧭 Warming Up

Task 1 Watch the video clip about how a helicopter takes off and fill in the blanks.

Helicopters are the true flying machines. They can take off and land without the need for a *1*_____. They can *2*_____ in the air. They can *3*_____ in any direction in a 360 degrees space. This video will unveil the complexity and science behind flying a helicopter. After going through the *4*_____ behind the helicopter flying, you will also understand why helicopter pilots are doing an incredibly *5*_____ job.

Helicopters use the airfoil principle to generate lift. When the *6*_____ rotate relative to the air, the special *7*_____ will generate lift force and make them fly. The blades derive rotation from the engine, more specifically, a turboshaft engine. The *8*_____ sucks the air in and pressurizes it. Fuel is burned in this *9*_____ and hot air. The hot exhaust leaves the combustion chamber, passes a series of turbine stages, and makes them turn. There're two sets of turbines. One turbine set turns the compressor, and the other set turns the helicopter's *10*_____. Jet engines of airplanes are used to generate *11*_____ force. However, the primary function of the helicopter's jet engine is to turn the rotor shaft.

The most challenging part in helicopter operation is its *12*_____. That means, how can it fly forward? How can it fly *13*_____, sideward, or how can it take a turn? The answer is quite simple. Just rotate the helicopter towards the direction you want to move and just fly. When the helicopter is at an angle, the force produced by the blade is not *14*_____. The horizontal component of this force will move the helicopter move in the desired direction. The vertical component of the blade force will balance the gravitational force.

Task 2 Discuss the following questions in groups.

1. How do helicopters become airborne?

2. How do the airplane's jet engine and the helicopter's jet engine function differently?

3. How can a helicopter fly forward or backward?

 TEXT A

Anatomy of a Helicopter

Marshall Brain & William Harris

The Basic Parts of a Helicopter

1   Igor Sikorsky[1] and a few of his contemporaries brought a technical **rigor** to the field that finally made vertical flight safe, practical and reliable. As the flight-crazy Russian continued to refine his helicopter designs, he

Sikorsky Logo

worked out a lightweight structural frame fundamental requirements that any such machine needed to have to be successful, including:

- a suitable engine with a high **power-to-weight ratio**;
- a **mechanism** to **counteract** rotor **torque** action;
- proper controls so the aircraft could be steered confidently and without catastrophic failures;
- a means to reduce **vibrations**.

2   Many of the basic parts seen on a modern helicopter **grew out of the need** to address one or more of these basic requirements. Let's look at these components in greater details.

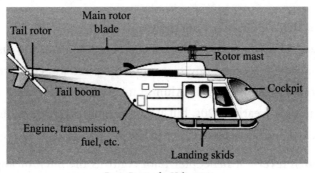

Basic Parts of a Helicopter

---

1 **Igor Sikorsky:** （1889—1972）伊戈尔·西科斯基，俄罗斯裔美国航空先驱，1939 年设计了美国第一架直升机。

3   Main rotor blade—The main rotor blade performs the same function as an airplane's wings, providing lift as the blades rotate—lift being one of the critical **aerodynamic** forces that keeps aircraft **aloft**. A pilot can affect lift by changing the rotor's **revolutions per minute (rpm)** or its angle of attack which refers to the angle of the rotary wing in relation to the oncoming wind.

4   **Stabilizer bar**—The stabilizer bar sits above and across the main rotor blade. Its weight and rotation **dampen** unwanted vibrations in the main rotor, helping to stabilize the craft in all flight conditions. Arthur Young, the **gent** who designed the Bell 47 helicopter, **is credited with** inventing the stabilizer bar.

5   **Rotor mast**—Also known as the **rotor shaft**, it is the mast connecting the **transmission** to the **rotor assembly**. The mast rotates the **upper swashplate** and the blades.

6   **Transmission**—Just as it does in a motor vehicle, a helicopter's transmission transmits power from the engine to the main and tail rotors. The transmission's main **gearbox steps down** the speed of the main rotor, so it doesn't rotate as rapidly as the engine shaft. A second gearbox does the same for the **tail rotor**, although the tail rotor, being much smaller, can rotate faster than the main rotor.

7   **Engine**—The engine generates power for the aircraft. Early helicopters relied on **reciprocating gasoline engines**, but modern helicopters use **gas turbine engines** like those found in **commercial airliners**.

Anatomy of a Helicopter: Working the Controls

8   **Fuselage**—The main body of the helicopter is known as the fuselage. In many models, a frameless plastic canopy surrounds the pilot and connects in the rear to a **flush-riveted** aluminum frame. Aluminum wasn't widely used in aeronautical applications until the early 1920s, but its appearance helped engineers make their helicopters lighter and, as a result, easier to fly.

9   **Cyclic-pitch lever**—A helicopter pilot controls the pitch or angle of the rotor blades with two inputs: the cyclic- and collective-pitch levers, often just shortened to the **cyclic** and the **collective**. The cyclic or "stick," comes out of the floor of the cockpit

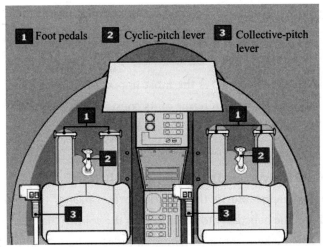

Inside a Helicopter cockpit

and sits between the pilot's legs, enabling a person to tilt the craft to either side or forward and backward.

10   **Collective-pitch lever**—The collective-pitch lever is responsible for up-and-down movements. For example, during takeoff, the pilot uses the collective-pitch lever to increase the pitch of all the rotor blades by the same amount.

11   **Foot pedals**—A pair of foot pedals controls the tail rotor. The control of the pedals affects the way that the helicopter points, so pushing the right pedal **deflects** the tail of the helicopter to the left and the nose to the right; and the left pedal turns the nose to the left.

12   **Tail boom**—The tail boom extends out from the rear of the fuselage and holds the tail rotor assemblies. In some models, the tail boom is nothing more than an aluminum frame. In others, it's a hollow carbon-fiber or aluminum tube.

13   **Anti-torque tail rotor**—Without a tail rotor, the main rotor of a helicopter simply spins the fuselage in the opposite direction. It's enough to make your stomach **heave** just thinking about all that endless circling. Thankfully, Igor Sikorsky had the idea to install a tail rotor to counter this torque **reaction** and provide directional control. In twin-rotor helicopters, the torque produced by the rotation of the front rotor is **offset** by the torque produced by a counter-rotating rear rotor.

14   **Landing skids**—Some helicopters have wheels, but most have skids, which are hollow tubes with no wheels or brakes. A few models have skids with two ground-handling wheels.

15   The **main rotor**, of course, is the most important part of a helicopter. It's also one of the most complex part in terms of its construction and operation. In the next section, we'll peer at the rotor assembly of a typical helicopter.

The Heart of the Helicopter: The Rotor Assembly

16   A helicopter's main rotor is the most important part of the vehicle. It provides the lift that allows the helicopter to fly, as well as the control that allows the helicopter to move **laterally**, make turns and change altitude. To handle all of these tasks, the rotor must first be incredibly strong. It must also be able to adjust the angle of the rotor blades with each revolution that they make. The pilot communicates these adjustments through a device known as the **swashplate assembly**.

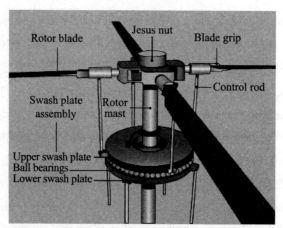

Basic Parts of a Helicopter Rotor

17   The swashplate assembly consists of two parts—the upper and **lower swashplates**. The upper swashplate connects to the mast or rotor shaft, through special linkages. As the engine turns the rotor shaft, it also turns the upper swashplate and the rotor blade system. This system includes **blade grips**, which connect the blades to a **hub. Control rods** from the upper swashplate have a connection point on the blades, making it

possible to transfer movements of the upper swashplate to the blades. And the hub mounts to the mast via the **Jesus nut**, so named because its failure is said to bring a pilot face-to-face with Jesus.

18   The lower swashplate is fixed and doesn't rotate. **Ball bearings** lie between the upper and lower swashplates, allowing the upper swashplate to spin freely on top of the lower swashplate. Control rods attached to the lower swashplate connect to the cyclic- and collective-pitch levers. When the pilot operates either of those two levers, his or her inputs are transmitted, via the control rods, to the lower swashplate and then, ultimately, to the upper swashplate.

19   Using this rotor design, a pilot can **manipulate** the swashplate assembly and control the helicopter's **motion**. With the cyclic, the swashplate assembly can change the angle of the blades individually as they revolve. This allows the helicopter to move in any direction around a 360-degree circle, including forward, backward, left and right. The collective allows the swashplate assembly to change the angle of all blades simultaneously. Doing this can increase or decrease the lift that the main rotor supplies to the vehicle, allowing the helicopter to gain or lose altitude.

Vocabulary

Special Terms

anti-torque tail rotor （直升机）尾桨，反扭尾桨
ball bearing 滚珠轴承
blade 桨叶，叶片
blade grip 桨叶板夹
control rod 操纵杆，变距拉杆
collective-pitch lever 总距杆，总距油门操纵手柄，油门变距杆
commercial airliner 民用客机
cyclic-pitch lever 周期变距杆，驾驶杆
flush-riveted 平齐铆接结构的
foot pedal 脚蹬，脚踏板，蹬舵

gas turbine engine 燃气涡轮发动机

gearbox 减速器；齿轮箱，传动机匣

hub 桨毂

Jesus nut 耶稣螺帽，主旋翼扣紧螺帽；主旋翼保险螺帽

landing skid 起落撬，着陆撬

lower swashplate 下倾斜盘，下（旋转）斜盘

main rotor 主旋翼

pitch （直升机）桨距，桨叶角

power-to-weight ratio 功率重量比，功重比；推重比

reaction 反作用力；反作用

reciprocating gasoline engine 活塞式汽油发动机

revolution per minute (rpm) 每分钟转数

rotor mast 旋翼主轴

rotor shaft 旋翼主轴；转子轴

rotor assembly 旋翼组件

stabilizer bar 稳定杆

swashplate assembly （旋翼）旋转倾转盘组件，倾斜盘组件

tail boom 尾梁，尾撑

tail rotor 尾桨，尾旋翼

torque 扭矩，转矩；旋转力矩

transmission 传动装置；变速器

upper swashplate 上倾斜盘，上（旋转）斜盘

vibration 振动；摆动

New Words and Expressions

aerodynamic	[ˌeərəʊdaɪˈnæmɪk]	*a.*	空气动力学的
aloft	[əˈlɒft]	*a.*	在高空的；离地的
counteract	[ˌkaʊntəˈækt]	*v.*	反作用
dampen	[ˈdæmpən]	*v.*	抑制，减少
deflect	[dɪˈflekt]	*v.*	使偏转，使转向
gent	[dʒent]	*n.*	绅士；男士
heave	[hiːv]	*v.*	恶心

laterally	['lætərəli]	*ad.*	横向地；侧向地
manipulate	[mə'nɪpjuleɪt]	*v.*	操控，操纵
mechanism	['mekənɪzəm]	*n.*	机械装置
motion	['məʊʃn]	*n.*	运动
offset	['ɒfset]	*v.*	抵消；抵偿
refine	[rɪ'faɪn]	*v.*	改进；提高
rigor	['rɪgə]	*n.*	严谨，严密

credit sb. with sth./doing sth.　　　　把（某成就）归于（某人）；认为（某人）
具有（某种好品质）

grow out of the need　　　　源自……需求
step down　　　　逐步降低

 Exercises

Comprehension of the Text

I. Answer the following questions according to the text.

1. How do modern helicopters meet the fundamental requirements proposed by Igor Sikorsky?

_____

2. How can a pilot change the lift of the helicopter?

_____

3. What is the function of a stabilizer bar?

_____

4. How does the transmission system work?

_____

5. How can a helicopter pilot control the AOA of the rotor blades?

_____

6. What motions can a helicopter perform if the pilot manipulates the cyclic-pitch lever?

_____

7. How does the collective-pitch lever get its name? What is it used for?

_____

8. What are the pedals used for?

_____

9. What would happen if there were no tail rotor on a helicopter? Why?

_____

10. How do the upper and lower swashplates work respectively?

_____

Vocabulary Practice

II. Match the descriptions in Column B with the special terms in Column A and translate the terms into Chinese.

Column A	Column B
1. collective _____	a. It helps give rigidity to the tail system, improving tail rotor control authority, and also helps to control any tail rotor vibration.
2. tail boom _____	b. It is a flat, wide section of an implement or device, such as a rotor or a propeller.
3. blade _____	c. It is attached to the main rotor blade or tail rotor blade and transfers the power from the engine to the blades.
4. shaft _____	d. It is used to control the main rotor in order to change the helicopter's direction of movement, such as flying forward, back, left and right.
5. cyclic _____	e. It is used to enable the helicopter to climb and descend. It does this by altering the pitch of the rotor blades together.
6. transmission _____	f. It refers to how much horsepower a vehicle has in relation to its weight.
7. power-to-weight ratio _____	g. It can transfer power from the engine to the main rotor, tail rotor and other accessories during flights.

Column A	Column B
8. swashplate _____	h. It is the small propeller at the end of the helicopter fuselage, spinning to create thrust in the opposite direction of the torque force.
9. Jesus nut _____	I. It is a device that translates input via the helicopter flight controls into motion of the main rotor blades.
10. anti-torque tail rotor _____	j. It is a slang term for the main rotor retaining nut which holds the main rotor to the mast of some helicopters.

III. **Complete each of the following sentences with a word or an expression from the box. Change the form if necessary.**

lower swashplate	reciprocating	turbine	skid	pedal
upper swashplate	counteract	offset	vibration	rotate
stabilizer bar	hub			

1. The _____ is a weighted, rotating unit mounted above and across the main rotor to provide a measure of stability for all flight conditions.

2. The two most common types of engines used in helicopters are the _____ engine and the _____ engine. The former is also called piston engine, generally used in smaller helicopters. The latter is more powerful and used in a wide variety of helicopters.

3. _____ are mainly used on light helicopters to provide for a smooth touch-down when landing, and to absorb energy in the case of ground resonance.

4. A swashplate has two sections. The _____, or moving star, can tilt in any direction. It _____ at the same speed as the rotor. The _____, or fixed star, can only tilt.

5. The _____ cause the helicopter to yaw or turn about a vertical axis. They do this by altering the pitch of the tail rotor.

6. The tail rotor is designed to _____ the torque produced by the engine and main rotor. If there is no tail rotor, the helicopter would spin uncontrollably on its main rotor axis.

7. In twin-rotor helicopters, the torque produced by the rotation of the front rotor is _____ by the torque produced by a counter-rotating rear rotor.

8. Due to the various moving parts and rotor system stress during operation, helicopters have a high level of _____, so left unchecked will cause machine failure or other serious damage to the aircraft in a short amount of time.

9. The helicopter rotor is powered by the engine, through the transmission, to the rotating mast, and at the top of the mast is the attachment point for the rotor blades called the _____.

IV. Complete the following short passage with the words or expressions in the box. Change the form if necessary.

gas turbine engine	counteract	tail rotor	main rotor	blade
angle of attack	transmission	tail boom	shaft	spin

A rotary motion is the easiest way to keep a wing continuously moving. You can mount two or more wings on a central *1*_____ and spin the shaft, much like the *2*_____ on a ceiling fan. The helicopter's rotating wing assembly is normally called the *3*_____. If you give the main rotor wings a slight *4*_____ on the shaft and *5*_____ the shaft, the wings start to develop lift. In order to spin the shaft with enough force to lift a human being and the vehicle, you need an engine, typically a(n) *6*_____ these days. The engine's driveshaft can connect through a(n) *7*_____ to the main rotor shaft. The *8*_____ produces thrust like an airplane's propeller does. By producing thrust in a sideways direction, this critical part *9*_____ the engine's desire to spin the body. Normally, the tail rotor is driven by a long driveshaft that runs from the main rotor's transmission back through the *10*_____ to a small transmission at the tail rotor.

Listening Practice

V. Watch the video clip about how to turn the helicopter in the desired way and fill in the blanks.

Now the real challenge is how to turn the helicopter in the desired way. To learn the science behind helicopter turning, we need to learn more about *1*_____. The lift produced by an airfoil varies with the *2*_____. Generally, the greater the angle of attack, the more the lift.

Now think for a moment. What happens if one blade was at one angle of attack and others were at a different angle? The lift forces acting on the *3*_____ would be different in this case. The *4*_____ in the lift forces would definitely result in a *5*_____ that can turn a helicopter. You can observe the beautiful blade motion required to achieve this non-uniform lift force distribution. It is clear that the blades must keep on changing angle of attack, so that at one particular *6*_____, the angle of attack is always the same. Such complex motion of the blades is easily achieved by a *7*_____ mechanism.

Let's get an exploded view and understand the basic *8*_____ first. The *9*_____ swashplate does not spin but it can move and tilt as shown. A *10*_____ swashplate is fitted on the bottom swashplate via a bearing, so that the top swashplate can inherit all the motions of the bottom swashplate while at the same time it can rotate independently. The top swashplate is attached to the *11*_____ with the help of a driver, so the top swashplate will always move with the blades. The blades are connected to the top swashplate with the help of *12*_____.

Translating Practice

VI. Translate the following sentences into Chinese.

1. A pilot can affect lift by changing the rotor's revolutions per minute (rpm) or its angle of attack which refers to the angle of the rotary wing in relation to the oncoming wind.

_____

_____

2. Just as it does in a motor vehicle, a helicopter's transmission transmits power from the engine to the main and tail rotors. The transmission's main gearbox steps down the speed of the main rotor, so it doesn't rotate as rapidly as the engine shaft.

_____

_____

3. The collective-pitch lever is responsible for up-and-down movements. For example, during takeoff, the pilot uses the collective-pitch lever to increase the pitch of all the rotor blades by the same amount.

_____

_____

4. A helicopter's main rotor is the most important part of the vehicle. It provides the lift that allows the helicopter to fly, as well as the control that allows the helicopter to move laterally, make turns and change altitude.

_____

_____

5. With the cyclic, the swashplate assembly can change the angle of the blades individually as they revolve. This allows the helicopter to move in any direction around a 360-degree circle, including forward, backward, left and right.

_____

_____

VII. Translate the following paragraph into English.

　　直升机常用于军事侦察和监视。部队会使用攻击型直升机对地面目标实施空中打击，这种直升机会装备导弹发射装置和小口径航炮。运输直升机用于运送部队和给养。海军会使用配备有吊放声呐的直升机进行反潜战。

_____

_____

_____

_____

⊘ TEXT B

How Helicopters Fly

Marshall Brain & William Harris

1   Imagine that we would like to create a machine that can simply fly straight upward. Let's not even worry about getting back down for the moment—up is all that matters. If you are going to provide the upward force with a wing, then the wing has to be in motion in order to create lift. Wings create lift by deflecting air downward and benefiting from the equal and opposite reaction that results.

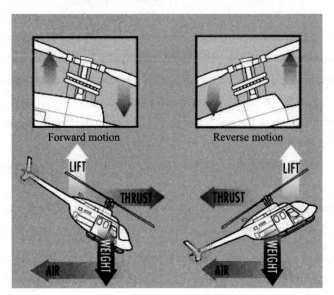

How Helicopters Fly

2   A rotary motion is the easiest way to keep a wing continuously moving. You can mount two or more wings on a central shaft and spin the shaft, much like the blades on a ceiling fan. In order to actually control the machine and, say, guide it into a canyon to complete the ultimate rescue, both the main rotor and the tail rotor need to be adjustable. The next three sections explain how pilots guide the helicopter into taking off, hovering or **buzzing** off in a particular direction.

Flying a Helicopter: Taking Off

3 The ability of helicopters to move laterally in any direction or rotate 360 degrees makes the pilots exciting to fly, but **piloting** one of these machines requires great skill and **dexterity**. To control a helicopter, the pilot grips the cyclic lever in one hand and the collective lever in the other. At the same time, his feet must operate the foot pedals that control the tail rotor, which allows the helicopter to rotate in either direction on its **horizontal axis**. It takes both hands and both feet to fly a helicopter!

4 During takeoff, the pilot works the collective lever and the foot pedals simultaneously. Before we discuss how to take off, you should know that the collective lever typically looks like a handbrake whose grip functions as the throttle. Twisting the grip controls the power output of the engine, increasing or decreasing the speed of the main rotor. With that in mind, we're ready to begin a typical helicopter takeoff.

- First, the pilot opens the throttle completely to increase the speed of the rotor.
- Next, he or she pulls up the collective lever slowly. The collective control raises the entire swashplate assembly as a unit. This has the effect of changing the pitch of all rotor blades by the same amount simultaneously.
- As the pilot increases the collective pitch, he or she depresses the left foot pedal to counteract the torque produced by the main rotor.
- The pilot keeps pulling up the collective lever slowly while depressing the left foot pedal.
- When the amount of lift being produced by the rotor exceeds the weight of the helicopter, the aircraft will get light on its skids and slowly leave the ground.

5 At this point, the pilot feels the cyclic lever become sensitive. He or she grips the cyclic lever and, in most cases, **nudges** the helicopter forward. Directional flight is the topic of the next section.

Flying a Helicopter: Directional Flight

6 In addition to moving up and down, helicopters can **fly forward**, **backward** and sideways. This kind of **directional flight** is achieved by tilting the swashplate assembly with the cyclic lever, which alters the pitch of each blade as it rotates. As a result, every blade produces maximum lift at a particular point. The rotor still generates lift,

but it also creates thrust in the direction that the swashplate assembly is tilted. This causes the helicopter to lean and fly in a certain direction. The pilot can **impart** much directional control by depressing or easing up on the foot pedals, which increases or decreases the counteracting thrust of the tail rotor.

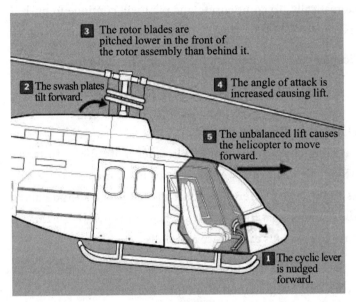

Directional Flight

7   Let's assume for a moment that the helicopter needs to fly forward. The following are the pilot's procedures:

- First, he or she nudges the cyclic lever forward.
- That input is transmitted to the lower swashplate and then to the upper swashplate.
- The swashplates tilt forward at an amount equal to the input.
- The rotor blades are pitched lower in the front of the rotor assembly than behind it.
- This increases the angle of attack and creates lift at the back of the helicopter.
- The unbalanced lift causes the helicopter to tip forward and move in that direction.

8   When the aircraft reaches about 15 to 20 knots of forward airspeed, it begins the transition from hovering flight to full forward flight. At this point, known as

Effective Translational Lift (ETL), the pilot eases up on the left foot pedal and moves closer to a **neutral setting**. He or she also feels a **shudder** in the rotor system as the helicopter begins to fly out of rotor wash (the turbulence created by a helicopter's rotor) and into the clean air. In response, the rotor will try to lift up and slow the aircraft automatically. To **compensate**, the pilot will continue to push the cyclic lever forward to keep the helicopter flying in that direction with increasing airspeed.

9   A helicopter that is flying forward can stop in mid-air and begin hovering very quickly.

Flying a Helicopter: Hovering

10   The defining characteristic of a helicopter is its ability to hover at any point during a flight. To achieve hovering, a pilot must maintain the aircraft in nearly motionless flight over a **reference point** at a constant altitude and on a constant heading (the direction that the front of a helicopter is pointing). This may sound easy, but it requires tremendous experience and skills.

11   Before we tackle the technique of hovering, let's take a moment to discuss **Nap-Of-the-Earth (NOE)** flight, another unique characteristic of helicopters. NOE flight describes a helicopter located just above the ground or any obstacles on the ground. Military pilots perfected the technique during Vietnam War as a means to become more **elusive** to **ground-based weapons**. In fact, film **footage** from the era often shows helicopters rapidly skimming the Earth's surface, machine-gunners firing from open rear doors or hovering with their skids just a few feet off the ground as troops **disembark** at a target location.

12   Of course, any helicopter taking off or landing must undertake NOE flight, if only for a few moments. It's a particularly critical time for a helicopter, because a wild attitude adjustment could tip the craft too far and bring the rotor blades in contact with an obstacle. Attitude, for our purposes, refers to the helicopter's orientation in relation to the helicopter's direction of motion. You'll also hear flight-minded folks talk about attitude in reference to an axis, such as the horizon.

13   With that said, here's the basic technique to bring a helicopter into a hovering position.

- First, the pilot must cease any directional flying. For example, if flying the helicopter forward, the pilot must ease back on the cyclic lever until the helicopter's forward motion stops and the aircraft remains motionless over a point on the ground.

- Next, it's important that the pilot can detect small changes in the aircraft's altitude or attitude. He or she accomplishes this by locating a fixed point outside the cockpit and tracking how the helicopter moves relative to that point.

- Finally, the pilot adjusts the collective lever to maintain a fixed altitude and adjusts the foot pedals to maintain the direction that the helicopter is pointing.

14   To maintain a stabilized hover, the pilot must make small, smooth, coordinated corrections on all of the controls. In fact, one of the most common errors of **novice** pilots is to **overcompensate** while trying to hover. For example, if the helicopter begins to move rearward, the pilot must be careful not to apply too much **forward pressure** on the cyclic lever because the aircraft will not just come to a stop but will start **drifting** forward.

 Vocabulary

Special Terms

buzz （口语）低空飞行；俯冲
directional flight （直升机）定向飞行
Effective Translational Lift (ETL) 有效过渡（状态的）升力
forward pressure 向前的杆力，推杆力
ground-based weapon 地面武器
horizontal axis 水平轴线
hover （直升机）悬停；（滑翔机）翱翔
Nap-Of-the-Earth (NOE) flight 掠地飞行，超低空飞行
neutral setting 中立设置；均势设置
overcompensate 过度补偿
reference point 参考点，基准点

New Words

axis	['æksɪs]	*n.*	轴，轴线
backward	[bækwəd]	*adv.*	向后地
compensate	['kɒmpənˌseɪt]	*v.*	补偿；平衡
dexterity	[dek'sterəti]	*n.*	灵活性
disembark	[ˌdɪsɪm'bɑːk]	*v.*	下飞机（车、船等）；上岸，登陆
drift	[drɪft]	*v.*	漂浮；飘移
elusive	[ɪ'luːsɪv]	*a.*	难以捉摸的
footage	['fʊtɪdʒ]	*n.*	片段
forward	['fɔːwəd]	*adv.*	向前地
impart	[ɪm'pɑːt]	*v.*	给予
novice	['nɒvɪs]	*n.*	新手，初学者
nudge	[nʌdʒ]	*v.*	推动
pilot	['paɪlət]	*v.*	驾驶（飞机）；为……引航，为……领航
shudder	['ʃʌdə]	*n.*	震动
tilt	[tɪlt]	*v.*	（使）倾斜 *n.* 倾斜

Exercises

Comprehension of the Text

I. Answer the following questions according to the text.

1. What controls does a helicopter pilot input during takeoff?

_____

2. Can you briefly describe a typical helicopter takeoff?

_____

3. Helicopters can carry out directional flight. What directional flight can you name?

_____

4. How can a helicopter pilot conduct directional flight?

_____

5. What is the typical procedure if a helicopter pilot needs to fly forward?

_____

6. What state must a helicopter experience from hovering flight to full forward flight?

_____

7. Why would a helicopter pilot feel a shake during the translational lift?

_____

8. How can a helicopter pilot accomplish hovering?

_____

9. What kind of flight must a helicopter undertake during takeoff and landing? Why is it so critical?

_____

10. How can a pilot bring a helicopter into a hovering position?

_____

Vocabulary Practice

II. Complete each of the following definitions with a special term from the box. Change the form if necessary.

Effective Translational Lift (ETL)	rotor wash	correction	attitude
Nap-Of-the-Earth (NOE) flight	forward flight	altitude	horizontal axis
flight control	reference point	hovering	

1. _____ is the most challenging part of flying a helicopter. This is because a helicopter generates its own gusty air which acts against the fuselage and flight control surfaces. This results in constant control inputs and _____ by the pilot to keep the helicopter where it is required to be.

2. A hovering turn is a maneuver performed at hovering _____ in which the nose of the helicopter is rotated either left or right while maintaining position over a _____ on the surface. Hovering turns can also be made around the mast or tail of the aircraft. The maneuver requires the coordination of all _____ and demands preciseness.

3. _____ is the air driven downwards by the main rotor of the helicopter as it turns.

4. _____ is a type of very low-altitude flight course used by military aircraft to avoid enemy detection and attack in a high-threat environment.

5. In _____, air flows opposite the aircraft's flight path, and the velocity of this airflow equals the helicopter's forward speed.

6. _____ is the translational lift advanced to the point where all air flowing through the rotor system of a helicopter is fresh or undisturbed air.

7. Pitch _____ control is the control of the movement of a helicopter about its _____.

Listening Practice

III. Watch the video clip about the function of a tailor rotor and fill in the blanks.

If you have ever seen a helicopter, you are all sure to have seen a *1*_____. Every single rotor helicopter needs this tail rotor for effective operation. Without the tail rotor, the helicopter *2*_____ would have spun as shown. This is due to a consequence of Newton's Third Law of Motion.

To understand it, let's focus on the force *3*_____ part of the rotor. We know the rotor gets the force of rotation via a bevel gear connected to the engine. The engine bevel gear transmits force to the rotor bevel gear as shown. However, according to Newton's Third Law of Motion, the rotor bevel gear should transmit an equal and *4*_____ force to the engine bevel gear. This *5*_____ would make the whole helicopter turn opposite to the blade rotation along the helicopter's *6*_____.

The function of the tail rotor is to prevent such *7*_____ by producing a force at the tail. By properly adjusting *8*_____ of the tail rotor blades, the pilot can easily manipulate the tail rotor force. This way with the help of the tail rotor, *9*_____ of the helicopter can also be achieved.

All the physics behind helicopter operation means that flying a helicopter is a truly challenging task. Minute variations in blade angles make huge variations in helicopter behavior. Often, the pilot has to do two or more operations together to achieve the desired motion. Moreover, the helicopter does not respond instantaneously to your inputs. So the pilot should possess a good sense of balance and *10*_____ to navigate the helicopter properly.

Translating Practice

IV. Translate the following sentences into Chinese.

1. To control a helicopter, the pilot grips the cyclic lever in one hand and the collective lever in the other. At the same time, his feet must operate the foot pedals that control the tail rotor, which allows the helicopter to rotate in either direction on its horizontal axis. It takes both hands and both feet to fly a helicopter!

_____

_____

2. During takeoff, the pilot works the collective lever and the foot pedals simultaneously. The collective lever typically looks like a handbrake whose grip functions as the throttle. Twisting the grip controls the power output of the engine, increasing or decreasing the speed of the main rotor.

_____

_____

3. In addition to moving up and down, helicopters can fly forward, backward and sideways. This kind of directional flight is achieved by tilting the swashplate assembly with the cyclic lever, which alters the pitch of each blade as it rotates.

_____

_____

4. When the aircraft reaches about 15 to 20 knots of forward airspeed, it begins the transition from hovering flight to full forward flight. At this point, known as Effective Translational Lift (ETL), the pilot eases up on the left foot pedal and moves closer to a neutral setting.

_____

_____

5. Before we tackle the technique of hovering, let's take a moment to discuss Nap-Of-the-Earth (NOE) flight, another unique characteristic of helicopters. NOE flight describes a helicopter located just above the ground or any obstacles on the ground.

🧭 TEXT C

How Apache Helicopters Work

Tom Harris

An Apache Helicopter

1   Apache helicopter is a revolutionary development in the history of war. It is essentially a flying tank—a helicopter designed to survive heavy attack and massive damage. It can **zero in on** (瞄准锁定) specific targets, day or night, even in terrible weather. As you might expect, it is a terrifying machine to ground forces.

2   In this text, we'll look at Apache's amazing flight systems, weapons systems, sensor systems and armor systems. Individually, each of these components is a remarkable piece of technology. Combined together, they make up an unbelievable fighting machine—the most lethal helicopter ever created.

3   At its core, an Apache works pretty much the same way as any other helicopter. It has two rotors that spin several blades. The newest Apache sports twin **General Electric T700-GE-701C turboshaft** (通用公司T700-GE-701C涡轮轴) engines, boasting about 1,700 **horsepower** (马力) each. With the powerful engine, the rotor is optimized to provide much greater agility than you find in a typical helicopter.

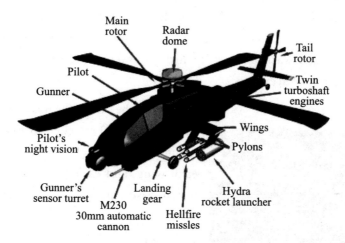

The Structure of an Apache Helicopter

4   The core structure of each blade consists of five stainless steel arms, called spars, which are surrounded by a fiberglass skeleton. The trailing edge of each blade is covered with a sturdy composite material, while the leading edge is made of **titanium** (钛). The titanium is strong enough to withstand brushes with trees and other minor obstacles, which is helpful in "Nap-Of-the-Earth" flight. Apaches need to fly this way to sneak up on targets and to avoid the attack.

5   You could say, based on all the information, that the Apache is just a high-end helicopter. But that would be like calling James Bond's Aston Martin just a high-end car. As we'll see in the next few parts, the Apache's advanced weaponry puts it in an entirely different class.

Apache Hellfire Missiles

6   The Apache's chief function is to take out heavily armored ground targets, such as tanks and **bunkers** (掩体). To inflict this kind of damage, the heavy fire power is needed, and to do it from a helicopter, an extremely sophisticated targeting system is expected.

7   The Apache's primary weapon, the **Hellfire**

The Armament of an Apache Helicopter

missile, meets these demands. Each missile is a miniature aircraft, complete with its own guidance computer, steering control and propulsion system. The **payload** (弹头) is a high-explosive **warhead** (弹头) which is powerful enough to burn through the heaviest tank armor in existence.

The Outboard Missile on a Apache Helicopter

8   Apache carries the missiles on four **firing rails** (发射导轨) attached to **pylons** (外挂梁) mounted to its wings. There are two pylons on each wing, and each pylon can support four missiles, so Apache can carry as many as 16 missiles at a time.

9   The original Hellfire design uses a **laser guidance system** (激光制导系统) to hit its mark. In this system, the Apache gunner aims a high-intensity **laser beam** (激光光束) at the target. Before giving the firing signal, the Apache computer tells the missile's control system the specific pulse pattern of the laser. The missile has a **laser seeker** (激光导引头) on its nose that detects the laser light reflecting off the target. In this way, the missile can see where the target is. The guidance system calculates the way that the missile needs to turn in order to head straight for the reflected laser light.

10   The laser-guided Hellfire system is highly effective, but it has some significant drawbacks.

- Cloud cover or obstacles can block the laser beam so it never makes it to the target.
- If the missile passes through a cloud, it can lose sight of the target.
- The helicopter (or a ground targeting crew) has to keep the laser fixing on the target until the missile makes contact. This means the helicopter has to be out in the open and vulnerable environment to be attacked.

11   The Hellfire II, used in **Apache Longbow** (阿帕奇长弓型) helicopters, corrects these flaws. Instead of a laser-seeking system, the missile has a **radar seeker** (雷达导引头). The helicopter's radar locates the target, and the missiles zero in on it. Since radio waves aren't obscured by clouds or obstacles, the missile is more likely to find its

target. Since it doesn't have to keep the laser focusing on the target, the helicopter can fire the missile and immediately find cover.

Apache Rockets and Chain Gun / Automatic Cannon

12   Apache usually fly with two **Hydra rocket launchers** (九头蛇火箭弹发射架) in place of two Hellfire missile sets. Each rocket launcher carries 19 **folding-fin** (折叠尾鳍) 2.75-inch **aerial rockets** (航空火箭弹), secured in **launching tubes** (发射管). The Apache gunner can fire one rocket at a time or launch them in groups.

The Outboard Rockets and Chain Gun on an Apache Helicopter

13   The gunner engages **close-range targets** (近距目标) with an M230 30-mm **automatic cannon** (机关炮) attached to a **turret** (炮塔) under the helicopter's nose. The gunner aims the gun using a sophisticated computer system in the cockpit.

Apache Controls

14   The Apache cockpit is divided into two sections, one directly behind the other. The pilot sits in the rear section, and the co-pilot/gunner sits in the front section. As you might expect, the pilot maneuvers the helicopter and the gunner aims and fires the weapons. Both sections of the cockpit include flight and firing controls in case that one pilot needs to take over full operation.

15   The pilot flies the Apache using collective and cyclic controls, similar to the ones that you would find in any other helicopter. The controls manipulate the rotors using both a mechanical **hydraulic** (液压) system and a digital stabilization system.

Apache Sensors

16   One of the coolest things about the Apache is its sophisticated sensor equipment. The Longbow Apache detects surrounding ground forces, aircraft and buildings using a **radar dome** (雷达天线整流罩) mounted to the mast. The radar dome uses

millimeter radio waves that can make out the shape of anything in range. The **radar signal processor** (雷达信号处理器) compares these shapes to a database of tanks, trucks, other aircraft and equipment to identify the general class of each potential target. The computer pinpoints these targets on the pilot's and gunner's **display panels** (显示板).

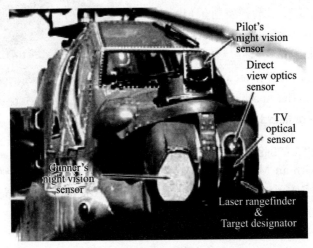

Sensors on an Apache Helicopter

17   The pilot and the gunner both use **night vision sensors** (夜视传感器) for night operations. The night vision sensors work on the **Forward-Looking Infrared (FLIR)** (前视红外线) system, which detects the infrared light released by heated objects.

18   The pilot's night vision sensor is attached to a rotating turret on top of Apache's nose. The gunner's night vision sensor is attached to a separate turret on the underside of the nose. The lower turret also supports a normal video camera and a telescope, which the gunner uses during the day.

Apache Evasion Tactics (规避战术) **and Armor**

19   Apache's first line of defense against attack is keeping out of range. As we saw earlier, the helicopter is specifically designed to fly low to the ground, hiding behind cover whenever possible. Apache is also designed to evade enemy's radar scanning. If the pilots pick up radar signals with the onboard scanner, they can activate a **radar jammer** (雷达干扰器) to confuse the enemy.

20   Apache is also designed to evade **heat-seeking missiles** (热导导弹) by reducing its infrared signature (the heat energy that it releases). The **Black Hole infrared suppression system** （"黑洞" 红外线抑制系统) **dissipates** (驱散) the heat of the engine exhaust by mixing it with the air flowing around the helicopter. The cooled exhaust then passes through a special filter, which absorbs more heat. The Longbow also has an infrared jammer, which generates infrared energy of varying frequencies to confuse heat-seeking missiles.

21   Apache is heavily armored on all sides. Some areas are also surrounded by **Kevlar** (凯夫拉尔，一种防弹材料) soft armor for extra protection. The cockpit is protected by layers of reinforced armor and **bulletproof glass** (防弹玻璃).

22   The pilot and gunner seats are outfitted with heavy Kevlar armor, which also absorbs the force of impact. With these advanced systems, the crew has an excellent chance of surviving a crash.

23   Flying an Apache into battle is extremely dangerous, to be sure, but with all its weapons, armor and sensor equipment, it is a formidable opponent to almost everything else on the battlefield. It is a deadly combination of strength, agility and firepower.

 Exercises

Comprehension of the Text

Answer the following questions according to the text.

1. What is the name for the Boeing AH-64?

_____

2. Why is Apache called a flying tank?

_____

3. What are the characteristics of the flight system making Apache so powerful?

_____

4. What is the primary weapon of Apache? How many Hellfire missiles can an Apache carry?

_____

5. How is Hellfire guided? What modifications are made to Hellfire II?

_____

6. What other weapons is an Apache armed with?

_____

7. What are the combat stations for Apache pilots and gunners?

_____

8. Can you name some of the major sensors equipped on an Apache?

_____

9. How can an Apache avoid ground or aerial attacks?

_____

10. What configurations make an Apache sturdy?

_____

🧭 UNIT PROJECT

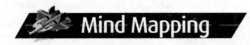
Mind Mapping

Work in groups and draw two mind maps respectively according to the following topics.

1. the basic parts of a helicopter
2. How helicopters fly?

Oral Practice

Work in groups, list some major types of helicopters served in PLA Navy or foreign navies, and missions that helicopters can conduct in naval aviation. And one student from each group will make a 3-minute oral presentation according to the discussion. You may refer to the texts of this unit and the relevant information from the Internet.

Writing Practice

After learning this unit, you have acquired some basic knowledge about helicopters and their major functions in military operations. Write a composition with at least 150 words on the topic of "Would you Choose to Be a Helicopter Pilot?" You may refer to the outline below.

1. your choice
2. the reasons for your choice
3. the efforts you have to make for your future career

Unit 10

Aviation Safety

🧭 Warming Up

Task 1 Watch the video clip about how an airplane usually copes with bad weather and fill in the blanks.

Nice and cozy. And that thunder? That's far away.

Well, did you know that you're just as safe in that storm as under your covers? Yep. Airplanes sometimes fly through storms like that and come out without a *1*_____.

How do they do it? A plane is made of *2*_____, like aluminum. It works like a *3*_____. When lightning strikes, it guides the *4*_____ off the plane again, protecting the space where we sit. You might feel a little *5*_____. But that's because *6*_____ are a bit bumpy.

Planes don't mind the rain as well. The *7*_____ just glide off when it flies. Wind is mostly an issue during takeoff and landing. But if it's too stormy, planes simply won't fly for a bit, until the storm passes.

The last weather forecast is ice. It gets *8*_____ on the wings and makes it a bit harder to fly and *9*_____. But of course, they have something for that too. Bleed air (引气), with the hot air that comes out of the engines—it heats up the wings and *10*_____ the ice.

No problem. So next time you are flying, you know that a little thunder is nothing to worry about.

Task 2 Discuss the following questions in groups.

1. What factors are related to aviation safety?
2. Can you list any aviation safety hazards?
3. What measures can be taken to prevent those hazards?

 TEXT A

Human Factors Related to Flight Safety

Overview of Human Factors

1   **Human factors** is a term that covers: (1) the science of understanding the properties of human capability (human factors science); (2) the application of this understanding to the design and development of systems and services (**human factors engineering**); (3) the art of ensuring successful application of human factors engineering to a program (sometimes referred to as human factors **integration**).

2   There is more to pilots than acquiring technical knowledge and gaining proficiency in aircraft control. Understanding how your mind and body function when you are flying is as important as knowing the operation of your airplane's system and equipment. The goal of human factors training for pilots is to increase aviation safety by **optimizing** human performance and reducing errors.

3   Instruction in human factors principles focuses on explaining how performance is affected by elements such as the interaction between individuals within the aviation environment, emotions and human **physiology**. Learning the human factors concept is essential to becoming a safe and effective pilot and is an important part of comprehensive pilot training.

4   It is estimated that **approximately** 75 percent of all aviation accidents are human factors related. Historically, the term **pilot error** has been used to describe the causes of these accidents. Pilot error means that an action or decision made by the pilot is the cause of an accident or the contributing factor which leads to the accident.

ADM and Influencing Factors

5   Problem definition is the first step in the decision-making process. Defining the problem begins with recognizing that a change has occurred or that an expected change did not occur. When the decision-making process is applied to flight operations, it is termed **Aeronautical Decision Making (ADM)**. The factors which

influence Aeronautical Decision Making can be organized into five elements: **pilot-in-command** responsibility, communication, resource use, workload management and situational awareness.

Pilot-In-Command's Responsibility

6   As pilot-in-command, you are the ultimate decision-maker and your choices determine the outcome of the flight. You are directly responsible for your own safety, as well as the safety of your passengers. An important pilot-in-command responsibility is to understand your own personal limitations. Your general health, level of stress or **fatigue**, attitude, knowledge, skill level and experience are several factors which affect your performance as pilot-in-command. Whether you are fit to fly depends on more than your physical condition.

- Self-assessment: Evaluating your condition to fly includes an awareness of your personal limitation.
- **Hazardous** attitudes: By learning to recognize hazardous attitudes, you can help prevent poor decision-making and actions which involve unnecessary risk.
- Interpersonal relationships: As pilot-in-command, you are responsible for establishing the proper relationship with other persons on board the aircraft.

7   Studies have identified five attitudes among pilots which are considered to be particularly hazardous. They are **anti-authority**, **impulsivity**, **invulnerability**, **macho** and **resignation**.

- Anti-authority: People with this attitude resent having someone tell them what to do, or they regard rules and procedures as unnecessary.
- Impulsivity: This is the attitude of people who feel the need to do something—anything—immediately. They do not stop to consider the best **alternative** but do the first thing which comes to mind.
- Invulnerability: Many people believe that accidents happen to others, but never to them. Pilots with this attitude are more likely to take chances and increase risks.
- Macho: By taking risks, these people attempt to prove that they are better than anyone else. While this pattern is thought to be a male characteristic, women are equally **susceptible**.

- Resignation: People with this attitude do not see themselves as making a great deal of difference in what happens to them. When things go well, they think, "That is good luck." When things go bad, they **attribute** it **to** bad luck or feel that someone is responsible. They leave the action to others, for better or worse.

Communication

8　　Communication is the exchange of ideas, information or instruction. The process of communication **is comprised of** three elements: the source (a sender, speaker, writer, instructor); the symbols used in composing and transmitting the message (words, illustrations, music); and the receiver (reader, listener, student). The relationship among these components is dynamic and each element influences the other.

9　　Effective communication requires that ideas are not only expressed but that they are conveyed in a clear and timely manner so that the message is received and understood with a minimum of confusion and misunderstanding.

10　　Exchanging information and ideas with your instructor is the first step in developing effective communication skills. If you are uncomfortable or are having difficulty in understanding something, do not hesitate to ask questions. Your instructor may not realize that you are having trouble unless you speak up.

11　　Communicative Concepts:
- Effective listening: This skill involves proper interpretation and evaluation of the message before responding.
- Barrier to communication: Barriers can include a lack of a common core of experience between the communicator and receiver, the overuse of abstractions, and the misuse of **terminology**.
- Verbal and **nonverbal** communication: It is essential to learn how to interpret both verbal and nonverbal cues during the communication process.

Resource Use

12　　Since useful tools and sources of information may not always be **readily** apparent, it is important that you learn to recognize and utilize the resources available to you. Resource use is an essential part of human factors training.

13   Resource Use Concepts:

- Resource recognition: Before you can effectively use resources, you must learn to identify potential sources of assistance and information.

- Internal resources: During pilot operations, these are sources of information found within the airplane, such as the pilot's operating handbook, checklists, aircraft equipment, **aeronautical charts,** your instructor, another pilot and passengers, as well as your own **ingenuity**, knowledge and skills.

- External resources: Many operational resources exist outside the cockpit, such as air traffic controllers, **maintenance technicians** and flight service personnel.

Workload Management

14   Effective workload management ensures that essential operations are accomplished by planning, prioritizing and **sequencing** tasks to avoid work **overload**. Effective workload management begins with preparation and planning before the flight, so that pilot operations can be performed more efficiently.

15   Workload Management Concepts:

- Planning and preparation: Work overload can be prevented by thorough planning and preparation, including the **delegation** of workload to others, if necessary.

- Prioritizing: As the pilot-in-command, you are responsible for determining the order in which tasks should be accomplished, so that items which are essential for safe operation of the aircraft are performed first.

- Work overload: Recognizing when you have become task **saturated** and how to prevent overload from occurring is necessary to effectively manage workload.

Situational Awareness

16   Situational awareness is the accurate **perception** of the operational and environmental factors which affect the aircraft, pilot and passengers during a specific period of time. The factors are the relationship between aircraft and **terrain**, traffic, weather and air traffic control.

17   Situational Awareness Concepts:

- Operational conditions: These include elements such as the status of aircraft systems and your own ability to function properly.
- Environmental conditions: These are elements which affect the flight such as the airplane's relationship to terrain, traffic and weather conditions.
- Obstacles to maintaining situational awareness: Stress, fatigue, distractions and emergencies can cause you to **fixate** on a single item and can **impair** situational awareness.

 Vocabulary

Special Terms

aeronautical chart 航图，航空地图
Aeronautical Decision Making (ADM) 飞行决策
human factor 人为因素
human factors engineering 人因工程学
maintenance technician 维护技师，维修技师
overload 超负荷；超载
pilot error 飞行员操纵错误
pilot-in-command 操控飞机的飞行员，责任机长

Words and Expressions

alternative	[ɔːl'tɜːnətɪv]	*n.*	可替代的选择
anti-authority	['ænti ɔː'θɒrəti]	*n.*	反权威
approximately	[ə'prɒksɪmətli]	*ad.*	大约地，近似地
delegation	[ˌdelə'geɪʃn]	*n.*	授权，委派；代表团
fatigue	[fə'tiːg]	*n.*	疲劳，劳累；（金属或木材的）疲劳
fixate	['fɪkseɪt]	*v.*	（使）注意；（使）固定下来
hazardous	['hæzədəs]	*a.*	有危险的；有害的
impair	[ɪm'peə]	*v.*	损害；削弱

impulsivity	[ɪmpʌl'sɪvɪti]	n.	冲动；冲动性
integration	[ɪntɪ'greɪʃn]	n.	整合，集成；综合
invulnerability	[ɪnˌvʌlnərə'bɪləti]	n.	刀枪不入；不会受伤害
ingenuity	[ˌɪndʒə'njuəti]	n.	独创性；创造力
macho	['mætʃəʊ]	n.	男子气概
nonverbal	[nɒn'vɜːbl]	a.	非言语的；不涉及言语的
optimize	['ɒptɪmaɪz]	v.	使最优化；完善
perception	[pə'sepʃn]	n.	［生理］感觉；看法；洞察力
physiology	[fɪzi'ɒlədʒi]	n.	生理学；生理机能
readily	['redɪli]	ad.	容易地；乐意地
resignation	[ˌrezɪg'neɪʃn]	n.	对逆境的接受，听天由命；辞职
saturate	['sætʃəreɪt]	v.	使充满；浸透
sequence	['siːkwəns]	v.	按顺序排列 n. 顺序，次序
susceptible	[sə'septəbl]	a.	易受影响的
terminology	[tɜːmɪ'nɒlədʒi]	n.	术语；术语学
terrain	[tə'reɪn]	n.	［地理］地形；领域
attribute... to			归因于……
be comprised of			包含，由……组成

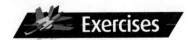

Exercises

Comprehension of the Text

I. Answer the following questions according to the text.

1. What does the term human factors cover?

_____

2. What is the goal of human factors training for pilots?

_____

3. Why is learning human factors concept essential to pilot training?

_____

4. What does the term pilot error refer to?

_____

5. What elements may influence aeronautical decision-making?

_____

6. What attitudes among pilots are considered to be particularly hazardous?

_____

7. What are the requirements for effective communication? How to develop effective communication skills?

_____

8. What do external resources include?

_____

9. What is the first step to have effective workload management?

_____

10. What is situational awareness? What do situational awareness concepts include?

_____

Vocabulary Practice

II. Match the definitions in Column B with the special terms in Column A and translate the terms into Chinese.

Column A	Column B
1. self-assessment _____	a. a systematic approach to the mental process used by pilots to consistently determine the best course of action in response to a given set of circumstances
2. checklist _____	b. a map used in air navigation containing all or part of the following: topographic features, hazards and obstructions, navigation aids, navigation routes, designated airspace and airports
3. terrain _____	c. a systematic and sequential list of all operations that must be performed to properly accomplish a task

Column A	Column B
4. overload _____	d. pilot knowledge of where the aircraft is in regard to location, air traffic control, weather, regulations, aircraft status and other factors that may affect flight
5. situational aware- ness _____	e. the process of judging your own progress, achievements, etc.
6. pilot-in- command _____	f. used to refer to an area of land when you are mentioning its natural features, for example, if it is rough, flat, etc.
7. ADM _____	g. that part of an aircraft's payload or useful load, either of cargo, fuel, bombs, etc., that is in excess of the maximum amount prescribed for the aircraft
8. aeronautical chart _____	h. the person who is in charge of the aircraft and is the final authority over all operations and safety throughout the flight

III. Complete each of the following sentences with a word from the box. Change the form if necessary.

readily	interpretation	optimize	alternative	utilize
susceptible	approximately	hesitate	attribute	terrain

1. The goal of human factors training for pilots is to increase aviation safety by _____ human performance and reducing errors.

2. It is estimated that _____ 75 percent of all aviation accidents are human factors related.

3. They do not stop to consider the best _____ but do the first thing which comes to mind.

4. While this pattern is thought to be a male characteristic, women are equally _____.

5. When things go bad, they _____ it to bad luck or feel that someone is responsible.

6. If you are uncomfortable or are having difficulty in understanding something, do not _____ to ask questions.

7. This skill involves proper _____ and evaluation of the message before responding.

8. The factors are the relationship between aircraft and _____, traffic, weather and air traffic control.

9. Since useful tools and sources of information may not always be _____ apparent, it is important that you learn to recognize and _____ the resources available to you.

IV. **Complete the following short passage with the words or expressions from the box. Change the form if necessary.**

unpredictable	mental	workload	insufficient	extended
significantly	pilot error	fatigue	limit	deprivation

The International Civil Aviation Organization (ICAO) defines *1*_____ as "a physiological state of reduced *2*_____ or physical performance capability resulting from sleep loss or *3*_____ wakefulness, circadian phase or *4*_____". The phenomenon places great risk on the crew and passengers of an airplane, because it *5*_____ increases the chance of *6*_____. Fatigue is particularly prevalent among pilots because of "*7*_____ work hours, long duty periods, circadian disruption and *8*_____ sleep." These factors can occur together to produce a combination of sleep *9*_____, circadian rhythm effects and "time-on task" fatigue. Regulators attempt to mitigate fatigue by *10*_____ the amount of hours that pilots are allowed to fly over varying periods of time.

Translating Practice

V. **Translate the following sentences into Chinese.**

1. Understanding how your mind and body function when you are flying is as important as knowing the operation of your airplane's system and equipment.

_____

_____

2. Historically, the term pilot error has been used to describe the causes of these accidents. Pilot error means that an action or decision made by the pilot is the cause of an accident or the contributing factor which leads to the accident.

_____

_____

3. Barriers to communication can include a lack of a common core of experience between the communicator and receiver, overuse of abstractions and misuse of terminology.

_____

_____

4. Effective workload management ensures that essential operations are accomplished by planning, prioritizing and sequencing tasks to avoid work overload.

_____

_____

5. Situational awareness is the accurate perception of the operational and environmental factors which affect the aircraft, pilot and passengers during a specific period of time.

_____

_____

VI. Translate the following paragraph into English.

机场的设计和位置对飞行安全有极大影响，特别是有些机场原来是为螺旋桨飞机所建造的，而且许多机场位于交通繁忙的区域，难以达到新的安全标准。例如，1999 年，联邦航空局（FAA）正式发布规则，要求设置跑道安全区。设置此区域的通常做法是向跑道两侧各延长 500 英尺，并且在跑道尽头增加 1000 英尺。这种做法旨在通过提供一个无障碍物的缓冲区来处理 90% 的飞机偏离跑道的情况。

_____

_____

_____

_____

🧭 TEXT B

Aviation Safety Hazards (I)

1   **Aviation safety** is a term encompassing the theory, investigation and categorization of flight failures, and the prevention of such failures through regulation, education and training. It can also be applied in the context of campaigns that inform the public as to the safety of air travel. Some common aviation safety hazards listed below will certainly enhance the safety awareness of pilots and those flight-related personnel.

Foreign Object Debris (FOD)

2   Foreign Object Debris includes items left in the aircraft structure during manufacture/repairs, debris on the runway and solids encountered in flight (e.g., hail and dust). Such items can damage engines and other parts of the aircraft. Air France Flight 4590 crashed after hitting a part that had fallen from another aircraft[1].

Foreign Object Debris

Misleading Information and Lack of Information

3   A pilot **misinformed** by a printed document (manual, map, etc.), reacting to a faulty instrument or indicator (in the cockpit or on the ground) or following inaccurate instructions or information from flight or ground control can lose **spatial orientation** or make another mistake, and consequently lead to accidents or **near misses**.

Lightning

4   Boeing studies showed that airliners are struck by lightning twice per year on

---

1 这里指法国航空公司 4590 号航班空难，又称协和客机空难。此次空难发生于 2007 年 7 月 25 日，事故原因为外来物损伤导致左侧发动机着火，飞机起飞后不久坠毁。此次事故共造成 113 人遇难。

Lightning

average and aircraft withstand typical lightning strikes without damage.

5   The dangers of more powerful **positive lightning** were not understood until the destruction of a glider in 1999. It has since been suggested that positive lightning might have caused the crash of Pan Am Flight 214 in 1963[1]. At that time, aircraft were not designed to withstand such strikes because their existence was unknown. The 1985 standard in force in the US at the time of the glider crash, Advisory Circular AC 20-53A, was replaced by Advisory Circular AC 20-53B[2] in 2006. However, it is unclear that whether adequate protection against positive lightning was incorporated.

6   The effects of typical lightning on traditional metal-covered aircraft are well understood and serious damage from a lightning strike on an airplane is rare. The Boeing 787 Dreamliner of which the **exterior** is **carbon-fiber-reinforced polymer** received no damage from a lightning strike during testing.

Ice and Snow

7   Ice and snow can be factors in airline accidents. In 2005, Southwest Airlines Flight 1248 slid off the end of a runway after landing in heavy snow conditions, killing one child on the ground. Even a small amount of icing or coarse frost can greatly impair the ability of a wing to develop adequate lift, that is why regulations prohibit ice, snow or even frost on the wings or tail, prior to takeoff. Air Florida Flight 90[3] crashed on takeoff in 1982, as a result of having ice/snow on its wings.

8   An **accumulation** of ice during flight can be catastrophic, as evidenced by

---

1 这里指泛美航空公司 214 号航班空难。此次空难发生于 1963 年 12 月 8 日，事故原因为飞机进近过程中左侧备用油箱被闪电击中。此次事故共造成机上 81 人遇难。

2 2006 年，美国联邦航空局 20-53B 号咨询通告替代了之前的 20-53A 号咨询通告，通告增加了关于航空器燃油系统油气雷击起火的防护。

3 这里指佛罗里达州航空公司 90 号航班空难。此次空难发生于 1982 年 1 月 13 日，事故原因为未有效除冰导致飞机起飞后不久坠入波托马克河。此次事故共造成 78 人遇难。

the loss of control and subsequent crashes of American Eagle Flight 4184 in 1994[1] and Comair Flight 3272 in 1997[2]. Both aircraft were **turboprop** airliners with **straight wings**, which tend to be more susceptible to in-flight ice accumulation, than **swept wing** jet airliners.

Aircraft Deicing

9   Airlines and airports ensure that aircraft are properly **deiced** before takeoff whenever the weather involves icing conditions. Modern airliners are designed to prevent ice **buildup** on wings, engines and tails (empennage) by either routing heated air from jet engines through the leading edges of the wing and **inlets**, or on slower aircraft by using **inflatable** rubber "boots" which can expand to break off any accumulated ice.

10   Airline flight plans require airline **dispatch** offices to monitor the progress of the weather along the routes of their flights, helping the pilots to avoid the worst of in-flight icing conditions. Aircraft can also be equipped with an **ice detector** in order to warn pilots to leave unexpected ice accumulation areas before the situation becomes critical.

Engine Failure

11   An engine may fail to function because of **fuel starvation, fuel exhaustion, foreign object damage, mechanical failure** due to **metal fatigue**, mechanical failure due to improper maintenance, mechanical failure caused by an original manufacturing defect in the engine, and pilot error.

US Airways Flight 1549's Ditching in the Hudson River

12   In a multi-engine aircraft, the failure of a single engine usually results in a **precautionary**

Metal Fatigue

---

1 这里指美鹰航空公司 4184 号航班空难。此次空难发生于 1994 年 10 月 31 日，事故原因为飞机盘旋等待降落时，机身结冰导致飞机失速坠毁。此次事故共造成机上 68 人遇难。

2 这里指康姆航空公司 3272 号航班空难。此次空难发生于 1997 年 1 月 9 日，事故原因为机翼积冰导致失去升力而失速坠毁。此次事故共造成机上 29 人遇难。

landing being performed, for example landing at a **diversion airport** instead of continuing to the intended destination. The failure of a second engine (e.g., US Airways Flight 1549[1]) or the damage of other aircraft systems caused by an **uncontained** engine failure (e.g., United Airlines Flight 232[2]) may, if an emergency landing is not possible, result in the aircraft crashing.

Structural Failure of the Aircraft

13　　Examples of the failure of aircraft structures caused by metal fatigue include the Havilland Comet accident in 1954[3] and Aloha Airlines Flight 243 accident in 1988[4]. Now that the subject is better understood, and **rigorous** inspection and **nondestructive testing** procedures are in place.

14　　**Composite materials** consist of layers of fibers **embedded** in a **resin matrix**. In some cases, especially when subjected to **cyclic stress**, the layers of the material separate from each other (**delaminate**) and lose strength. As the failure develops inside the material, nothing is shown on the surface; instrument methods (often **ultrasound-based**) have to be used to detect such a material failure. In the 1940s, several Yakovlev Yak-9 experienced the delamination of **plywood** in their constructions.

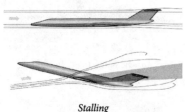

Stalling

Stalling

15　　Stalling an aircraft (by increasing the angle of attack to a point at which the wings fail to produce enough lift), is dangerous and can result in a crash if the pilot fails to make a timely correction.

1　这里指全美航空公司 1549 号航班迫降事件。此次事件发生于 2009 年 1 月 15 日，飞机起飞后遭遇鸟击而双发失效，萨林伯格机长以高超技术迫降纽约哈德逊河，事故无人伤亡。此次事件被称为哈德逊奇迹。

2　这里指联合航空公司 232 号航班空难。此次空难发生于 1989 年 7 月 19 日，事故原因为机件失灵导致液压系统损坏而失控，此次空难共造成 285 名乘客中 110 人丧生。因发生在爱阿华州苏城，事故又名"苏城空难"。

3　这里指哈维兰彗星型客机事故。此次事故发生于 1954 年 4 月 8 日，飞机起飞 6 分钟后，由于在空中解体而坠毁，此次事故共造成 43 人遇难。

4　这里指阿罗哈航空公司 243 号航班事故。此次事故发生于 1988 年 4 月 28 日，飞机在飞行途中遭遇爆炸性失压，但奇迹般安全迫降。

16   Devices used to warn the pilot when the aircraft's speed is decreasing close to the **stall speed** include stall warning horns (installed on virtually all **powered aircraft** now), **stick shakers** and **voice warnings**. Most stalls are a result of the allowing of the airspeed to be too slow for a particular weight and configuration at the time. Stall speed is higher when ice or even frost has attached to the wings and/or tail stabilizer. The severer the icing is, the higher the stall speed is. That is not only because the obstruction of the smooth airflow over the wings, but also because of the added weight of the accumulated ice.

Special Terms

carbon-fiber-reinforced 碳纤维增强的，碳纤维强化的

composite material 复合材料

cyclic stress 周期应力，循环应力

deice 除冰

diversion airport 备降机场

foreign object damage 外来物损伤

Foreign Object Debris (FOD) 外来物碎片

fuel exhaustion 燃油耗尽

fuel starvation 燃油不足

ice/icing detector 结冰传感器

mechanical failure 机械疲劳

metal fatigue 金属疲劳

near miss 几乎相撞；靠近弹；近距脱靶

nondestructive testing 非破坏性测试

plywood 胶合板，层板

polymer 丙烯酸聚合物

positive lightning 正闪电

powered aircraft 有动力装置的航空器

resin matrix 树脂基体

stall speed 失速速度

stick shaker 振杆器，抖杆

straight wing 平直机翼

swept wing 后掠翼；箭形机翼；斜掠翼

turboprop 涡轮螺旋桨发动机

ultrasound-based 基于超声波的

voice warning 语音警告

Words and Expressions

accumulation	[əkjuːmjəˈleɪʃn]	*n.*	堆积物；积聚
buildup	[ˈbɪldʌp]	*n.*	形成；增强；发展
debris	[dəˈbriː]	*n.*	碎片；残骸
delaminate	[dɪˈlæmɪneɪt]	*v.*	脱层，分层
dispatch	[dɪspætʃ]	*n./v.*	派遣；签派
embed	[ɪmˈbed]	*v.*	使嵌入；栽种
exterior	[ɪkˈstɪərɪə]	*n.*	外部 *a.* 外部的；外在的
inflatable	[ɪnˈfleɪtəbl]	*a.*	膨胀的；可充气的
inlet	[ˈɪnlet]	*n.*	入口，进口
misinform	[ˌmɪsɪnˈfɔːm]	*v.*	误报；误传
orientation	[ˌɒrɪənˈteɪʃn]	*n.*	方向；方位
precautionary	[prɪˈkɒʃnrɪ]	*a.*	预防的；预先警戒的
rigorous	[ˈrɪɡrəs]	*a.*	严格的；严密的
spatial	[ˈspeɪʃl]	*a.*	空间的；太空的
uncontained	[ˌʌnkənˈteɪnd]	*a.*	不受控制的；不加制约的

Comprehension of the Text

I. Answer the following questions according to the text.

1. What does Foreign Object Debris include?

_____

2. What kind of situation may make a pilot lose spatial orientation?

_____

3. What are the potential dangers of positive lightning?

_____

4. Why do regulations prohibit ice, snow or even frost on the wings or tail prior to takeoff?

_____

5. How are the modern airliners designed to prevent ice buildup on wings, engines and tails?

_____

6. What is an ice detector used for?

_____

7. What may cause engine failure?

_____

8. What kind of engine failure can result in aircraft crashing?

_____

9. What methods should be used to detect the composite materials failure? Why?

_____

10. Can you list the devices used to warn the pilot when the aircraft's speed is decreasing close to the stall speed?

_____

Vocabulary Practice

II. Match the definitions in Column B with the special terms in Column A and translate the terms into Chinese.

Column A	Column B
1. glider _____	a. the acute angle between the direction of airflow and the line linking the leading and trailing edges of an aircraft
2. stick shaker _____	b. the problem that no fuel is available for an engine to burn
3. positive lightning _____	c. an aircraft without an engine that flies by riding air currents
4. stall _____	d. a mechanical device to rapidly and noisily vibrate the stick of an aircraft to warn the pilot of an imminent stall
5. angle of attack _____	e. the distribution of forces that change over time in a repetitive fashion
6. fuel starvation _____	f. any airfoil or any combination of airfoils considered as a single unit, the primary function of which is to give an aircraft stability
7. cyclic stress _____	g. a rare form of lightning that carries a positive charge to the ground
8. spatial orientation _____	h. a complex material made up of two or more complementary substances
9. composite materials _____	i. the action or behavior of an airplane when by the separation of the airflow, as in the case of insufficient airspeed or of an excessive angle of attack, the airplane or airfoil tends to drop
10. stabilizer _____	j. the ability to identify the position or direction of objects or points in space

Vocabulary Practice

III. Complete each of the following sentences with a word or an expression from the box. Change the form if necessary.

metal fatigue	catastrophic	deice	precautionary	glider
swept wing	inflatable	spatial	voice warning	rigorous

1. The advent of _____ jets meant ever-higher landing speeds, which reduced the narrowing safety margin for carrier aircraft.

2. The system optimization between human and machine is achieved by the _____ system in the airplanes.

3. The pilots waited while the ground crew _____ the plane before takeoff.

4. The company has taken _____ measures to cope with the bad weather.

5. He said that if both engines of the plane had failed, the aircraft would like a _____.

6. This submarine was spotted bobbing in the East River near Brooklyn along with a(n) _____ boat.

7. _____ is an essential consideration for engineers looking at factors that cause metals to fail through stress.

8. GIS (Geographic Information System) can acquire and process _____ data describing the Earth's surface.

9. The minister warned that if war broke out, it would be _____ for the whole world.

10. Traveling through airports nowadays can be very _____, especially when trying to pass through the security checkpoints.

Listening Practice

IV. Watch the video clip about Airbus's new autonomous management system and fill in the blanks.

Every day, millions of people fly through the world's airspace smoothly and safely.

But keeping our skies safe is a *1*_____ job and a vital mindset for thousands of aviation professionals.

Certified mechanics regularly check planes and professional ground crews ready the aircraft before each departure. Pilots follow *2*_____ to make sure everything is set before takeoff. They count on controllers to keep them safely separated from everything else in the air.

Everyone in aviation knows they can trust one another to work with safety top of mind. This *3*_____ culture means admitting mistakes and learning from them, so that a dangerous situation doesn't repeat itself. That mindset allows us to manage unexpected situations, such as avoiding severe *4*_____ along a flight route.

Today, when pilots need to deviate around weather, the controller gives instructions to one plane at a time, making sure none of these aircraft come into *5*_____ with each other or the nearby thunderstorms can be a big *6*_____.

There is no doubt that our world is on the cusp (前沿) of exciting technological advances in aviation, like autonomous vehicles that will make it easier for us to visit family and friends or deliver lifesaving *7*_____ supplies to remote areas.

But with so many more flights in our skies, it won't be possible for people to track each and every vehicle. An *8*_____ management system overseen by air traffic control must be put in place.

Airbus's *9*_____ risk service will be a key part of this new system, aggregating and analyzing vast amounts of data, identifying risks and safety trends across the airspace, monitoring capacity, and smoothly keeping countless vehicles on *10*_____ routes. Afterwards, Airbus's risk service analyzes the flight data to learn from subtle *11*_____ that a human might not notice.

Air traffic controllers will play a vital role and be better equipped to keep our airspace safe, orderly, and efficient. A quantitative approach to risk *12*_____ is critical. It will enable the growing number and diversity of aircraft taking to our skies. With that system in place, we can enjoy safe, connected and evolving airspace for the future.

Translating Practice

V. Translate the following sentences into Chinese.

1. The effects of typical lightning on traditional metal-covered aircraft are well understood and serious damage from a lightning strike on an airplane is rare.

_____

_____

2. Airline flight plans require airline dispatch offices to monitor the progress of the weather along the routes of their flights, helping the pilots to avoid the worst of in-flight icing conditions.

_____

_____

3. Aircraft can also be equipped with an ice detector in order to warn pilots to leave unexpected ice accumulation areas before the situation becomes critical.

_____

_____

4. In a multi-engine aircraft, the failure of a single engine usually results in a precautionary landing being performed, for example landing at a diversion airport instead of continuing to the intended destination.

_____

_____

5. Stalling an aircraft (by increasing the angle of attack to a point at which the wings fail to produce enough lift), is dangerous and can result in a crash if the pilot fails to make a timely correction.

_____

_____

🧭 TEXT C

Aviation Safety Hazards (II)

Fire

1   Safety regulations control aircraft materials and the requirements for **automated** (自动的) fire safety systems. Usually, these requirements take the form of required tests. The tests measure the **flammability** (可燃性) of materials and the **toxicity** (毒性) of smoke. When the tests fail, the material will be used as a prototype in an engineering laboratory rather than in an aircraft.

2   Fire and its toxic smoke have been the cause of accidents. An electrical fire on Air Canada Flight 797[1] in 1983 caused the deaths of 23 of the 46 passengers, resulting in the introduction of **floor level lighting** (地板照明) to assist people to **evacuate** (撤退) a smoke-filled aircraft. In 1985, a fire on the runway caused the loss of 55 lives, 48 from the effects of **incapacitating** (丧失能力的) and subsequently **lethal** (致命的) toxic gas and smoke in the British Airtours Flight 28M[2] accident which raised the serious concerns relating to **survivability** (存活能力)—something that had not been studied in such detail. The swift **incursion** (侵入) of the fire into the fuselage and the layout of the aircraft impaired passengers' ability to evacuate, with the areas such as the forward **galley** (厨房) area becoming a bottle-neck for escaping passengers with some dying very close to the exits.

3   Much research into evacuation, cabin and seating layouts was carried out at Cranfield Institute[3] to try to measure what makes a good evacuation route, which led to the change of the seating layouts at **overwing exit**s (翼上紧急出口) by the **mandate** (授权) and the examination of the evacuation requirements relating to the

---

1   这里指加拿大航空公司 797 号航班事故。此次事故发生于 1982 年 6 月 2 日，飞机着火迫降，大火共造成 23 名乘客遇难。

2   这里指英国空旅航空公司 28M 号航班空难。此次事故发生于 1985 年 8 月 22 日，事故原因为起飞时发动机起火，此次事故共造成 55 人遇难。

3   **Cranfield Institute:** 全称为 Cranfield Institute for Safety, Risk and Reliability，克兰菲尔德安全、风险和可靠性学院，此学院隶属英国克兰菲尔德大学。

design of the galley areas. The use of the **smoke hoods** (防烟罩) or **misting systems** (喷雾系统) were also examined although both were rejected.

4   At one time, **fire fighting foam paths** (灭火泡沫通道) were laid down before an emergency landing, but the practice was considered only **marginally** (少量地) effective, and concerns about the **depletion** (消耗) of the fire fighting capability due to pre-foaming led the United States **FAA** (联邦航空局) withdraw its recommendation in 1987.

5   One possible cause of fire in airplanes is wiring problems that involve **intermittent** (间歇的) faults, such as wires with breached **insulation** (绝缘) touching each other, having water dripping on them or short circuits. These problems are difficult to detect once the aircraft is on the ground. However, there are methods, such as using **spread-spectrum time-domain reflectometry** (扩频时域反射仪), that can feasibly test live wires on aircraft during flight.

Bird Strike (鸟击，撞鸟)

6   Bird strike is an aviation term for a collision between a bird and an aircraft. Fatal accidents have been caused by both engine failure following bird **ingestion** (吸入) and bird strikes breaking **cockpit windshields** (驾驶舱风挡).

7   Modern jet engines have the capability of surviving an ingestion of a bird. Small fast planes, such as military jet fighters, are at higher risk than heavy multi-engine ones. This is due to the fact that the fan of a **high-bypass turbofan engine** (高涵道涡轮风扇发动机), typical on transport aircraft, acts as a **centrifugal separator** (离心式分离器) to force ingested materials (birds, ice, etc.) to the outside of the fan's disc. As a result, such materials go through the relatively **unobstructed** (无阻挡的) **bypass duct** (外涵道), rather than through the core of the engine, which contains the smaller and more delicate **compressor** (压缩机) blades. Military aircraft designed for high-speed flight typically have pure turbojet, or **low-bypass turbofan engines** (低涵道涡轮风扇发动机), increasing the risk that ingested materials will get into the core of the engine to cause damage.

8   The highest risk of bird strike is during the takeoff and landing, in low altitudes, which is in the vicinity of the airports. Some airports use **active countermeasures** (主动干扰), ranging from employing a person with a shotgun through playing recorded sounds of **predators** (捕食性动物) to employing **falconers** (养鹰者). Poisonous grass can be planted, which is not **palatable** (美味的) to birds, nor to insects that attract **insectivorous** (食虫的) birds. **Passive countermeasures** (被动干扰) involve sensible land-use management, avoiding conditions attracting flocks of birds to the area (e.g., landfills). Another tactic found effective is to let the grass at the airfield grow taller (approximately 12 inches) as some species of birds won't land if they cannot see one another.

Ground Damage

9   Various ground support equipment operates in close proximity to the fuselage and wings of the aircraft for service and occasionally cause accidental damage in the form of scratches in the paint or small dents in the skin. Because aircraft structures (including the outer skin) play such a critical role in the safe operation of a flight, all damage should be inspected, measured and possibly tested to ensure that any damage is within safe tolerance.

10   An example problem was the **depressurization** (失压) incident on Alaska Airlines Flight 536[1] in 2005. During ground services, a baggage handler hit the side of the aircraft with a tug towing a train of baggage carts. This incident damaged the metal skin of the aircraft, but it was not reported. When the plane departed and climbed through 26,000 feet (7,900 m), the damaged section of the skin gave way under the difference in pressure between the inside of the aircraft and the outside air. The cabin depressurized explosively necessitating a rapid descent to denser (breathable) air and an emergency landing. Post landing examination of the fuselage of the aircraft revealed a 12 inch (30 cm) hole on the right side of the airplane.

1　这里指阿拉斯加航空公司 536 号航班事故。事故发生于 2005 年 12 月 26 日，事故原因为飞机在高空经历座舱失压，机组启动紧急下降，成功着陆。

Volcanic Ash

11   Plumes of volcanic ash near active volcanoes can damage propellers, engines and cockpit windows. In 1982, British Airways Flight 9[1] flew through an ash cloud and temporarily lost power from all four engines.

12   Prior to 2010, the general approach taken by airspace regulators was that if the ash concentration rose above zero, then the airspace was considered unsafe and was consequently closed. Volcanic Ash Advisory Centers enable the liaison between meteorologists, **volcanologists** (火山学家) and the aviation industry.

Controlled Flight into Terrain (CFIT) (可控飞行撞地)

13   Controlled Flight into Terrain is a class of accidents in which an aircraft is flown under control into terrain or man-made structures. CFIT accidents typically result from pilot error or navigational system error. The failure to protect ILS critical areas can also cause CFIT accidents. In December 1995, American Airlines Flight 965[2] tracked off course while approaching Calí, Colombia and hit a mountainside, although the **Terrain Awareness and Warning System (TAWS)** (地形感知与告警系统) sounded a terrain warning in the cockpit and the desperate pilot attempted to gain altitude after that warning. Crew position awareness and monitoring of navigational systems are essential to the prevention of CFIT accidents. As of February 2008, over 40,000 aircraft installed enhanced TAWS, and they had flown over 800 million hours without a CFIT accident.

14   Another anti-CFIT tool is the **Minimum Safe Altitude Warning (MSAW) system** (最低安全高度警告系统) which monitors the altitudes transmitted by aircraft transponders and compares that with the system's defined minimum safe

---

1 这里指英国航空公司 9 号航班事故，又称"雅加达事件"。事故发生于 1982 年 7 月 24 日，飞机途经印度尼西亚时飞入火山灰云，四台发动机全部熄火，但最终飞机平安降落。

2 这里指美国航空公司 965 号航班空难，事故发生于 1995 年 12 月 20 日，飞机着陆前 5 分钟撞山坠毁，机上 163 人仅 4 人生还，这是波音 757 飞机的首宗坠机事故。

altitudes for a given area. When the system determines that the aircraft is lower or might soon be lower than the minimum safe altitude, the air traffic controller receives an **acoustic** (听觉的) and visual warning and then alerts the pilot that his aircraft is too low.

Electromagnetic Interference (电磁干扰)

15 The use of certain electronic equipment is partially or entirely prohibited as it might interfere with aircraft operation, such as causing compass deviations. The use of some types of personal electronic devices is prohibited when an aircraft is below 10,000 meters, taking off, or landing. The use of a mobile phone is prohibited on most flights because in-flight usage creates problems with ground-based cells.

Runway Safety

16 The following are the types of runway safety incidents.

- **Runway excursion** (跑道偏离)—an incident involving only a single aircraft making an inappropriate exit from the runway.
- **Runway overrun** (跑道冲出)—a specific type of excursion where the aircraft does not stop before the end of the runway (e.g., Air France Flight 358[1]).
- **Runway incursion** (跑道入侵)—the incorrect presence of a vehicle, person or another aircraft on the runway (e.g., Tenerife airport disaster[2]).
- Runway confusion—crew **misidentification** (误认) of the runway for landing or taking off (e.g., Comair Flight 5191[3]).

---

1 这里指法国航空公司 358 号航班事故, 事故发生于 2005 年 8 月 2 日, 飞机着陆时冲出跑道起火, 所幸人员及时逃出, 无人遇难。

2 这里指特内里费空难, 事故发生于 1977 年 3 月 27 日, 在加纳利群岛的洛斯罗迪欧机场, 由于大雾和无线电干扰, 两架波音 747 航班在跑道相撞, 事故造成 583 人丧生, 是航空史上死亡人数最多的空难。

3 这里指康姆航空公司 5191 号航班事故。事故发生于 2006 年 8 月 7 日, 飞机由于错用跑道, 导致起飞跑道太短而冲出跑道起火爆炸, 事故造成机上 49 人遇难, 仅 1 人生还。

 Exercises

Comprehension of the Text

Answer the following questions according to the text.

1. How did engineers deal with the materials which failed the test?

_____

2. Why did the United States FAA withdraw its recommendation for fire fighting foam paths in 1987?

_____

3. What is one possible cause of fire in airplanes and how to deal with this problem?

_____

4. Why are small fast planes, such as military jet fighters, at higher risk of bird strike than heavy multi-engine ones?

_____

5. Can you list some active countermeasures that some airports used to avoid bird strike?

_____

6. What was the general approach to the plumes of the volcanic ash taken by airspace regulators prior to 2010?

_____

7. What may cause CFIT accidents?

_____

8. What is MSAW system?

_____

9. What may cause runway incursion?

_____

10. Can you list some other types of runway safety incidents?

_____

⊘ UNIT PROJECT

Mind Mapping

Work in groups and draw two mind maps respectively according to the following topics.

1. human factors related to flight safety
2. aviation safety hazards

Oral Practice

Work in groups and discuss the measures that should be taken for aviation safety. And one student from each group will make a 3-minute oral presentation according to the discussion. You may refer to the texts of this unit and the relevant information from the Internet.

Writing Practice

Based on the discussion above, write a composition with at least 150 words on the topic of "What should Be Done for Aviation Safety". You may refer to the outline below.

1. the brief introduction to an air crash in history
2. the lessons that can be learned from the crash
3. the measures that can be taken to prevent such crashes

Appendix 1
Commonly Used
Aviation Abbreviations

ACC: Area Control Center 区域管制中心

ADF: Automatic Direction Finder 自动侧向仪

ADIZ: Air Defense Identification Zone 防空识别区（发音为 AY-DIZ）

ADR: Advisory Route 咨询航路

ADS: Automatic Dependent Surveillance 自动相关监视

AEW: Airborne Early Warning 空中预警

AEWACS: Airborne Early Warning and Control System 空中预警与指挥系统

AFIS: Aerodrome Flight Information Service 机场飞行情报业务

AGL: Above Ground Level 离地高度

AGSM: Anti-G Straining Maneuver 抗荷预紧动作

AIP: Aeronautical Information Publication 航空资料出版物

AIS: Aeronautical Information Service 航空情报业务

AMSL: Above Mean Sea Level 距平均海平面高度

AOA: Angle of Attack 攻角，迎角

AOR: Area of Responsibility 责任区

ARTCC: Air Route Traffic Control Center 航路交通管制中心

ASR: Airport Surveillance Radar 机场对空监视雷达

ATC: Air Traffic Control 空中交通管制

ATD: Actual Time of Departure 实际离场时间

ATIS: Automatic Terminal Information Service 自动终端情报服务（简称"通播"）

ATS: Air Traffic Services 空中交通服务

ATZ: Aerodrome Traffic Zone 机场交通区域

BDHI: Bearing-Distance-Heading Indicator 方位距离航向指示器

BKN: broken, 5 to 7 Oktas 多云，5~7 个量的云

BR: mist 轻雾

BVR: Beyond Visual Range 超视距

CAS: Close Air Support 近距空中支援

CAT: Clear Air Turbulence 晴空湍流

CAVOK: Ceiling and Visibility OK 天气良好，云底高度和能见度很好

CB: cumulonimbus 积雨云

CDI: Course Deviation Indicator 航线偏航指示仪

CTR: Control Zone 管制区域（权）

CG: Center of Gravity 重心

DA: Danger Area 危险区

DEP: departure 离场

DH: Decision Height 决断高度

DI: Direction Indicator 方向指示器，方向标

DME: Distance Measuring Equipment 测距装置，测距仪

ECM: Electronic Countermeasures 电子对抗

EET : Estimated Elapsed Time 预计经过时间

EFD: Electronic Flight Display 电子飞行显示器

EGTI: Exhaust Gas Temperature Indicator 排气温度指示表

ETA: Estimated Time of Arrival 预计到达时间

ETB: Estimated Time of Boundary 预计到达边界时间

ETD: Estimated Time of Departure 预计离场时间

ETE: Estimated Time Endurance 预计途中时间

FAC: Forward Air Controller (airborne) 空中前进管制员

FEW: few clouds, 1 to 2 Oktas 少云

FIC: Flight Information Center 飞行情报中心

FIR: Flight Information Region 飞行情报区

FIS : Flight Information Service 飞行情报服务

FSS: Flight Service Station 飞行勤务站

FW Aircraft : Fixed Wing Aircraft 固定翼飞机

GHz : gigahertz 千兆赫

G-LOC: Gravity Induced Loss of Consciousness 加速度诱发意识丧失

GPS: Global Positioning System 全球卫星定位系统

GS: Glide Slope 下滑道；下滑坡度

GBU: Guided Bomb Unit 制导炸弹

GCA: Ground Controlled Approach 地面控制进近

GCI: Ground Controlled Interception 地面引导拦截

H24: continues day and night service 24 小时服务

HF: High Frequency (3 to 30 MHz) 高频

HIWAS: Hazardous Inflight Weather Advisory 空中危险天气咨询服务

HOTAS: Hands on Throttle-and-Stick 手不离杆，握杆控制

HSI: Horizontal Situation Indicator 水平位置指示器

HUD: Head-Up Display 平视显示仪

ICAO: International Civil Aviation Organization 国际民航组织

IFF : Identification Friend or Foe 敌我识别器

IFR: Instrument Flight Rules 仪表飞行规则

ILS: Instrument Landing System 仪表着陆系统

IM: Inner Marker 近距指点标，内指点标，近台

IMC: Instrument Meteorological Condition 仪表气象条件

INFO: information 信息，情报

IP: Instructor Pilot 飞行教官

IR: Instrument Routes 仪表飞行航线

LOC: localizer 着陆航向；定向台

LGW: Laser-Guided Weapons 激光制导武器

MDA: Minimum Descent Altitude 最低下降高度

MET: meteorology 气象

METAR: Aviation Routine Weather Report 航空例行气象报告

MFD: Multi-Function Display 多功能显示器

MHz: megahertz 兆赫

MLS: Microwave Landing System 微波着陆系统

MM: Middle Marker 中距指点标

MNPS: Minimum Navigation Performance Specifications 最低导航性能规范

MOA: Military Operations Area 军事飞行训练空域

MTR: Military Training Route 军事训练航线

NATO: North Atlantic Treaty Organization 北大西洋公约组织（简称"北约"）

NATOPS: Naval Air Training and Operating Procedures Standardization 海军航空兵训练与操作程序标准化

NAVAIDs: Navigational Aids 导航设备；助航方法

NDB: Non-Directional Radio Beacon 无方向性信标，全向信标，导航台

NIL: None or I Have Nothing to Send You 无或无可发送

NOTAM: Notice to Airman 航行通告

NOZ: Normal Operating Zone 正常运行区

NSA: National Security Area 国家安全区域

NSC: No/Nil Significant Cloud 无显著云层

NTZ: No-Transgression Zone 非侵入区

PAPI: Precision Approach Path Indicator 精密进近航道指示器

PAR : Precision Approach Radar 精密进近雷达

PDR: Predetermined Route 预定航线

PIREP: Pilot Weather Report 飞行员气象报告

QFE: Query Field Elevation（航空通信代码）机场标高（跑道段）地点大气压（简称"场压"）

QNH: Query Nautical Height（航空通信代码）修正海平面气压拨正值（简称"修正海压"）

RCC: Rescue Coordination Center 救援协调中心

RNAV: Area Navigation 区域导航

RTB: Return to Base 返回基地，返航

RVR: Runway Visual Range 跑道视程

RVSM: Reduced Vertical Separation Minimum 缩小垂直间隔

SELCAL: Selective Calling System 选择性呼叫系统

SID: Standard Instrument Departure 标准仪表（程序）离场

SIGMET: information concerning en-route weather phenomena which may affect safety of aircraft operations 航路重要天气情报

SNA: Student Naval Aviator 海军飞行学员

SNOWTAM: a special series NOTAM notifying the presence or removal of hazardous conditions due to snow, ice, slush or standing water associated with snow, slush and ice on the movement area, by means of a special format 雪情通告

SPECIAL: special meteorological report 特选报

SRA : Surveillance Radar Approach 监视雷达进场

SSR: Secondary Surveillance Radar 二次监视雷达

SST: Supersonic Transport 超音速运输机

STAR: Standard Instrument Arrival 标准仪表（程序）进场

TACAN: UHF tactical air navigational aid 超高频战术空中导航设备，塔康

TAD: Tactical Air Direction 战术空中指导

TAF: Terminal Area Forecast 机场天气预报

TCAS/ACAS: Traffic Alert and Collision Avoidance System / Airborne Collision Avoidance System 机载防撞系统

TMA: Terminal Control Area 终端管制区

TRSA: Terminal Radar Service Area 终端雷达服务区

UAV: Unmanned Aerial Vehicle 无人机

UHF: Ultra-High Frequency 超高频

UIR: Upper Flight Information Region 高空情报区

UTC: Coordinated Universal Time 国际标准时

UWS: Urgent Weather SIGMET 紧急重要气象变化预报

VASIS: Visual Approach Slope Indicator System 目视进近坡度指示系统

VDF : Very High Frequency Direction Finding System 甚高频定向台

VFR: Visual Flight Rules 目视飞行规则

VHF: Very High Frequency 甚高频

VMC: Instrument Meteorological Condition 目视气象条件

VOLMET: Meteorological Information for Aircraft in Flight 对空天气广播

VOR: VHF Omnidirectional Radio Range 甚高频全向无线电信标

VORTAC: VHF Omni-Directional Range/Tactical Air Navigation 甚高频全向无线电信标，战术导航台（伏尔/塔康）

VSI: Vertical Speed Indicator 升降速度表，爬升率指示器

V/STOL: Vertical/Short Takeoff and Landing 垂直/短距起降

VTAS: Visual Target Acquisition System 目视目标捕捉系统，目视目标截获系统

WP: waypoint 航路点

Appendix 2
Transmission of Letters

Transmission of Letters

Letter	Code word	Pronunciation
A	Alpha/Alfa	**AL** FAH
B	Bravo	**BRAH** VOH
C	Charlie	**CHAR** LEE or **SHAR** LEE
D	Delta	**DELL** TAH
E	Echo	**ECK** OH
F	Foxtrot	**FOKS** TROT
G	Golf	GOLF
H	Hotel	HOH **TELL**
I	India	**IN** DEE AH
J	Juliett	**JEW** LEE **ETT**
K	Kilo	**KEY** LOH
L	Lima	**LEE** MAH
M	Mike	MIKE
N	November	NO **VEM** BER
O	Oscar	**OSS** CAH
P	Papa	PAH **PAH**
Q	Quebec	KEH **BECK**
R	Romeo	**ROW** ME OH
S	Sierra	SEE **AIR** RAH
T	Tango	**TANG** GO
U	Uniform	**YOU** NEE FORM or **OO** NEE FORM
V	Victor	**VIK** TAH
W	Whiskey	**WISS** KEY
X	X-ray	**ECKS RAY**
Y	Yankee	**YANG** KEY
Z	Zulu	**ZOO** LOO

注：1. 黑体部分为重读部分，特别重点发音：Juliet、Papa、Quebec、Sierra。

2. 发音中的空格代表发音分读。例如，"Sierra: SEE AIR RAH"的发音为：SEE、AIR、RAH。

3. 在印度尼西亚，字母"L"的代码不是Lima，而是London。

4. 在陆空无线电通话中，英文字母皆按国际民航组织（ICAO）规定发音，即按以上字母表发音，但在不影响电文准确接收和理解的前提下，有下列例外：

1）一些日常使用的字母组合仍按英文字母发音，例如，ILS、NDB、GPS、QFE、QNH、RVR等；

2）航空公司呼号按注册规定发音，例如，CCA读作Air China等；

3）飞机型号按飞机制造厂注册型号发音，例如，B777读作Boeing777等。

Appendix 3
Transmission of Numbers

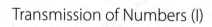

Transmission of Numbers (I)

Number	Word	Pronunciation (English)	Pronunciation (Chinese)
0	Zero	**ZE**-RO	洞
1	One	**WUN**	幺
2	Two	**TOO**	两
3	Three	**TREE**	三
4	Four	**FOW**-ER	四
5	Five	**FIFE**	五
6	Six	**SIX**	六
7	Seven	**SEV**-EN	拐
8	Eight	**AIT**	八
9	Nine	**NIN**-ER	九
.	Decimal / Point (US)	**DAY**-SEE-**MAL** / Point (US)	点
100	Hundred	**HUN**-DRED	百
1000	Thousand	**TOU**-SAND	千

注：黑体部分重读。

Transmission of Numbers (II)

Number	Pronunciation (English)	Pronunciation (Chinese)
10	WUN ZE-RO	幺洞
75	SEV-EN FIFE	拐五
200	TWO HUN-DRED	两百
450	FOW-ER FIFE ZE-RO	四五洞 / 四百五
2500	TOO TOU-SAND FIFE HUNDRED	两千五
5000	FIFE TOU-SAND	五千
11000	WUN WUN TOU-SAND	一万一千
25000	TOO FIFE TOU-SAND	两万五千
38143	TREE AIT WUN FOW-ER TREE	三八幺四三

注：1. 数字组合的汉语读法通常为，根据数字的汉语发音按顺序逐位读出数字；整百、整千或整万组合的数字通常读出数字，后面加上百、千或万，也可按数字顺序读出。

2. 数字组合的英语读法通常为：根据数字的英语发音按顺序逐位读出数字；整百或整千组合的数字通常读出数字，后面加上百或千。具体示例如下。

三位数以下的整数数字按照单数字读法分开认读。

三位数百整数读为"单数字+hundred"；

四位数百整数读为"单数字+thousand+单数字+hundred"；

五位数千整数读为"单数字+单数字+thousand"；

五位数全为非 0 数读为"单数字+单数字+单数字+单数字+单数字"。

References

高培新 . 2013. ICAO 民航飞行员专业英语 . 天津：天津科技翻译出版有限公司 .

卢小萍 . 2011. 飞行专业英语 . 空军军事职业大学 .

王传经等 . 2013. 军事英语听说教程（修订版）. 北京：外语教学与研究出版社 .

吴土星等 . 2016. 无线电陆空通话教程（第二版）. 北京：中国民航出版社 .

Francis, A. C. 1988. *The Language of the Air Force in English.* NY: Regents Publishing.